YVES MONTAND

The Passionate Voice

JOSEPH HARRISS

UNIVERSITY PRESS OF KENTUCKY

A note to the reader: This volume contains discussions of domestic violence, alleged sexual abuse, and other sensitive topics. The opinions and interpretations are solely those of the author. In addition, the author has documented several instances of racially insensitive language to provide full historical context for the events under discussion. Discretion is advised.

Scholarly publisher for the Commonwealth,
serving Bellarmine University, Berea College, Centre College of Kentucky, Eastern Kentucky University, The Filson Historical Society, Georgetown College, Kentucky Historical Society, Kentucky State University, Morehead State University, Murray State University, Northern Kentucky University, Spalding University, Transylvania University, University of Kentucky, University of Louisville, University of Pikeville, and Western Kentucky University.

Editorial and Sales Offices: The University Press of Kentucky
663 South Limestone Street, Lexington, Kentucky 40508-4008
www.kentuckypress.com

Library of Congress Cataloging-in-Publication Data

Names: Harriss, Joseph, author.
Title: Yves Montand : the passionate voice / Joseph Harriss.
Description: Lexington : The University Press of Kentucky, 2024. | Series: Screen classics | Includes bibliographical references and index.
Identifiers: LCCN 2023023313 | ISBN 9780813198606 (hardcover) | ISBN 9780813198620 (pdf) | ISBN 9780813198613 (epub)
Subjects: LCSH: Montand, Yves, 1921–1991. | Singers—France—Biography. | Actors—France—Biography.
Classification: LCC ML420.M56 H37 2024 | DDC 782.42164092 [B]—dc23/eng/20230620
LC record available at https://lccn.loc.gov/2023023313

This book is printed on acid-free paper meeting the requirements of the American National Standard for Permanence in Paper for Printed Library Materials.

Manufactured in the United States of America

Member of the Association of University Presses

For Claudie and Christopher

Contents

Introduction

We can thank Benito Mussolini and his Blackshirt fascist goons for the felicitous fact that Ivo Livi didn't spend his life as a dirt-poor Italian peasant. Instead, as Yves Montand he became to our benefit a top film actor on both sides of the Atlantic, an important political activist—first a youthful, Soviet-leaning communist fellow traveler, then a rueful, outspoken humanist condemning totalitarianism wherever it arose—and arguably the best-ever French balladeer whose deceptively simple songs about life and love conveyed, for much of the world, the essence of Paris. The undercurrent of passion in his resonant baritone both expressed joie de vivre and, when he chose, projected his uncompromising support for individual freedom and social justice.

I felt that immediately after I came across one of his albums in a music shop many years ago. Songs such as "À Paris," "Les grands boulevards," "Le temps des cerises," "Les feuilles mortes," and, of course, "C'est si bon," with their mixture of contagious gaiety, intense romanticism, and poetic resonance, personified the city I had come to love after studying there. They have stayed with me ever since, snatches of certain refrains popping unbidden into my head as I walk the streets of my adopted home.

The irony is striking: this quintessential Frenchman who performed those haunting songs had not a drop of French blood. He was French only by an accident of history. For that matter, it was due to another fortuitous twist of fate that he barely missed growing up American. Instead, he became a twentieth-century French icon recognized throughout the world, successfully juggling both singing and acting careers for nearly fifty years.

An American critic partially explained his universal appeal in the early 1980s, finding that his songs "have an arresting simplicity and a knowing, ironic seductiveness. With his special kind of romanticism, his nonchalance and his intensity, he created his own persona and a brand of eroticism that have resisted changing fashions."[1] Women were especially vulnerable to his velvety, caressing tremolo. As his wife of thirty-four years, Simone Signoret, once said, his singing acted on women's nervous systems, sparking a million fantasies. She made a point of posting herself backstage to ward off overly enthusiastic groupies. Women polled by a French magazine voted him the man they most wanted to, shall we say, father their child. As London's *Times* put it in an obituary, he was "an idol who captured their hearts with effortless ease for more than four decades."[2]

During an equally busy acting career that spanned more than fifty films, he won praise for powerful performances in films such as Henri-Georges Clouzot's *Salaire de la peur / Wages of Fear* (1953, US 1955) and Costa-Gavras's courageous antitotalitarian films *Z* (France and US 1969), and *L'aveu / The Confession* (1970). His American films included George Cukor's scandalous *Let's Make Love* (1960)—scandalous more for Marilyn Monroe and Montand's behavior off-set than for anything in the film. He was still maturing and burnishing his acting at the age of sixty-five, when he gave some of his best performances in *Jean de Florette* and *Manon des sources / Manon of the Springs* (both 1986), in which he played a wily, unscrupulous paysan in the film versions of Marcel Pagnol's novels set in Provence.

The case can be made that Montand became the most successful and popular French entertainer ever to cross the Atlantic. In America, recognition took the form of invitations to perform at the Kennedy White House in 1963 and at New York's Metropolitan Opera House in 1982, the first time a popular singer was given that honor, one that was repeated in 1984. In 1988, the city's prestigious Film Society of Lincoln Center gave him a special tribute, the Chaplin Award, for his contribution to film, an honor given to the biggest names in filmdom.

The technical reasons for his success were no secret. Preparing for his films, he worked so hard at getting into character that it often astonished his directors. For his one-man shows, he repeatedly rehearsed the numbers with his small orchestra, insisting on including new, often difficult songs that would surprise and sometimes discomfit the audience. Every dance step, every expressive gesture of his oversize hands were repeated until they became a reflex. Indeed, when critics cast about for something negative to say of a new show, they often faulted him for excessive perfectionism, as if a sort of amateurish awkwardness would be preferable. Introverted and shy by nature despite his public persona of passionate Mediterranean exuberance, he was hagridden by doubt and never got over gut-wrenching stage fright before every performance or film shoot. Thus the need to keep trying ever harder.

You know the value of hard work when you are the third child of a penniless Italian peasant farming the rocky soil of Tuscany. His father, Giovanni Livi, strongly believed there must be a better way for a man to live; he found hope in the new secular religion called communism sweeping Europe in the early twentieth century. He made no attempt to hide his beliefs, and that got him in big trouble with Mussolini's National Fascist Party militants. Deciding to leave for America, he made it only as far as Marseilles. The Livis' frugal, precarious life in the tawdry slums of the port city marked Ivo for life and goes far to explain his passionate left-wing politics as a young adult. As for so many then as now, the way out of poverty was show business. Ivo Livi became Yves Montand.

His budding career seemed condemned with the fall of France in 1940, but he managed to avoid being sent to the front or to forced labor in Germany. After he surreptitiously made it to Paris, his lucky break came when he met Edith Piaf, then one of the biggest stars of Paris music halls. She recognized in Montand a fellow proletarian, reaching, as she had, for the brass ring of the big time. Many claimed it was Piaf who launched his career, that without her he would have remained nothing but a gawky kid with a thick Marseilles accent doing the same imitations of Charles Trenet and Donald Duck he began with. That claim underestimates Montand's native intelligence and show business instincts. More likely, his ability to learn fast from her and his willingness to work hard simply saved him several years' apprenticeship.

Montand loved women, many of them, not wisely but too well, and they were often key to his professional and personal development. (There were, however, several allegations made of sexual aggression and abuse.) Piaf was the first of several who helped him bloom into a show business star of the first magnitude and a mature, multifaceted human being. In August 1949, Montand visited the scenic Provençal village of Saint Paul de Vence and met another woman who changed his life forever. She was the actress Simone Signoret—who in 1960 would become the first French person to win an Oscar, for the British film *Room at the Top*—and the coup de foudre between her and Montand was immediate, mutual, and ardent.

The importance of Signoret in Montand's development cannot be overestimated. She was able to articulate the inchoate political ideas he had had since his youth about the plight of the working class and introduced him to the political activism that became so important in his life. He, in turn, put her in touch with a social reality absent from her intellectual debates in the cafés of Saint Germain des Près. He and Signoret became active fellow travelers of the French Communist Party, though they never formally joined it, as had many other artists and intellectuals of the period, from Jean-Paul Sartre and Simone de Beauvoir to Pablo Picasso and countless others. High-profile darlings of the left, they were anathema to the US State Department, which refused them visas for years, fearful of contamination by the communist virus.

Their most controversial act came during the depth of the Cold War, when he accepted a weeks-long concert tour of the Soviet Union and eastern Europe beginning in December 1956. It's an open question who profited most from the tour. Besides the income it represented, Montand had the satisfaction of singing before huge audiences of ordinary, working-class Russians, Poles, Czechs, and other eastern Europeans. The Soviet organizers got their payoff by triumphantly parading the famous couple from the West like a trophy.

What is certain is that when word of his critical remarks to Soviet leaders about the Communist Party's human rights violations reached Paris, many fellow travelers, shocked that he dared question the party's infallibility, considered him a traitor. Montand, however, was satisfied he had remained true to his values, although this first taste of the reality of life under communism came as a rude awakening to him. His attitude toward communism continued to evolve until, following the Soviet invasion of Czechoslovakia in 1968, he publicly turned against it. It was a painful conversion that meant abandoning the political ideals of the father he idolized and bitterly alienating him from his beloved older brother, Julien.

His most important films of that period, from *La guerre est finie / The War Is Over* (1966, US 1967) and *Z* to *L'aveu / The Confession,* were protests against totalitarianism. Soon he would be saying that the main threat to world security was the Soviet Union and that President Ronald Reagan, scorned by the French Left on orders from Moscow, was right to oppose it. Unwittingly, Montand became the symbol of a generation struggling with conflicting political beliefs, a virtual seismograph of the ideological conflicts of the second half of the twentieth century.

Montand, very macho Mediterranean, never pretended to be a faithful husband. Signoret seemed to accept that. By all appearances, she agreed to turn a blind eye to what he called his "little adventures" as long as he didn't damage their marriage or involve her close friends. But his well-publicized affair with Marilyn Monroe at the Beverly Hills Hotel in 1960 hurt Signoret badly and broke their relationship irrevocably. His attempts to explain that it was spontaneous and unintentional were to no avail. Both tried to shrug it off as Montand just being Montand, but the fact is that it was more than just a simple fling.

Despite the stress of his deteriorating marriage and Signoret's declining health and death in 1985, his later years were among the most productive of his career. Besides touring the world with his music hall act from New York to Brazil, London to Tokyo, he found the time and energy to take politics more seriously than ever, both with his films and his public statements. In one of the more bizarre episodes in modern French political history, it seemed for a while that an entertainer rather than a professional politician or a certified member of the country's elite might run for president in 1988 against the socialist incumbent François Mitterrand.

Despite working with top French directors of his generation, such as Alain Resnais, Claude Lelouch, and Jean-Pierre Melville, as well as with Costa-Gavras, he was never awarded an Oscar or even a César, France's equivalent of the Oscar. Nor did the Cannes Film Festival jury ever declare him best actor for any of his films. His two appearances at the Met and his award from the Film Society of Lincoln Center consecrated his status in America, making him something of a prophet without honor in his own country. Many in the United States compared him to Frank Sinatra and Dean Martin. They, too, went from singing to acting—and they, too, were of Italian origin. The reason for the ungenerous French treatment of Montand likely lay in his controversial political stands, which rocked many of the country's conventional, politically correct boats.

The last few years of his personal life were enhanced by a new companion, his former assistant Carole Amiel, with whom he fathered his only child, a son named Valentin, in 1989 at the age of sixty-eight. They never married, Montand seemingly remaining faithful to the memory of Signoret to the end. But that year was also marred by a paternity suit brought by a minor actress who claimed he was the father of her daughter. Suits and countersuits resulted in Montand's body being exhumed in 1998, to much public outrage, for DNA testing. Forensics concluded he was not the father, but the whole sorry episode with its screaming headlines tarnished his image in the minds of many in France.

By then, Montand had lain for seven years beside Signoret in Paris's famous Père Lachaise Cemetery, not far from the tomb of Edith Piaf, becoming a tourist attraction among other French culture icons from Molière to Marcel Proust, Balzac, and Bernhardt. Even right before he died, never satisfied that he had done all he could, he was rehearsing for a big new show in Paris for the following spring. He especially wanted to do it for Valentin, so he could see his *papa* sing at least once. The posters were already up all over the city, showing him in jaunty silhouette with top hat and cane.

Montand's untimely death at seventy deprived Valentin and us of that final show. But in his albums and films we can still get glimpses of the France he incarnated, when the Champs-Élysées really was the most beautiful avenue in the world, it seemed that ideas passionately held could change things for the better, and there were still troubadours to sing ballads written by poets.

1

The Blackshirts Come

It was an unfortunate choice of birthplace. Only a few miles away was the larger and more prosperous Monsummano Terme, a handsome spa known for the healing qualities of its saline waters that attracted those hoping for a cure for their rheumatism, syphilis, and other ailments. Or it could have been nearby Florence, the glorious capital of Tuscany, home to the great Renaissance blooming of art and literature whose geniuses ranged from Giotto to Botticelli, Leonardo da Vinci to Michelangelo and Dante. But no, it was to be in Monsummano Alto, a hardscrabble hilltop hamlet made up of a few small fieldstone houses, where life was grim and hopes were low, that Ivo Livi was born in 1921, youngest of the three children of Giovanni and Giuseppina Livi.

The Livis had been peasants there for generations, their name deriving from Roman antiquity, "Livius" or perhaps "Livie." Giovanni, who was born there in 1891, lost his father when he was two years old; the poor man died, exhausted, in the hole he was digging for a cherry tree. After his mother ran off with a local boy, Giovanni and his two brothers, Virgilio and Giuseppino, were raised by their grandfather Carlo. Carlino, as he was known, was an exception among the peasants of Monsummano because he was able to read and write. His little library included literary works by Tasso, Dante, and Victor Hugo.

Though Giovanni worked in the fields from age seven, Carlino insisted he attend a few years of elementary school. Giovanni stayed on the land, hacking at the hard ocher earth, while his brothers used their talents to better advantage: Virgilio went to Livorno on the Ligurian coast and eventually became manager in a truck factory; Giuseppino sang and played guitar and mandolin at regional festivals. In 1912, Giovanni, now a short, stocky, muscular man of twenty-one, was drafted for service in the army. He fought in the pacification campaign in Italian-occupied Libya against anticolonialist resistance fighters led by the Lion of the Desert, Omar Mukhtar. He served nearly three years, became a corporal, contracted chronic conjunctivitis, and returned home disgusted by the inhuman violence of warfare.

A local young woman named Giuseppina Simoni caught his eye. They had first met in elementary school and had had similarly impoverished childhoods. They began seeing each other, and the inevitable happened: Giuseppina became pregnant before they had had time to make it official. They weren't ready for parenthood: Giuseppina tried everything to abort, even climbing a tree and jumping down, hard. All that accomplished, the family says, was to knock her unconscious for a few minutes. The child, a girl, was born in 1915 and named Lidia. When Giovanni was drafted again in 1916 for the Great War, his bad eyesight kept him from serving in the trenches. On his leaves home, he found time to father a son, Giuliano.

On October 13, 1921, a third child was born after a painful, thirteen-hour labor during which four men had to hold Giuseppina. When the baby finally came, it was clear why the birth was difficult: the boy weighed nearly twelve pounds. He was, according to family legend, an exceptionally beautiful bambino, admired by friends and neighbors who came to visit. Giovanni named him "Ivo," hoping he would make something of himself and become a lawyer, Saint Ivo of Kermartin being the patron saint of that trade.

It would be an understatement to say that life for the growing family was frugal. Everybody pitched in to produce food, the parents plowing and harvesting a small plot of wheat, the children scrounging for wild vegetables. They raised rabbits to sell at the local market, using the money to buy salt cod, which could be served many different ways. They mostly ate the northern Italian staple, cornmeal polenta, with meat reserved for occasional feast days. In an attempt to better their lives, Giovanni built himself a ramshackle workshop where he and a few coworkers made brooms with sorghum grass.[1]

It was probably during bull sessions in the army that Giovanni became interested in politics. Back home, he learned that an increasing number of Italian peasants and workers were joining the Socialist Party, especially in northern Italy, where it was mobilizing against the country's severe postwar economic problems. With soldiers returning from the front, unemployment ballooned to 2 million as they sought jobs. Factory workers were striking and taking over plants; peasants, organized by trade unions and war veterans' groups, were spontaneously occupying the land they worked and threatening landlords. Shopkeepers were hit by looting and riots. The lira plummeted in value, making savings practically worthless. Even the Catholic Left was advocating revolution and leading strikes. These years were the *biennio rosso,* the two Red Years of 1919 and 1920 when Italy seemed on the verge of nationwide insurrection or even revolution.[2]

The Socialists split into hard- and soft-line factions. During a party congress in Livorno, the hard-liners, grouped in the Ordino Nuovo, or New Order, under the radical Marxist theorist and writer Antonio Gramsci, broke away to found the Italian Communist Party on January 15, 1921. This party joined Lenin's Communist International in calling for "struggle by all available means, including armed force, for the overthrow of the international bourgeoisie and the creation of an international Soviet republic."[3] This call resonated with Giovanni's search for more social justice and a better life. He became an active member, creating the party's local cell in Monsummano and distributing propaganda. On May Day, he proudly marched with the red flag, singing the revolutionary anthem "Bandiera rossa." Giuseppina, a pious Catholic, respected his ardent new secular faith, but only so far. She surreptitiously sneaked Ivo out to be baptized by the parish priest.

But not only the Left was organizing for political battle. A former schoolteacher, journalist, and fervent member of the Socialist Party suddenly turned against socialist ideals in the face of Italy's burgeoning postwar problems. As Italy threatened to descend into civil war, Benito Mussolini declared that what it needed was a strong, authoritarian leader to save the country from chaos. In 1919, he created the Fasci di Combattimento, tightly bound militant groups, to advance his ideals, which included some measures that today would be considered democratic socialism, such as an eight-hour workday, the vote for women, and confiscation of war profits. Moving quickly, the Fascists held their first national congress on November 7, 1921, which formally created the Partito Nazionale Fascista.[4]

The party's militias, known as Camicie Nere, or Blackshirts, because of their uniforms, rapidly increased in number. They began strong-arming Socialists and Communists, burning their local offices and harassing or killing party members. In Tuscany alone, their marauding *squadristi* destroyed eleven community centers, fifteen employment exchanges, twenty-four workers' clubs, and seventy Socialist or Communist Party local headquarters. One much-used method to convince recalcitrants to change their politics was to make them drink castor oil, forcing them to vomit and soil themselves until they shouted "Viva Mussolini!" Disciplined squads, claiming to be fighting the Bolsheviks, marched in lockstep through villages, singing "To arms, to arms, Fascists!" After thousands marched on Rome in October 1922,

Mussolini became prime minister, in effect the country's dictator, a post he would hold as the self-proclaimed "Il Duce" until 1943.[5]

Giovanni Livi's active promotion of communism in Monsummano caught the attention of Blackshirt *squadristi.* One night in November 1921 they ambushed him as he was returning home from a Communist Party meeting and horsewhipped him badly. "My mother and I heard him calling for help," Ivo's sister, Lidia, recalled. "Then he appeared. His eyes were starting out of his head. There were purple marks like fat worms all over his face and neck. He looked insane. What shocked him the most was that he had recognized two of his attackers . . . two former fellow Socialists who had joined Mussolini."[6] The harassment continued to make life miserable for the Livis. The Blackshirts returned and burned down the little workshop where Giovanni made brooms. Later on, they summoned him to Fascist headquarters in town and told him that they would be glad to have a man like him on the team. They would even help build a new, better workshop for him. What would he have to do? Just join our night raids.

Giovanni asked for a little time to think it over, but he knew he would never join the Fascists. Despite his communist faith, he, like many Italians of that period, felt that America was a country of freedom where anyone who wanted to work could make a good life. He had often bucked up the family when things were difficult by saying, "Wait until we get to America!" It was time to act on that claim. In early 1924, he called Giuseppina and the children together and announced his decision. He would leave for Marseilles, where he would get his visa to America. It should be easy to find a job in the United States because everybody knew it needed foreign workers for its postwar boom. As of 1920, more than 4 million Italians had passed through Ellis Island and other ports, amounting to fully 10 percent of the country's foreign-born population. Once he was settled—probably in Pittsburgh, where one of Giuseppina's relatives had gone—he would send for them.

Besides a few clothes, Giovanni packed only one other thing: a red-bound copy of Tasso's late-Renaissance poetry he had from his grandfather Carlino. Clandestine travel to France—he had no visa for there, either—would have been difficult in the best of times, entailing as it did crossing the Maritime Alps on foot. Now, in the winter, it meant crossing those Alpine passes and summits, some as high as 10,000 feet, in freezing weather. He borrowed enough lire to buy a third-class train ticket to the border at Ventimiglia. There he paid a smuggler to get him across the mountainous terrain, dodging customs patrols, and down to Marseilles, a trip of some 150 miles. It took him two arduous months to make the trip, arriving in Marseilles in early April. He called on an aunt named Lizena, who had settled there with her husband. They let him sleep on the floor while waiting for his visa and departure on the first America-bound ship.

Then his best-laid plans went awry. When he went to the US consulate, he was told there were no more visas available. He couldn't have known that on April 12, 1924, the US Congress had passed the Immigration Act, also known as the Johnson-Reed Act, establishing a quota system for immigrants. Only 2 percent of the number of persons of any given nationality in the United States (except Asian nations, which were mostly excluded) according to the national census of 1890, were eligible for visas. This act, as one senator proudly claimed, would freeze the racial composition of the nation at its current level. It was to be enforced by creation of the US Border Patrol.[7] As Yves Montand once mused, "By just twenty-four hours, I might have been a De Niro character or a Sinatra from Hoboken."[8]

Undaunted, Giovanni decided to make do with Marseilles. Even if it weren't Pittsburgh, it was at least better and much safer than Monsummano and its Fascist patrols. He stayed on with his aunt and found work as a manual laborer. Meanwhile, life was even worse than before for Giuseppina and the children. Money was scarce, food was still harder to come by, and the *squadristi* were determined to find her husband. Several times they banged on the door in the middle of the night, forced their way in, and ransacked the house looking for letters or anything else that might give them a clue to Giovanni's whereabouts. Even when interrogated by her older brother Luigi Simoni, who had become a Fascist and led a group of *squadristi*, Giuseppina and the children refused to talk.

After receiving a note from Giovanni in May 1924 telling her to join him, she threw a few things into burlap bags, rounded up Lidia, age nine, Giuliano, six, and Ivo, three, and caught the night train to Marseilles (again, probably on borrowed money). At times during the night, Blackshirts roamed through the coaches checking for anyone who might be suspicious. Anticipating this, Giuseppina had Ivo wear a cap that resembled those worn by the militias. The ploy worked: they found this amusing enough to leave the Livis alone. Montand, reflecting later on his family's odyssey, compared it to a Western. "The people who crossed the United States in covered wagons, facing the worst difficulties, became tough and stubborn. . . . [A]ll things being equal, it was the same with Italian peasants, or with peasants anywhere in the

Mediterranean basin: if you weren't very tough you went under. . . . [A]s a small child I learned about oppression, humiliation, struggle, and dignity."[9]

⊙ ⊙ ⊙

Unintentionally, the Livis had plunged into France's Mediterranean melting pot. For centuries, Marseilles had been its door open to the world, welcoming trade, adventurers, and refugees from southern Europe, North and Black Africa, the Middle East and Asia. As it happened, Giovanni and family were joining its largest wave of immigrants of the twentieth century. During the 1920s and 1930s, some 5,000 Greeks seeking opportunity, 20,000 Armenians escaping from the Turkish genocide, and 120,000 Italians fleeing fascism made up nearly 25 percent of the city's total population of 790,000. This ethnic diversity made it something like the New York of France.[10]

It's a role Marseilles has long played. This oldest of France's large cities was a thriving cosmopolitan center when Paris was no more than a village of huts huddled on an island in the Seine. Vestiges of human settlement in Marseilles date back thousands of years. Greek explorers from Phocaea in Asia Minor founded Massalia around 600 BCE; it's possible that Phoenicians had settled there even earlier. The ancient Greeks and Romans praised it, Aristotle observing that it was a democracy with elected officials, while for Cicero it was the Athens of the Gauls. In more recent French history, it rallied to the revolution in 1789. Hundreds of volunteers marched to Paris to support it, singing a martial song that became known as "La marseillaise."

If it was the New York of France, it was also the Chicago of the Al Capone days. Even the ancients tended to look askance at its mores, with the Greek writer Athenaeus noting around the third century that the Marseillais were pusillanimous and given to vice. By the time the Livis arrived in the 1920s, it was a hotbed of criminality dominated by Corsican syndicates, Neapolitan Camorra, and Sicilian Mafia. While the Corsicans held a corrupt city hall and turned a blind eye, the gangs ran trafficking in everything from drugs and guns to women. That made it an appropriate place for the assassination of the Yugoslavian king Alexander I and the French prime minister Jean-Louis Barthou in October 1934, right on La Canebière, the city's main thoroughfare.[11]

Paris might be where romantic films are made, but Marseilles's well-earned reputation for corruption and violence made it a natural setting for thrillers. Such films started with Maurice Tourneur's story of gang warfare among drug traffickers, *Justin de Marseille* (1935), with its location shots showing crime and its high-flying padrones as a part of quotidian life. Jacques Deray's two-hour film *Borsalino* (France and US 1970), about two small-time crooks memorably played by Alain Delon and Jean-Paul Belmondo, is set there, as is Luc Besson's *Taxi* (France and US 1998). Then there are William Friedkin's *The French Connection* (1971) and its sequel, John Frankenheimer's *French Connection II* (1975), both with Gene Hackman as the New York narcotics detective Popeye Doyle, who traces drug smugglers' Marseilles connection. Audiences seemingly couldn't get enough of Marseilles crime films, so Cédric Jimenez directed a sequel of sorts, *La French* (2014, US 2015), with Jean Dujardin as a judge assigned to deal with organized crime there in the 1970s.

The first home Giovanni found after getting a job on the night shift in an olive oil plant was a small tumble-down house in the Verdron-Haut neighborhood well north of the city. It was one of a potpourri of villages that, altogether, spread over an area several times that of Paris. The living quarters were spartan: though there was cold running water in the kitchen sink, packing crates had to serve as furniture. Everybody got used to being hungry constantly. Meals often consisted of a bowl of watered milk with scraps of bread floating in it. When they were lucky, the children would get a fried egg—one for the three of them, which big sister Lidia divided as evenly as possible, with the bits of bread used to soak up the yolky cooking oil. One day Ivo marveled at a watermelon that Giovanni brought home. When it had cooled in a bucket of water, Giovanni pulled it out and ceremoniously sliced it on the packing-crate dining table.

After three years of that, they moved to an apartment in a slum called Les Crottes, near the tough docks area closer to the city. Located between a chemical factory that produced an ill-smelling fertilizer and a drainage ditch full of refuse, it merited its name, which denotes droppings of excrement. Still, it was a lively social scene that gave Ivo his first taste of ethnic Marseilles. Populated by Spaniards, Arabs, Poles, Russians, and of course lots of Italians, it gave him the chance to pick up bits of their languages, phrases that he still could speak as an adult. In the evenings, his parents pulled cane-bottom chairs out into the street to enjoy the cool air and socialize with the neighbors, gossiping and complaining about their often back-breaking jobs. The good news was that Giovanni was starting a little broom business again; the bad news was that it meant he and Giuseppina left the apartment early in the morning to make brooms by hand in the workshop and didn't return until evening, leaving the children alone all day. Lidia grew up fast, assuming much of the responsibility for the household.

Bit by bit, things were looking up for the Livis. The broom business was producing enough revenue to allow another move, this time to the nearby village of La Cabucelle. This neighborhood near the docks was no better, being a labyrinth of wandering streets, alleys, and malodorous rivulets formed by the ad hoc drainage system. Their new address, the impasse des Mûriers, was a dead-end alley surrounded by the sort of operations that no one wants in their backyard: a chemical depot, a slaughterhouse, a soap factory, and a garbage-treatment plant. But it was a four-room house of sorts with the luxury of a small patch of grass in front, a washroom on the ground floor, and bedrooms upstairs. The neighbors were mostly Italian, with an admixture of Greeks, Maltese, Levantines, and still more Armenians. The latter were so numerous that they built an Armenian church that still stands in the neighborhood.

Relations were not always cordial. Ivo got used to being called a dirty Macaroni, a Mussolini, and other racist slurs. But there were compensations, such as the nearby sea. Ivo's first childhood memory was of holding tight to his big brother's hand as he stared, mesmerized, at a great expanse of brilliant blue where enormous ships moved majestically amid a forest of cranes; later he would learn that it was the Old Port, the beating heart of Marseilles then as now.

⊙ ⊙ ⊙

Also, good news came in early 1929. When Giovanni opened the letter from Paris, he found a reason for celebration: the Livis had been granted French nationality. Ivo was a French citizen at the age of eight.

2

Amateur Night

He had started school, at least nominally, for he mentally wasn't there. Ivo, bored to tears as the teacher expounded on something like the Paris Commune of 1871, developed a technique for getting through the school day. He would sit with his gaze fixed on the teacher, apparently listening intently, while he gave free rein to his mind to wander far and wide. One day a baffled teacher came to the Livi house to explain Ivo's bad grades. "He pays attention, no doubt about that," he told Lidia. "But he understands nothing, nothing at all." Giovanni took up the question when he got home, trying to convince his son of the importance of education if he didn't want to end up as poor as he was.[1]

That didn't work. Soon Ivo was playing hooky, heading in the morning for the Old Port a few hundred yards away as soon as he was out of his parents' sight. He preferred getting his education amid the swarming activity of the docks, dreaming of the open sea, planning to slip aboard a ship bound for America. He couldn't manage that, but with other young ruffians he found opportunities to steal fresh produce such as bananas, oranges, and spices. When trucks laden with unrefined sugar lumbered away, they ran alongside, stabbing holes in the burlap bags and scooping up the sugar as it spilled out. When not at the docks, Ivo and friends played what they called the tunnel game: entering a railway tunnel just before a train and running through it with the locomotive fast gaining on them. One slip or misstep, and they would finish under the train's wheels. As an adult, Montand identified with James Dean as his car raced toward the cliff in *Rebel without a Cause*.

Came the Great Depression, and the fun ended. The Wall Street crash of 1929 took two years to hit France, but when it did, it hit hard. Bankrupt businesses laid off workers, filling the streets with jobless men, many of whom blamed immigrants, in particular Italians, for stealing French jobs. Giovanni's business went bust in 1932. That left him unable to reimburse the 15,000 francs (about $600) he had borrowed in 1931 to buy a machine to produce more brooms, plus other sums loaned by friends and acquaintances. With his total debt amounting to 32,000 francs (about $1,280) and little or no revenue in sight, everyone had to contribute to the family finances. Giuliano went to work as a bartender on the docks. Lidia had been cutting friends' hair at home for a few francs; now she took a course in hairdressing and opened a little makeshift salon in a corner of the living room.

As for Ivo, he quit school definitively at eleven and, big for his age and lying about his birthdate, found a job in a pasta factory. He stuffed vermicelli, macaroni, and spaghetti into cellophane bags ten hours a day for 50 francs (about $2) a week. After several months at that, he was switched to deliveries, making the rounds in a truck, carrying heavy bags of pasta on his back, downing the glasses of strong, anis-flavored pastis occasionally offered by storekeepers. Already showing signs of the explosive temper that would be one of his troublesome traits as an adult, he had a row with the boss one day and got fired.

Fortunately, Lidia's little salon was doing well—even if customers often paid in eggs, meat, and potatoes—and she had a growing clientele. She took on Ivo to help with shampooing. It wasn't much of a job, but it had its fringe benefits. As he washed the women's hair, they threw their heads back and gave him a plunging view down their décolleté. Even better was when he scrambled on the floor picking up hairpins, letting him sneak a view up their dresses. He credited those visions of forbidden pleasure, plus eavesdropping on intimate female conversations about their love lives, with being his first impromptu lessons in sex education.

Having developed a taste for the work, he went to hair-dressing school, got his professional diploma, and was hired by a big salon, Chez Yvonne et Fernand, on rue Pavillon, near the port. (As an adult, he could tell instantly whether a politician or entertainer on television had dyed hair.) There, most of the clientele were prostitutes who worked the port area. Their uninhibited conversations about their trade and the quirks of their customers continued his sex education and added to the pleasure of the job. It was beginning to look as if, at sixteen, he had found his lifelong vocation.

Moreover, the adolescent Ivo, now known as Yves to be more French (Lidia also became Lydia, and Giuliano was Julien) had fallen in love. Not with Bruna, the pretty, flirtatious waitress in an Italian-owned café just down the street from home, on whom he had had a juvenile unrequited crush. This time it was real passion, one that cost him every spare franc he had; he even economized on his transport budget, walking three miles to the salon every morning rather than taking a streetcar. "I fell into movie madness the way you fall in love," he once explained. "Just like that, a chance encounter that seemed of no importance at the time. Movies were an open door on a world full of hope, where the heroes were in a state of contagious euphoria." He spent all his free time at the Star, a little theater where American films were projected in the undubbed original version. He was so crazy about them that one day he deliberately burned a hand with a curling iron at the salon so he could take the rest of the day off and head to the Star.[2]

He could have been watching some of the great French classics, such as Julien Duvivier's *Pépé le Moko* (1937, US 1941), Jean Renoir's *La grande illusion / Grand Illusion* (1937, US 1938), Marcel Carné's *Le quai des brumes / Port of Shadows* (1938, US 1939), or many others of the country's golden age of cinema. But he instead fell for Gloria Swanson, Clara Bow, Greta Garbo. He tried to imitate the male virility of Humphrey Bogart and Gary Cooper. He gorged on films such as William Wyler's *Dead End* (1937) with Joel McCrea and Sylvia Sydney; Michael Curtiz's *Angels with Dirty Faces* (1938) with James Cagney, Pat O'Brien, and the Dead End Kids; and William Keighley's *The Right to Live* (1935) with Josephine Hutchinson and George Brent. Above all, he wondered at the way Fred Astaire seemed to float when he danced with Ginger Rogers in *Top Hat* and *Roberta* (both 1935). He spent a few francs for tap-dancing lessons from an Armenian, who taught him to use not only his feet but his whole body.

He had to admit that he was a long way from looking like Bogart or Cooper. At seventeen, he was over six feet tall, with long skinny arms and legs and narrow shoulders. He was still smarting from the taunting he had received at school, where they called him Bouche (Mouth) because of his thick lips and wide mouth and little girls had mocked him and laughed at his big nose and ears. That had convinced him early on that he was hopelessly ugly. Now, as a gawky adolescent, he hated even to see himself in a mirror at the salon. Almost pathologically shy, he avoided meeting new people. When he took a streetcar, he would stand outside on the platform rather than take a seat inside, the better to avoid being looked at. Not the least of this young introvert's paradoxes was that, despite his painful shyness, he dreamed of a career as an actor on the big screen.

⊙ ⊙ ⊙

His start in show business was unexpected, roundabout, and had nothing to do with acting. It was due to a neighborhood candy vendor named Francis Trottobas, known locally as "Berlingot" because he sold sugary, colored bonbons by that name from a cart at street markets and fairs. He was a flamboyant, exuberant type with a mouth full of gold teeth, who liked to organize Saturday amateur nights outside a café near the Livi house. It was a jerry-rigged poor-man's music hall. The stage was fashioned from planks laid on trestles, sacks and tarpaulins served as the curtain, a corner of the café was the dressing room, lights on the ground provided faint illumination for the acts. If the entertainment wasn't professional quality, it was at least highly varied, ranging from singers of operetta to comics, storytellers to flamenco dancers and contortionists. A few of the night's amateurs found enough favor with the rowdy, beer-drinking audience to merit applause. Most received jeers and derisive whistles for their stammering efforts.

One summer evening in 1938, Yves and Julien were leaning out their bedroom window watching the show when Yves sneered at a youngster's efforts to sing. Big Brother Julien, annoyed, retorted that if he was so smart, why didn't he try it himself? Yves had never sung anything beyond choral numbers at school. Besides, he wanted to be an actor, not a singer. But he was stung by the challenge. Like most people in the neighborhood, he had a nodding acquaintance with Trottobas. They agreed that he would choose two or three songs for an act, popular things from Charles Trenet that he already knew by heart, and go take a few lessons from a music teacher in Marseilles whom Trottobas knew, Marguerite Fancelli.

The choice of songs was easy, the first music lesson a humiliation. With the severe, gray-haired Madame Fancelli sitting in audience and her daughter Mado at the piano, he launched into his first song, only to realize after the first few measures that he knew absolutely nothing about singing technique. He staggered on, Madame Fancelli rolling her eyes until she heard him out. The verdict: he sang off-key, he couldn't keep time, and she didn't understand a word he was saying. Did he really want to be a singer? Seeing his disappointment, she tempered her critique and encouraged him to practice at home. Being big gave him a certain presence, at least he knew the words, and he was clearly burning with ambition. The important things were to articulate clearly and to sing, as she put it, with his heart in his mouth, sincerely.

Soon he was going to her regularly for free lessons, taking meals there, and dating Mado on the side. Sometimes he slept in Lydia's salon, where he could rehearse his singing and Donald Duck routine in front of a mirror until three or four in the morning. When he spent the night in the bedroom he shared with Julien, he kept him awake practicing his Fred Astaire tap dancing. Seeing his protégé's progress, Trottobas told him to find a better stage name than "Yves Livi," something that would look good on music hall programs and posters. His own awkward suggestion was "Yves Trechenel," composed from "TREnet," "CHEvalier," and "FernandEL." Yves countered with something that he remembered from his childhood, when his mother called him up to dinner in Italian: "Ivo, monta!" He would be Yves Montand.

His first performance was set for a September evening. By then, Trottobas had located a vest-pocket theater with a few dozen seats in the Vallon des Tuves quarter north of the city center. Montand selected five numbers for his act—two by Trenet, one by Chevalier, one by Fernandel, and a Donald Duck imitation—the idea being that their variety would prevent monotony and show his range. He rejected his first notion of wearing something wildly colorful and eccentric in favor of a conservative gray suit, white shirt, blue tie, and blue-and-white shoes. He glued a gob of white paste over a broken front tooth and waited in the dressing room for his cue in a sweating state of utter panic, his legs buckling, his face ghostly pale. He begged Trottobas to let him off, announce that he was sick, anything to avoid facing that audience in the dark that was sure to laugh at him.

Afterward, he barely remembered going on stage. He had performed in a benumbed trance, but somehow he had done it. The loud applause, and Trottobas's lavish praise, proved that his first try at being an entertainer was a success. But it had come at a surprising cost. As he mused years later, "Singing looked like a good way of getting ahead by doing what you enjoyed. But nobody had told me about the terrible pain that went with it, churning your bowels, making you nauseated, the panic that dries your throat, makes your legs wobble, paralyzes you. There are no words to convey that pain. And no cure for it."[3]

No cure either for the show business virus that now infected him. There was, after all, the easy money—Trottobas gave him 50 francs (about $2) a show, not much but enough to keep him in cigarettes and impress his parents as he spread the banknotes out on the kitchen table. He would never shampoo another head or clip a lock of hair. Acting as his manager, Trottobas got him gigs at local movie houses as intermission entertainment, including as a special attraction at the Ritz cinema near the Old Port at Christmas 1938: "A magnificent movie, Clark Gable and Myrna Loy in *Test Pilot,*" blared the poster, "and during intermission, by popular demand, Yves Montand, accompanied by Mlle Mado Fancelli."[4] After following that up during the spring of 1939 with more performances at little theaters all around the city, he was ready for the Alcazar.

The 2,000-seat theater just off La Canebière was known as nothing less than Marseilles's music hall temple. Built in 1857 in a lavish Moorish style reminiscent of the Alhambra palace in Grenada, the Alcazar was where you had to make it if you wanted to become a professional entertainer. A seventeen-year-old Maurice Chevalier had auditioned there in 1905; Tino Rossi, Fernandel, and many others synonymous with French entertainment had sought the applause of the Alcazar's notoriously irreverent, hard-to-please audiences. There was a saying in the business: if you can sing at the Alcazar, you can sing anywhere. For Montand, the test was to come on the evening of June 21, 1939. "When we heard he was going to appear at the Alcazar, the whole family shook in its boots," recalled Elvire, Julien's fiancée. "For a beginner, the Alcazar was terrifying."[5]

On that first day of summer, it was a Marseilles tradition to hold a talent show for amateur and young professional entertainers at the Alcazar. This year it featured the usual lineup of monologists, tap dancers, mimes, and contortionists but also, the posters announced, "the light-hearted mimic and singer Yves Montand." Preparing his act with the meticulous attention to detail that would be the hallmark of his career, he went to see Charles Humel, a blind composer who lived in Marseilles, for some fresh material. Remembering all the Westerns he had seen at the Star, Montand told him he wanted something about cowboys in the American West. The result was a ditty called "Dans les plaines du Far West" about cowpokes around a campfire singing of "their beautiful Texas." It was a risky departure from the usual crooner fare at the Alcazar. To put it over, Montand used some instinctive showmanship. He found a wide-brimmed hat and painted it white, put on a checked shirt and neck scarf, and walked on stage on the outside edge of his shoes, making him look bandy-legged, as if he had just spent a hard day on horseback.

The audience loved it. He took two bows, and they called for more, but, having nothing else for an encore, he retreated to his dressing room to enjoy his success.

> All I wanted was to be alone with myself and savor that incredible reception. That was the moment when I said to myself: This is what I want to do. There is no more reason for it not to work. My fear had gone, and it was easier to think straight after the event. My

> manager, with typical Mediterranean exuberance, was raving. I had "knocked them flat," Trottobas kept saying. "Do you hear me? Knocked them flat!" But I was still worried. Had I really climbed onto that stage and taken on that audience? I couldn't sleep all that night. I kept wondering if the guy who had sung was really me.[6]

It was, indeed, and his triumph at the Alcazar made him much in demand all that summer at movie houses and small theaters in the region. By October, he had signed his first show business contract. It guaranteed him about $2 a day—with a 10 percent commission going to Trottobas as his agent—for eighteen days to do three songs and one imitation every evening and matinees. Rail transportation in third class for him and his baggage was provided, though the contract could be suspended in case of floods, wars, or epidemics. That was a good contract, but it blithely overlooked the fact that France had just gone to war with Germany.

Montand, entirely concentrated on his budding career, might be forgiven for ignoring the German invasion of Poland on September 1, 1939, which triggered French and British declarations of war against Germany on September 3. No one in France was ready to die for Dantzig. There followed nearly ten months of what everybody called the "phony war." The French were assured by their generals that they were safe behind the impregnable Maginot Line, defended by an 800,000-man standing army, thought to be the most potent in Europe. Life went on almost normally. People still wanted to be entertained by an eighteen-year-old phenomenon billed as "the revelation of the year" in a revue called *Un soir de folie*. The *Crazy Evening* road show had dates all over the region, from Istres to Saint Rémy, Orange to Sète.

Then in May and June of 1940, the French learned a new word: *blitzkrieg*.

The German army simply went around the northern end of the Maginot Line. They struck through Belgium and the Somme with a combination of fast, mobile panzer divisions and dive-bombing Luftwaffe Stukas, their eerie sirens howling. The French army disintegrated in the face of the mechanized onslaught. On June 10, the National Assembly voted to abolish itself and, at the same time, the Third Republic. Two days later, Premier Paul Reynaud broadcast a call to Parisians to flee as fast as they could; Paris was declared an open city to avoid bombardment as the first German troops entered it without resistance.

Eighty-four-year-old Marshal Philippe Pétain, the heralded hero of the Battle of Verdun in the First World War, who declared in his dotage that "what I have really loved in my life were infantry and love-making," replaced Reynaud as head of government.[7] His first move was to sign an armistice with Germany on June 22, allowing it to occupy northern and eastern France, with a new capital established in the spa city of Vichy. It hardly seemed to matter that a little-known general named Charles de Gaulle had issued a plea from his new base in London on June 18 to all Frenchmen to join him in a resistance movement. A pitiful few did so. In Marseilles, a Resistance leader named Henri Frenay was disheartened when he saw how little his countrymen were inclined to fight back. "The general drift of French public opinion was profoundly disappointing," he remembered. "Aside from the few friends whom we recruited, there was not a hint of the spirit of revolt. People had made themselves comfortable in defeat just as they would have done in victory."[8]

That criticism applied to Montand, as it did to the vast majority of his compatriots. The country had been bled white by the slaughter of 1914–1918. Now its people were disgusted with their feckless leaders of the *entre deux guerres*. The reaction was simply to accept defeat—when they didn't actively collaborate with their conquerors. As the caustic writer André Gide noted in his diary, "Oh incurably frivolous people of France! You are going to pay dearly for your lack of application, your heedlessness, your smug lolling among so many charming virtues."[9]

3

"I Discover My Career"

Of the millions of civilians who began the mass exodus starting in June 1940 from Belgium, northern France, and then Paris, as many as 150,000 sought refuge in Marseilles, hugely increasing its population of 650,000. In August, the American literary journalist Varian Fry arrived in the city with $3,000 in cash strapped to his legs to set up an operation funded by the American Emergency Rescue Committee in New York. Its goal was to try to help the escape to the United States of mainly German and Austrian intellectuals and artists as well as wealthy Jews from Paris under threat of deportation to Germany by Marshal Pétain's puppet regime. With local newspapers calling attention to his operation, Fry and his Centre américain de secours were quickly inundated by requests for help; within a few months he had taken on 1,800 cases concerning 4,000 persons.[1] As the Russian poet and novelist Victor Serge, who lived in Belgium and France after being ostracized for his criticism of Soviet policy, noted on his arrival in Marseilles, "In our ranks are enough doctors, psychologists, engineers, educationalists, poets, painters, writers, musicians, economists and public men to vitalize a whole great country."[2]

Fry's group helped these people by getting them to Portbou on the Spanish border and then, if they could procure Spanish transit visas, across the Pyrenees to Barcelona, Madrid, and Lisbon, where they boarded ships for America. Among those who got out were the German novelist Heinrich Mann, the psychiatrist Bruno Strauss, the Nobel laureate in medicine Otto Meyerhof, the writer Hannah Arendt, and the harpsichordist Wanda Landowska. However, some refused Fry's help. Gertrude Stein and her companion, Alice B. Toklas, both Jews, decided to stay put in France, as did André Gide, Henri Matisse, and André Malraux.

Others who might have sought to escape, in particular show business people, found the good life on the Riviera instead. The actress Michèle Morgan, for example, had a contract with RKO and could have left for the United States when she wanted but decided to join friends for some fun in Cannes. "It was like a vacation," she recalled. "Swimming, tennis, cycling around town, and at the hotel in the evening we joked around like college students, laughing, shouting, dancing and improvising operas. . . . We needed to erase, to wash out the filth of the defeat, the world of our elders. The present helped us forget our fear of having no future."[3] Her friend Danielle Darrieux, also a prominent actress, put it succinctly: "We were very young, very pretty and fashionable stars, and we didn't give a damn about what was happening up north."[4] Rare indeed were the French stars such as Jean Gabin, who saw combat as a tank commander with the Free French; Raymond Aimos, who did more than one hundred films in the 1930s and died during the liberation of Paris; and Jean-Pierre Aumont, who fought with the Resistance in the South of France. Most fled to freedom or reached an accommodation with the Nazis and enjoyed a comfortable life.

Montand wasn't so lucky even though he evinced remarkably little interest in his adopted country's tragic situation. Unlike Julien, who was drafted into the army, captured, and spent several years as a prisoner of war in Germany, he made no attempt at any form of resistance to the Nazis. Still, he had to face the unpleasant fact that suddenly there was no more demand for what he did. His singing career abruptly halted; he had to find other employment to support himself and help with family finances. In May 1940, he hired on as an assistant boilermaker at the Marseilles shipyard Chantiers & Ateliers de Provence.

For a song-and-dance man, this job was a brutal introduction to the world of harsh, grimy factory work. His task was to help make buoys to anchor undersea cables. He had to squeeze his six-foot frame into three-by-nine-foot cylinders and, squatting, hammer them into final shape from the inside. Rusty dust flew as he hammered at the steel, making him cough when it entered his lungs. As an antidote, he had to drink milk, lots of it. It was small comfort that his company ID card gave him the right to a special rate on Marseilles tramways on Sundays and holidays. Yet instead of detesting the job, Montand felt for the first time that he was actually doing something useful, that he was part of the comradeship of the working class felt by his father. "In ancient times, it would have been the work of slaves," he recalled. "But it was there that I discovered the feeling of solidarity and human warmth with others, those who have to earn a living with so little money and so much effort."[5]

France's capitulation and armistice with Germany at least had the effect of freeing Montand from a job that might have resulted in lung disease. Defense production at the shipyard halted, and he was laid off, joining many others that summer standing in line for the dole. After a few months of that, he went back to his former playground, the docks, but this time as a longshoreman. At nineteen, he was still skinny and lanky, and the work involved the sort of heavy lifting he had never done. He began to fill out in his shoulders, back, and legs, developing the lithe, muscular physique that would become an important part of his stage presence later. He also learned the dockers' techniques of keeping his back straight, walking smoothly, and breathing evenly to keep the load carefully balanced. These techniques, too, were to serve him well. Whether on stage or in film, he moved only his legs, keeping his upper body still. As Catherine Deneuve, who made two films with him, said, "No one moved on a movie set like Montand."[6]

France's situation as a noncombatant and its division into the German-occupied North and the relatively free Vichy France of the South also had its advantages for Marseilles. The city went back to living much as before, with cinemas and theaters again open and filled with a public that craved whatever amusement and distractions it could get. The enterprising Francis Trottobas, seeing a window of opportunity after the first shock of war wore off in southern France, got Montand off the docks and back on stage with a lineup of engagements in Marseilles and the surrounding region. The self-styled bandy-legged cowboy in the white hat was back on "les plaines du Far West."

⊙ ⊙ ⊙

It may fairly be said that Yves Montand's career as an entertainer really began that spring of 1941. With one brief exception due to the war, it would not pause for the next fifty years.

Now he started on an intense three months of touring in the South of France, doing his cowboy number, tap dancing, miming, and singing his versions of Trenet and Chevalier numbers to increasing applause and critical notice. Spelling his new last name with a final *t,* perhaps as a play on the word *montant,* "rising," the important local show business magazine *Artistica* described him as "a born mimic. Just 19, tall, likable, a sharp dresser, energetic and adaptable, this excellent variety artist has a wide range of perfect imitations. One of the best of our tap dancers, Yves Montant is climbing the ladder to stardom with giant strides."[7] He was convinced that this time he was on his way.

He began keeping a scrapbook of clippings. On the first page he wrote: "I began one evening in 1938, what stage fright . . . but what satisfaction, what joy, I finally discover my career, my real life! What will it bring? But what I didn't know was that it's a career of hard work, determination, and above all, above all, constant renewal. My only consolation, despite numerous obstacles, is to have been successful so far. But what does the future hold?"[8] To keep improving, he took dance lessons from an old teacher said to have been a member of the Saint Petersburg Ballet before the Bolshevik Revolution; he would work at the barre all his life to keep limber.

He was soon back at the Alcazar for a second consecration. He was noticed by Émile Audiffred, one of France's best-known impresarios and agent for major stars such as Josephine Baker, Maurice Chevalier, Fernandel, Mistinguett, and Edith Piaf. When Audiffred approached him with an exclusive contract, Montand quickly dumped Trottobas and signed on July 1, 1941. Immediately he began doing warm-up acts for music hall stars such as Rina Ketty, who had recorded the popular song "J'attendrai," the Second World War French equivalent of "We'll Meet Again" in Britain or "Lili Marleen" in Germany. In October, Audiffred put together a big three-hour show with fifteen acts, of which Montand, for the first time, was the star, on stage for fully thirty minutes. "You like Gary Cooper or Maurice Chevalier?," asked the master of ceremonies. "Well, tonight we offer you something even better, a genuine theater bombshell: Yves Montand!"[9]

That promising year almost saw even the start of a movie career.

Marcel Pagnol, the bard of Provence who described the region's rich character and traditions in Marseilles-centered novels and films such as *Marius* (1931), *Fanny* (1932), and *César* (1936) gave Montand a walk-on role in his film *La prière aux étoiles* in mid-1941. But before Pagnol could finish filming, Joseph Goebbels, Hitler's culture czar, heard of it and demanded he do it for the German-controlled French production company Continental Films, the only one authorized to make films under the Occupation. Established in October 1940, Continental Films was bankrolled entirely by the German government, its finances, production, and distribution integrated with the German film industry. Any French actor or director who did films for it represented a great propaganda coup for the Germans and for Vichy. A few refused to work for Continental Films—for example, Jean Gabin, who turned down an offer even when the studio proposed to free a nephew who was then a prisoner in Germany. Pagnol, too, refused. He pretended that the rolls of film he had used for *La prière aux étoiles* were of bad quality, and he was going to destroy them. Goebbels insisted on seeing him do it. Pagnol duly took a hatchet and hacked the offending rolls to pieces as Goebbels watched. That was the end of the project and with it Montand's first chance to act in a film—but the loss of this role saved him from the dishonor of working for the enemy.[10]

Vichy laws passed in January 1941 requiring all twenty-year-old males to perform service in work camps interrupted Montand's quick climb to stardom. The Chantiers de la jeunesse (Youth Work Camps) were a disguised way of replacing the draft, which had ended because of the Occupation, with a sort of Boy Scout organization designed to inculcate the Pétainist values of *travail, famille, patrie* (work, family, country) that had replaced France's traditional values *liberté, égalité, fraternité.* With paramilitary-style discipline and wearing uniforms, the young men were to do public-service work such as road maintenance, forestry, and the like. Montand was assigned to the Culture and Music section, whose task was to entertain the troops with improvised shows in the evening.

He reported to the camp on marshland near Hyères, about fifty miles east of Marseilles, in mid-March 1942 for eight months of futility and boredom. He did little actual singing for his comrades besides the "Marseillaise." He spent his days learning parade-ground drills and doing plenty of push-ups, his nights fighting off mosquitos and bedbugs in the spartan wooden huts that served as barracks. The only danger he faced came one day when he was summoned to the commandant's office with three others. The officer asked suspiciously about his name being "Levy": Surely he must be Jewish? Montand corrected the record: it was "Livi." Luckily for him, the officer accepted this. The three others, Jews, were never seen again in the camp.

Released from the Chantiers in November, Montand went back to his show with bigger billing and better fees than ever. But life was about to change for the worse for Marseilles. With the Allied invasion of North Africa on November 8, Hitler abrogated the terms of the armistice with Pétain and ordered the occupation of France's southern zone. The city would learn what it was like to live under ruthless Nazi military governance until its liberation in August 1944 by US and French troops in Operation Dragoon. Launched on the Riviera near Saint Tropez by General Dwight Eisenhower, that operation quickly routed the German troops ordered to defend Marseilles to the last man.

On orders from Waffen SS chief Heinrich Himmler in Berlin, assiduously pursuing Hitler's Final Solution, the Germans' first move as occupiers of southern France was to search out and arrest all Jews, including the many who had fled there from Paris and the North. The infamous Marseilles Roundup of January 1943 was shamefully carried out on the orders of René Bousquet, the chief of the Vichy government's own police. Operation Sultan, as it was called, was supervised on the spot by SS major general Karl Oberg, known as the "Butcher of Paris" for organizing the mass arrest and deportation of more than 13,000 Jews in the notorious Vélodrome d'Hiver Roundup in Paris in July 1942.

On January 23, beginning at dawn, 12,000 French police and gendarmes cordoned off the Panier district near the Old Port with barbed wire and armored vehicles and started checking everyone's identity papers. By the end of the day, 6,000 persons had been arrested. Of the 1,642 culled for deportation, including Roma, homosexuals, undocumented immigrants, vagabonds, and anyone else the Nazis considered undesirable, nearly 800 Jews were sent to death camps at Sobibor in Poland and Sachsenhausen in Germany.[11]

But to be complete, Operation Sultan had to rid Marseilles of what Oberg declared was "a lair of international bandits . . . the canker of Europe."[12] The Germans believed that the Panier, Marseilles's oldest quarter, known for its criminal hideouts and numerous brothels in its narrow, twisting streets, was also home to members of the Resistance. On January 3, Resistance attacks at two hotels and a brothel had killed several German soldiers. Oberg, incensed, announced that the neighborhood would have to be purged. The cleanup was radical. Twenty-five thousand persons were expulsed from the district with whatever belongings they could carry, and for the next nine days some 1,500 buildings were systematically dynamited, emitting clouds of billowing dust and hordes of fleeing rats.[13]

Then or later, Montand never showed any sign that he was affected by all this. Yet it was impossible for him not to know what was happening, with his parents still living in La Cabucelle, not far from the Panier district. His father was participating in the Resistance by clandestinely printing and distributing anti-Nazi propaganda prepared by his communist comrades, who spearheaded the Resistance after Hitler violated the Nazi–Soviet Nonaggression Pact and attacked the Soviet Union in 1941. Julien was doing forced labor in a German aircraft plant. But Montand unhesitatingly went back to his road show. His mind was on developing his career—and on girls. "I had no regular girlfriend, no stable relationship," he recalled. "Naturally, I met girls when I was on tour. It was wartime, I was just twenty, I was beginning to enjoy a bit of a reputation, and I took advantage of it. I sang in one club called Maxim's, where I met a wonderful blonde. Another time, in Cannes I remember, there was a gorgeous, warm-hearted lady announcer in fishnet stockings."[14]

When some suggested that he ought to join the Resistance fighters known as maquis in the hills around Saint Raphael, he claimed he didn't understand what that was all about, that for him the word *maquis* simply meant the fragrant, heatherlike vegetation of Provence and Corsica. Forming battalions in the hills of Provence sounded to him "like the movies." (In fact, American commanders later praised the maquis fighters for having made the invasion of southern France one of the most successful Allied campaigns of the war.) "I had no wish to go and hide in the hills. I was singing. It was going well, and I wanted to keep on doing it."[15] Montand was a lover, not a fighter.

His behavior during that catastrophic period in his adopted country's history raises difficult questions. Instead of concentrating exclusively on his singing career, should he have served in the French army, as Julien did? Joined the underground Resistance fighting the Nazi occupier, as many patriotic young men and women did? Made the clandestine trip to London to heed Charles de Gaulle's call to form the Free French? Given the complexity of his situation in the prevailing chaos of war, it would be presumptuous to cast the first stone. Suffice it to say that this does not appear to have been Montand's finest hour. It is not impossible that some residue of guilt about this period helps explain his passionate stands against totalitarianism later in life.

In any case, there was no way he could escape entirely the dangers of life under the Occupation. As Hitler tightened his grip on France in the face of Allied advances, the Vichy government decreed in February 1943 that all men older than eighteen report for Service du travail obligatoire (STO, Compulsory Labor Service) for the Third Reich. Within a few months, more than 600,000 men would be forced to perform this compulsory labor service for the Nazi war effort under the STO program, many of them never returning home. In September, Montand answered a summons to appear before a selection board in its office at the train station to learn where he would be sent. He showed up, thinking it was only a first contact to discuss his situation, and was stunned by the immediate decision: he was assigned to the salt mines of Silesia at Wieliczka, southern Poland.

He was herded into a holding center at the station with other conscripts to await their train to the East. When he didn't return home, Lydia, fearing the worst, worked her contacts from the hairdressing salon to meet a local politico, a collaborationist with ties to the Kommandantur (Commander's Office) of Marseilles. The politico got her an urgent appointment with a German officer there who, after checking Montand's nationality papers and looking over the copious press clippings about him that Lydia had brought, signed off on letting him go free after six days in the holding center. It was a close call, and not the last for Montand. A few weeks later, French and German police began nighttime house-to-house searches to catch STO dodgers. They forced their way into the house in La Cabucelle, but by sheer luck they overlooked the door half-hidden by a quickly drawn curtain that led to the room where he was hiding. When interrogated about her son, Giuseppina said he was away somewhere doing a show; she didn't know exactly where.

With the clampdown on occupied Marseilles tightening, his situation as, essentially, a draft dodger was becoming more untenable by the day. His identity papers showed that he had not done his STO duty. Any French policeman or German soldier in the street could see this during a routine check and arrest him on the spot. It was then that Montand had another of the many lucky breaks that would distinguish his life and his career.

Émile Audiffred thought his protégé had proved himself in the provinces and was ready for the big time. In centralized France, that could only mean Paris, which sucked the artistic and intellectual oxygen out of every other city, large or small. As one of the country's top agents, Audiffred was able to obtain a prize contract for the relatively unknown provincial entertainer named Yves Montand to perform at the ABC, then one of the most famous music halls in the capital. It was a tremendous opportunity and a highly risky one.

In effect, it meant that he, a criminal in the eyes of the Nazi occupier, would be hiding out in broad daylight or, rather, in the glare of Parisian footlights. Having left his family and their warm support for the first time, he would be alone in unknown territory, with no friends and, given his spendthrift ways, with very little money in his pocket despite his recent big fees. After discussing the idea with the family, who were both fearful that the venture could end in a fiasco—or worse—and hopeful that it was his big chance, he decided to go for it. A skeptical Giovanni told him to give it six months; if he flopped, he could always come back home and take a real job, like at a factory. With the heedlessness of youth, a few francs in his pocket, and a change of clothing in a cheap cardboard suitcase, he went to the Saint Charles station and bought a third-class ticket on the night train to Paris. One way.

4

Edith

It was an awkward, disoriented provincial who got off the train at the Gare de Lyon on the morning of February 17, 1944. He found a room at a cheap, Greek-owned hotel near Montmartre. Montand had barely had time to unpack when he was startled by a banging on the door. The two uniformed members of the Feldgendarmerie military police he faced demanded his papers. As the flustered Montand pretended to search for them in his pockets, the Greek owner came rushing up to the room and, with arm-waving Mediterranean volubility and in a nearly incomprehensible mix of pidgin French and broken German, explained at eye-glazing length that this was his cousin. The youngster had just arrived in Paris to help him with the hotel and, of course—wink-wink, nudge-nudge—have a little fun in the big city. The police, bored and lubricated with numerous glasses of cognac on the house, finally threw up their hands and left.

Following a turbulent night during which Montand repulsed a drunk who claimed he had taken his room and ministered to a waif who knocked at random on his door after being beaten by her lover, he set out to explore the city. The first problem was to master the Metro. The Paris subway is a marvel of engineering and intelligent layout dating from the Paris World's Fair of 1900; on it, you can go nearly everywhere in the city with one ticket and a maximum of two changes. It is, however, a labyrinth of interconnecting tunnels where you can easily get lost. The names of the stations, too, make little sense until you know the city's geography. Montand therefore spent part of his first day in Paris learning the Metro map and the names of the stations, riding and walking miles through the system, carefully noting Abbesses to Anvers, Barbés to Bourse. The last train he caught was to the station Bonne Nouvelle, the closest to 11, boulevard Poissonière, where he got off and checked in at the ABC music hall.

Created in 1934 by the Rumanian-born impresario Mitty Goldin, who named it that so it would be listed first in newspaper show rubrics, the 1,200-seat ABC was one of Paris's premier entertainment palaces, along with the Casino de Paris, the Folies Bergère, the Lido, and the Bobino. It was here that Edith Piaf became a star in 1937, followed by other big-name singers such as Charles Trenet, Jean Sablon, Tino Rossi, Les Frères Jacques, and Patachou. It could have been an intimidating place to start for a young newcomer to Paris, whom the theater's personnel called everything from "Jacques Morand" to "Yves Montana," but he plunged into rehearsal that first afternoon. His act was scheduled for the bottom of the program, after performances by the popular operetta singer André Dassary, the peppy actress Betty Spell, and variety numbers ranging from the Renati Clowns to the Gasty Acrobats.

When his cue came, he bounded on stage in a splashy maroon-and-red jacket and yellow polka-dot tie of dubious taste and launched into a new song, "Je m'en fous" (I Don't Give a Damn), a sort of Bronx cheer to all the difficulties of life under the Occupation. He followed this up with a tap-dance number, during which he couldn't help noticing with a pang of panic that many in the audience were getting up and leaving. (He later learned that they were afraid of missing the last metro home before curfew.) He quickly went into the wings, grabbed his white cowboy hat, and came back bandy-legged to keep on doggedly with "Dans les plaines du Far West."

Suddenly patrons stopped making for the exit and began to sit down. He did another song about America, "Il sortit son revolver" (He Took out His Revolver), about Chicago thugs, sprinkling it with what he hoped sounded like American slang: "Hello boys," "Oh baby, oh sweetheart," "Oh man, I got the blues." When he finished, there was disconcerting silence for a heart-stopping moment. When the applause finally came, it was thunderous. Here was someone actually singing about America, right under the noses of the Nazi occupiers, many of them sitting in the audience. He hadn't planned it that way, but the audience saw Montand as someone who was doing something refreshingly daring, different, and rebellious. It was the first time they had seen that since June 1940.

That was what alarmed the German Propaganda-Staffel, whose job, besides Nazi propaganda, was censorship of the arts to ensure that there was nothing on show in France and especially in Paris that might be considered subversive to the values of the Third Reich. The next day, they called him on the carpet at their main offices at 52, avenue des Champs-Élysées and strongly recommended that he stop singing those "American" songs. And while he was at it, it would be wise to eliminate the Yankee slang. It was just a suggestion, of course, but since he seemed to like the West so much, maybe he could sing some Mexican cowboy songs. Then they sent him on his way, free to get on with his job. Incredibly, they had not even checked his papers.

Paradoxically, Paris night life during the Occupation was booming. There were an estimated 102 nightspots at one time or another during that period, 49 of them in Montmartre. German soldiers posted in the city or on leave were welcome, as they were at the restaurants where menus were conveniently in German and at the many flourishing brothels, with separate ones for officers and men, of course. French entertainers were therefore in the morally ambiguous position of performing for the pleasure of their enemy, who most evenings made up the majority of the audience. Most of these entertainers did so unhesitatingly, some doing several shows a night, racing from one place to another by bicycle. Others, such as the American-born dancer and singer Josephine Baker, refused to be part of that scene.

Montand, as we have seen, was determined not to let the war interfere with his career. He could and did surf on the lively entertainment scene as the hot new ticket. He ended his run at the ABC in March and went on to shuttle for the next few months among the top music halls, such as the Bobino, the Européen, and the Folies Belleville, sometimes with guest-star billing. Often he doubled up, doing both the big theaters and chic cabarets such as the Beaulieu or the Night Club the same evening. Then came the dramatic days of August 1944.

Troops of General Philippe Leclerc's Second Armored Division were speeding their half-tracks and tanks toward the city—one tank commander compared sighting Paris to the Crusaders seeing the walls of Jerusalem.[1] Every able-bodied man-jack was pressed into service to rout the last of the occupiers. To Montand's surprise, members of the Resistance sought him out and supplied him with a rifle and four grenades. Because he was a performing artist, they told him to go guard the Comédie-Française. With Allied Shermans and German panzers firing rounds point-blank at each other on place de la Concorde, the Wehrmacht had other things on its mind than attacking theaters. He dutifully took up his position but saw no action, which was just as well because he had had no training in how to handle either a rifle or a grenade. General Dietrich von Choltitz, commander of the German garrison, surrendered the city to Leclerc, Charles de Gaulle marched in triumph down the Champs-Élysées, and Montand could go back to doing what he did best.

Only two weeks later, he was to have another life-changing lucky break. Émile Audiffred learned that the famous Belle Époque institution the Moulin Rouge was going to return to its vocation as a music hall after a period as a movie theater. The second purpose-built music hall in Paris after the Folies Bergère opened in 1869—adopting the idea from impresario Charles Morton's Oxford Music Hall in London, where patrons could have a drink and a meal while watching a variety show—the Moulin Rouge had opened in October 1889, the year that the Paris World's Fair featured the new Eiffel Tower.

For the pleasure-loving Parisians of the Belle Époque, the grand premiere of the theater with the revolving red windmill on its facade was one of the year's great social occasions. "Last evening the Tout Paris inaugurated it and the show was as much in the theater as on stage," a local paper reported breathlessly, "with His Highnesses Prince Stanislas de Poniatowski and Troubetzkoï, the Count de la Rochefoucauld, Monsieur Elie de Talleurand and the *fine fleur* of the arts." And when the scandalous dance that became known as the French cancan concluded the show with shrieking girls doing splits, cartwheels, and high kicks to Offenbach's frenzied tune "Galop Infernal," the audience reaction was nothing less than "collective delirium."[2] Many of the great entertainers of the 1930s and 1940s had done acts there, including Mistinguett, known for having the most beautiful legs in Paris, and her very public lover Maurice Chevalier as well as Charles Trenet and Jean Gabin.

What Audiffred also learned was that with opening night scheduled for August 30, 1944, Edith Piaf was signed as the main attraction, but the actor Roger Dann, slated to be guest star, had dropped out at the last minute to concentrate on his film career. His departure left the show without a "comic entertainer." Audiffred was quick to sell the theater's management on the young phenomenon from Marseilles. The problem was selling him to Piaf.

On its face, it looked like a hard sell. Piaf had been an established cabaret and music hall star since the 1930s; just weeks before this opening night at the Moulin Rouge, she had done a recital at the important Salle Pleyel concert hall with full orchestra and chorus. She had never heard Montand sing. As far as she knew, he was a yokel from the Marseilles hinterland who was unlikely to add luster to her show. What she didn't know was that they had at least one thing very much in common: a hard, impoverished childhood. Compared to Piaf's *Les misérables*–like infancy, Montand's early years were a bed of roses.

While Ivo was being cared for by a poor but loving family, Edith Giovanna Gassion was abandoned by her flighty mother, a cabaret singer, and left malnourished and covered with sores by her grandmother, a street entertainer whose specialty was a flea circus she kept in a matchbox; while he shared a bedroom with his brother, she was living in a trailer or shabby hotels with her father, a traveling contortionist-acrobat who performed in circuses or in the street and who clouted her when he was drunk on rotgut wine; while he day-dreamed in school, she was learning about life in a provincial brothel where women were treated as sexual objects; while he was working in a pasta factory, she was singing in the streets of Paris and picking up coins thrown from apartment windows; while he was watching American films and nourishing ambitions to become an actor, she got pregnant at sixteen and saw her baby girl die of meningitis; while he was singing in Marseilles theaters, she was hanging out with hoodlums, pimps, and streetwalkers at rough, louche night-clubs in the lower depths of Pigalle.

Her story might have ended there, with her as just another anonymous body in the Paris morgue, if she had not been noticed by the owner of an upscale Champs-Élysées cabaret named Louis Leplée when she was twenty. She sang there regularly, developing a small repertory of hard-bitten, nostalgic chansons about working-class life, until Leplée was found dead in his bed one day with a bullet through an eye, an occupational hazard of the Paris nocturnal world. By then, her big, throaty voice was enough to attract the aid of the lyricist Raymond Asso. He not only provided her with important songs such as "Mon Légionnaire," which became one of her signature numbers, but also persuaded her to avoid the Pigalle milieu and go straight. From there, her talent, innate sense for songs that suited her style, and gutsy street smarts sufficed to start the climb to success.

Maybe she sensed that Montand, with his similarly proletarian origins, was a kindred spirit who only needed a break to blossom. Maybe she simply had to find an act to replace Roger Dann, and time was short before opening night. Whatever her motivation, she agreed to having him in the show on one condition: that he give her an audition so she could judge his talent. Montand bridled at this demand. Except for a few random recordings, he had never heard Piaf sing, and what he had heard, he didn't like. He called her songs *cafardeuses,* "depressing," mainly about lost love, down-and-outers, destitution, the tragedy of existence among the dregs of society—just the opposite of the mimes, grimaces, and tap dancing that he considered *entertainment.* Who was this minuscule tearjerker—at four feet ten inches, she barely came up to his chest—a woman to boot, to stand in judgment of him? Audiffred tactfully explained that it was a mere formality; the contract was a done deal. Montand reluctantly agreed to sing for her on the stage of the empty, darkened Moulin Rouge auditorium.

What happened next depends on which of the extant versions you believe.

According to Simone Berteaut, a childhood friend from Piaf's days singing in the streets who pretended to be her half-sister, "We saw a tall guy with dark hair, an Italian type, come onstage, good-looking but badly dressed in a loud checked sports jacket and a little hat like Trenet wore. What's worse, he sang old American stuff, fake Texas songs." In *Piaf: A Biography* (1972), Berteaut writes that Piaf asked him to come around later to her hotel room in Montmartre for a talk. There, she told him that he was good-looking with expressive hands and a low warm voice that would bowl women over. He had to get rid of the loud clothes and the Marseilles accent and change his repertory. But she was ready to work with him if he would follow her guidance. After he left, Berteaut recalled, Piaf told her, "The fathead's so good looking he's a dream. That guy's going to revolutionize singing. He's the one the public's been waiting for."[3]

In her first autobiography, *Au bal de la chance,* dictated to the journalist Louis-René Dauven in 1958, Piaf gives a more complete account of their encounter:

> On the day of the audition I was nearly all alone in the vast hall of the Moulin, lost in the darkness. Yves sang, and right away I was conquered. He had a terrific personality that made an impression of strength and solidity, his hands were eloquent, powerful, admirable, his face was handsome and tormented, his voice deep and, miraculously, with little trace of a Marseilles accent. By dent of hard work, he had gotten rid of it. But his songs were impossible: facile and vulgar cowboy songs, a phony Americanism that would work with some publics because the Liberation was near, but which to my eyes were an error. Yves Montand was worth better than that. When his fourth song was over, I left my seat and went to the edge of the stage. He came over to me. I'll always remember how small I felt, almost crushed by this tall, lanky boy toward whom I lifted my face at the level of his ankles. I told him he was *formidable* and that he could be sure of a magnificent career. After that, I joined him on the stage and added the essential point: he absolutely had to change his repertoire and get some better material, songs that would let

> him take on different characters and express something. He looked at me with surprise, probably thinking that I was sticking my nose into something that was none of my business, and then said "Yes" without conviction. I realized that he was just saying that to make me happy and to have some peace. He wasn't going to contradict the star of the show, of course, but he wasn't interested in her advice.[4]

In her second autobiography, *Ma vie,* which was cobbled together in 1964 by the journalist Jean Noli from a series of articles he had done for the weekly *France-Dimanche* from 1961 to 1963 (and published in English as *My Life* in 1990), she says, "At first I couldn't stand him. I saw him as one of those minor performers without any style who came up to Paris in 1944. He sang cowboy songs and imitated Charles Trenet. I thought he looked like a would-be tough guy. He seemed so pleased with himself that he made me angry." She says she told friends, "He sings badly, he dances badly, he's got no sense of rhythm. That man's just nothing." After she heard him sing, she says she went to his dressing room and admitted she had been wrong. She told him that if he worked hard and agreed to follow her advice, "within a year you'll be the great revelation of the postwar music hall."[5]

Montand also had two versions of that first meeting. In his initial memoir published in 1955, *Du solieil plein la tête* (A Head Full of Sun), he recalled:

> When I had to sing before Edith Piaf in the Moulin Rouge theater, I had a particularly bad case of stage fright. I tried to reason with myself, but that small, attentive, impassive spectator lost in the middle of the seats intimidated me more than 300 noisily impatient members of an audience. I summoned my male pride: I wasn't going to beat a retreat from a woman. I went to work and sang four songs. By the last one, I had completely forgotten Edith. I saw her come to me out of the dark. She stopped at the edge of the stage. She just said that she thought I was terrific, that she was very glad we would be on the same program. The stage lighting modeled her face lifted toward me. She was sincere. She promised me a great future.[6]

Thirty-five years later, in *Tu vois, je n'ai pas oublié,* featuring interviews, letters, and other personal materials edited by the journalists Hervé Hamon and Patrick Rotman in 1990 (and published in English as *You See, I Haven't Forgotten* in 1992), he described the event somewhat differently:

> I didn't find out till later how determined Edith had been not to like me. But Roger Dann had spoken well of me, and Audiffred wasn't going to let me be condemned without a hearing. . . . Someone had said to Piaf: "Montand? Are you crazy? Not him, you don't know him. If he goes on before you, he'll kill you!" Exactly what you should never say to Piaf. "Well, let's see this man who's going to kill me!" There was a strong element of challenge at our first meeting. . . . There she was in her flowered dress, very pretty, very delicate, with that left-hand-side part in her hair. She had a peculiar way of giving you her hand, with the thumb tucked in. . . . I sang "Les Plaines du Far West," "Je m'en Fous," "Je vends des hot dogs à Madison," and she got up. But as I recall, it was only later, after my first performance, that she heaped praise on me. "Well done, bravo, well done!" She looked adorable, beautiful, with that high forehead, those big blue eyes, and that delicately proportioned body—tiny breasts, narrow hips.[7]

Despite these contradictory accounts, it is clear that Montand and Piaf were smitten. Within a week, she took him into her act, under her wing, and into her bed. For nearly two years, they were France's most famous lovers, while she polished his stage manner, his education, and his repertory. Montand was six years younger than Piaf and new to the worldly temptations of Paris, but he must have known her reputation. Still, his initial reaction shows that he saw the purity in her that she herself felt, a childlike innocence that appealed to him. Within days of that first meeting, he was in love with her: "I had fallen in love without even knowing it," he remembered. "I was head over heels in love with Edith's charm, her admiration for me, her loneliness. . . . She was fresh, flirtatious, both funny and cruel, passionately devoted to her profession. . . . I was 23. It was my first true love. Edith was one of those people who made you think you were God, that you were irreplaceable."[8]

At first, however, it was to be a ménage à trois, for Piaf had been having an affair with her main librettist, Henri Contet, for three years. An engineer by training, a journalist by choice, Contet discovered a talent for songwriting under Piaf's influence and eventually wrote more than thirty songs for her among the more than thousand he wrote from the 1940s to the 1960s, including the popular "Padam, padam . . . ." He could see there was something between her and Montand, and he didn't like it. But for the sake of Piaf, he accepted the situation. Soon both Contet and Piaf were writing material for Montand that changed his style from variety show impersonator to recitalist—love songs such as "Ma gosse, ma p'tite môme" (My Kid, My Little Kid), with its promise of beautiful meadows and perfumed beds for making love. Contet had originally written it for Chevalier, but Piaf persuaded him to give it to Montand. There were also surprisingly poignant songs such as "Ce monsieur-là," about an ordinary, comfort-loving married man who kills his wife's lover and spends the rest of his unhappy days running from the police.

Piaf honed and burnished Montand's act, showing him how to keep the audience's attention by alternating movement and quiet, the light and the dark. She instructed him to stop swinging his arms like windmills, to come on stage slowly instead of sprinting. She got him to take lessons: tap dancing, voice exercises, rhythm, stretching to keep limber and lithe. She told him his diction was awful: he corrected it by reciting poetry and singing before a mirror with a pencil in his mouth. She was amazed at how hard he worked to improve, practicing his routine for hours in her apartment.

A month after they met, Montand took a hotel room in rue de Richelieu, not far from the Moulin Rouge, and she joined him there. As she liked to do with all her lovers, she poured gifts on him: gold watches, rings, cufflinks and cigarette cases, bespoke suits, alligator-skin shoes. More important, she introduced him to an intellectual and artistic world that he had never had the time, opportunity, or inclination to explore. (Henri Contet, perhaps spitefully, said Montand's ignorance was abysmal when he reached Paris; he couldn't write a few lines without making gross grammar and spelling errors.[9]) Through her, Montand met cultural figures such as her great friend the writer Jean Cocteau, the playwright Sacha Guitry, the poet Jacques Prévert.

She explained to him that he had to interest both the masses and the educated. He discovered an unsuspected hunger for culture that would last the rest of his life. He devoured writers from Rabelais to Anouilh, Steinbeck to Hemingway. A visitor to his hotel room saw on his bookshelves Bergson's *On Laughter,* Malraux's *La condition humaine,* Sartre's *L'existentialism est un humanism,* side by side with *English without Tears.* His intellectual awakening included his first serious religious doubts. Although never a practicing Catholic despite Giuseppina's efforts, he began to consider questions such as the existence of evil in a world created by a good God. After seeing newsreels of Nazi death camps in early 1945 with Piaf, he turned to her angrily and said,

"What about your God now? How can you believe in a being who tolerates such a horror?"[10]

After their show at the Moulin Rouge ended its run, they began a tour of the South of France in the fall, ending up in Marseilles in December at the Variétés-Casino, a theater where Montand felt very much at home. However, the homecoming revealed how much he had changed in the year since he left for Paris—and the audience didn't like it. Instead of welcoming his new repertory of songs put together by Piaf and Contet, they responded with catcalls and insulting small change thrown on the stage. They wanted the Montand they had known, the amusing local boy who used American slang and sang about Western cowboys and Chicago thugs, not the sophisticated Parisian who had adopted *chansons réalistes* about lost love and poor souls.

The reception was better when he took Piaf to meet his family in La Cabucelle. They arrived at impasse des Mûriers by limousine, to the delight of neighbors leaning out of their windows to see the stars. Giuseppina and Lydia had laid out a feast. Piaf was briefly confused by all the excited chatter, much of it in Italian, but with the aid of the free-flowing wine soon responded to the warm family atmosphere that enveloped her. It was a novel experience for the waif from Pigalle by way of Belleville. She felt adopted; they assumed that she and Montand were engaged to be married. She developed a friendship with them that lasted long after her breakup with him, visiting La Cabucelle and calling his parents "Papa and Mama Livi."

The public was growing accustomed to seeing Piaf and Montand on the same billing—with his name now nearly as big as hers. In February 1945, they opened for a month at the elegant Théâtre de l'Étoile near place de l'Étoile and the Arc de Triomphe. With its 1,500 seats, pink-and-silver décor, and marble main staircase, it had specialized in operettas and revues since opening in 1928. It would become associated with Montand, who appeared there several times over the next decade. Following that, they undertook another tour of the provinces, including a ten-day return to Marseilles. This time the audiences were more receptive to his repertory. They applauded "La grande cité" (The Big City) about life in the metropolis, where men churn all their lives in factories that spew clouds of smoke, but there are still girls with soft skin and love to be found. They applauded "Elle a. . ." (She Has . . .), about a girl who has marvelous eyes and hands "and so many other things just for me."

With her protégé going from strength to strength, Piaf was getting worried. When they were on tour, he scored such a hit every evening that they kept calling him back for encores, and she had the gnawing feeling that he was putting her in the shade. She told Henri Contet that Montand was getting too big to be on the same program. To her friend Simone Berteaut, she put it more bluntly: she was getting tired of his "new self-importance, pomposity and money-consciousness. . . . In a year's time, I'll only be good enough to clean his shoes."[11] Piaf and Montand agreed that in October he would get prominent billing when they returned to the Étoile, but she would still do the first half of the show.

The billing was indeed impressive, with "Yves Montand, the New Fantasist," printed in large characters separately from the other performers. He beefed up his onstage time to fourteen songs, plus encores. There were still the Spanish dancer, a contortionist, a "comic cyclist," and "the trapezists of death,"[12] but the result was more of one man's recital rather than a balanced music hall show. He was doing something no one but first-magnitude stars such as Maurice Chevalier had done before. He was aware enough of the challenge it represented to ask Piaf to go to the Sacré Coeur Basilica on Montmartre and light a votive candle for his success, which she did. She also invited Lydia and Julien, recently released from the army and come to Paris to see his kid brother, to sit in her box seats.

He need not have worried. The audience raved, as did the critics. "Beyond a doubt, Yves Montand is the strongest personality to have emerged in music-hall since Charles Trenet's now distant beginnings," said one in *La dépêche de Paris*. His unusual way of mixing serious songs such as "La grande cité" with lighthearted numbers such as "Luna Park" unsettled some. The critic for *Opéra* wrote, "This disconcerting young singer is the doorkeeper to a new world . . . the voice of youth."[13] In his dressing room afterward, he thanked Piaf and said he owed it all to her: "This time, Edith, it worked! I got them!" But Piaf thought she felt a change in him. After she left the theater, she turned to Berteaut and said, "It's all over now. He doesn't need me any more [*sic*]."[14]

5

First Films

Piaf's intuition was right: there *was* a change in Montand's feelings for her. But what she seemed unwilling to acknowledge to herself was that she, too, was tiring of their relationship. Over the next few months, they did a pas de deux in which they told each other it was over, but neither was ready to make it final. Shortly after his opening-night success at the Étoile in October, he sent a cryptic telegram to her in Brussels, where she had an engagement. "Maybe you're right," it said. "I'm too young for you. With all my heart I wish you the happiness you deserve." She described her feelings in a letter to a friend in her stream-of-consciousness prose, saying that the break was just as well if he thought no more of her than the abrupt, unfeeling cable implied. "A telegram . . . is easier than a letter, a letter takes too long, you dictate a telegram, what thoughtfulness, what a way to think about love."[1]

Still, the end of the affair would not come decisively until the following spring. While on tour in Alsace and Germany with Les Compagnons de la Chanson, Piaf had fallen in love with Jean-Louis Jaubert, the leader of the nine-man choral group. On the day she was due to return, Montand waited for her in the apartment they shared on rue de Berri, near the Champs-Élysées. When she didn't show up, he called her secretary. She confirmed that Piaf had indeed returned from tour but that she didn't want to see him. Montand got the point, packed up, and left for a hotel room.

He always admitted that the way Piaf dumped him left him in a depressive state for nearly two years. He vowed never again to let himself get so involved with a woman. (That vow did not, however, stop him from immediately having an affair with Gisèle Pascal, a film starlet his age and also from the South of France.) Piaf, on the other hand, seemed no more affected by the breakup than she would have been with one of her Foreign Legionnaires. She went on to play Pygmalion—and sometimes much more than that—to many other popular singers, including Eddie Constantine, Gilbert Bécaud, Georges

Moustaki, and Charles Aznavour (whom she convinced to get a nose job), while eventually selling 40 million copies of her records and making ten concert tours of the United States. As Montand described the breakup to the *New York Times* in 1982, "For a little while I was Piaf's man. Then suddenly she left me. She went on a short tour and then, clack! She was gone. It was enormously cruel. But that was her temperament. She knew instinctively that when she was in love she sang marvelously. So when she got bored, she would leave." In the same interview, he dealt with the frequently heard notion that it was Piaf who launched his career and made him what he was. "Don't destroy the legend," he said and then proceeded to do so by setting the record straight. "The truth is Piaf did not make me. I had a bit of a name already when I met her. But when a woman like Piaf comes near you, of course you are put in the spotlight, and learning from her saved me five years' work."[2]

The breakup also led to his first film role since Marcel Pagnol's aborted *La prière aux étoiles* in 1941. A friend of Piaf's, Marcel Blistène, a journalist turned director, had written a screenplay for her while as a Jew he was hiding from the Nazis during the war. However, this was his first film, so he was having trouble finding a producer. Piaf suggested a trade-off: if he would write in a small part for a friend of hers named Yves Montand, she would use her contacts to get financing. The result was *Étoile sans lumière / Star without Light* (1946, US 1947). The shoot began in July 1945, well before they parted, with Piaf the female lead as Madeleine, a simple housemaid with a talent for singing, and Montand as her gauche, jealous boyfriend. The rest of the cast included the veteran Jules Berry as an unscrupulous impresario, the rising young actor Serge Reggiani as a supportive friend, and the beauteous Mila Parély as a silent-film actress threatened by the transition to talkies.

The film received a polite reception at best, but the plot involving a declining actress whose singing voice has to be dubbed (by Piaf) was good enough to be a precursor to Gene Kelly's film *Singin' in the Rain* in 1952, which had the same storyline. Thanks to Piaf, Montand received good billing in the credits, but the part was a mere token; he was on-screen for only a few minutes, and his lines were minimal. As with many of his later films, the director emphasized more his size and agile, muscular physicality than his acting ability, with shots showing him leaping acrobatically into the driver's seat of a convertible and engaging in a water fight in a locker-room shower. Although Montand was obviously ill at home on the set and let himself be completely dominated by Piaf, Blistène was impressed by how involved he wanted to be in making the film, hanging around and questioning him about everything from props and lighting to camera angles and sound engineering. "He spent a lot of time on the set, much more than was required by his minor role," Blistène recalled. "He was always with Edith, who dominated him completely. He was a model of docility and conscientious application, full of curiosity about how movies were made."[3]

He didn't have to wait long for his next film role, his first with a top director, thanks to both Piaf and Blistène. In the summer of 1945, Marcel Carné and Jacques Prévert had gone to see a new ballet by the brash young choreographer Roland Petit, who had just founded the Ballet des Champs-Élysées. With a haunting musical score by the Hungarian-born composer Joseph Kosma, it was about a tragic love affair that had been foretold by a character suitably named Fate. Carné and Prévert had done two great films of the 1930s with Jean Gabin, *Le quai des brumes / Port of Shadows* (1938, US 1939) and *Le jour se lève / Daybreak* (1939, US 1940), both considered prime examples of France's new *réalisme poétique* and precursors of the American film noir style of the 1940s and 1950s. They were eager to do another with Gabin, who they knew was looking for a role after a long dry period due to the war.

The planets lined up nicely. RKO and Pathé, which agreed to coproduce a film based on the ballet, also saw it as a vehicle for Gabin's return to the screen. He was involved in the project for several weeks, even agreeing to do screen tests with other actors. In thrall to Marlene Dietrich, with whom he had been having an affair since their meeting in Hollywood in 1941, he agreed to sign on condition that she be given the female lead.

It was a done deal, and everybody was happy, especially the producers, who felt they had a winner: Carné was again going to direct Gabin, and the rest of the cast, besides Dietrich, comprised other stars, such as Pierre Brasseur, Saturnin Fabre, and Serge Reggiani. Prévert went to work in earnest on a screenplay set in France's *glauque* postwar period peopled by former collaborators, Resistance members, and black marketeers. Kosma wrote the music for a song with lyrics by Prévert called "Les feuilles mortes" (The Dead Leaves) to be sung by Dietrich. The talented set designer Alexander Trauner, who had done the imaginative sets for *Le quai des brumes* and *Le jour se lève,* began constructing an entire neighborhood in Northeast Paris.

Then the whole project began to curdle.

To start with, Dietrich was carping about the script. She didn't like being cast as an unglamorous housewife. She didn't see how, with her German accent, she could play the daughter of a French collaborator married to a racketeer. She suggested dozens of changes—How about paying a taxi driver by pulling her dress up and plucking the franc notes from her thigh-high stocking, which would let her show off her famous legs?[4] And she really didn't want to sing Prévert's "Les feuilles mortes," decreeing "that song is *merde*."[5] Gabin, too, had his reservations. He wasn't comfortable playing a former Resistance fighter. He had in fact taken part in the liberation of France as a tank commander with Leclerc's Second Armored Division, but many French ignored this and criticized him for spending time in Hollywood before that.

He especially wanted to keep Dietrich happy. Every time there was a script change, he would ask, "What will La Grande think?," referring to her by his pet name. Prévert got so tired of it that he said he would throw up if he heard any more about La Grande. Unfortunately, her contract gave her script approval. She finally withdrew, and Gabin followed suit, refusing to do the film without her, even if he did have to pay a penalty for breach of contract.[6]

All this preproduction squabbling alarmed RKO. Besides, its executives got squeamish over the fact that the story involved an extramarital affair, which might be offensive to American audiences of the day. They decided to pull the plug on RKO's participation, so Pathé had to find other financing. To make matters worse, the defection of Gabin and Dietrich left Carné without his two lead stars. Then he remembered that Montand was having a very successful music hall run and that he had acted in *Étoile sans lumière*. He called Blistène, who, knowing Piaf was lobbying Carné insistently, praised him highly. "Piaf continued to call me every day to say that Montand had a great future in films," Carné recalled in his memoirs. "He was going to be tomorrow's big star. My film could be his chance of a lifetime. So much friendly pressure annoyed me, and I was tempted to say no. But I had to admit that there was no one else I could try, and time was passing."[7] He signed Montand. To replace Dietrich, he decided on a promising young actress named Nathalie Nattier.

Les portes de la nuit / Gates of the Night (1946, US 1950) was, predictably, a flop for many reasons. Asking young beginners in their twenties such as Montand and Nattier to replace the heavyweights Gabin and Dietrich in parts obviously written for forty-year-olds was careless, not to say absurd, on the face of it. Montand tried hard to please his dictatorial director, who was known for ruling his actors and crew with an iron hand. He sought advice and criticism from everyone, but he was obviously still uncomfortable on a film set. When he saw the rushes, he was appalled by his gangly body—he thought he looked like a big bird—and could hardly recognize his voice. Moreover, he was still in the dumps from the recent breakup with Piaf; the other actors and the film crew were alarmed to see that he often wept uncontrollably between takes. In Carné's post mortem of the film, he said Montand was handicapped by a slack presence and by an accent that made him seem to be speaking with his mouth half-full.[8]

But to be fair to Montand, the biggest cause of the film's failure was that Carné was out of touch with the temper of France at the time. He was attempting to repeat his successes of the 1930s, while audiences had moved on. With the privations and horrors of the war finally behind them, the French wanted to feel good about something; they wanted to laugh. They weren't interested in seeing a film noir complete with dark streets and lurking shadows about a sad postwar Paris with all the problems they were only too familiar with daily. Nor did they want to be reminded of how sordidly many of them had acted during the Occupation. The film was mocked as *Les portes de l'ennui,* so boring was the plot filled with unlikely coincidences and Prévert's portentous dialogue.

The critics were merciless toward the music hall singer turned actor. "Montand is at his ease when he dances, croons, or says nothing," snidely noted the film magazine *L'ecran français.*[9] *Le Monde,* coining a new term, found that "Yves Montand is neither photogenic nor phonogenic, and he lacks experience more than he lacks talent. He has a lot to learn."[10] They were no harder on him than he was on himself. "It wasn't a question of whether I was good or bad," he commented later, summing up his performance. "I was nothing. I understood neither what I was saying nor what I was doing. The critics massacred me. Still, I think I can plead attenuating circumstances. I had no experience, and you don't replace Gabin just like that."[11]

Overall, it was an experience that left Montand bruised and doubtful about a possible career in films, in retrospect considering that it set his acting career back by twenty years. The film had one undeniable success, however, in Kosma's music. "Les feuilles mortes" was to become "Autumn Leaves" thanks to Johnny Mercer's English rendition in 1947 and as such one of the world's most popular standards. Contrary to a common belief, Montand sang only a brief snatch of it during the film. He didn't sing it in its entirety until 1949, when it entered his permanent repertory.

Clearly, he was still more comfortable doing music hall, even if it was a high-wire act every evening without a director or scriptwriter to blame for failure. In September, even before the film was released, he was back at the Étoile for another show. He continued to add new songs and to confirm his style of surprising audiences, moving deceptively between moods. "Battling Joe" starts off seeming to mock just another boxer who dreams of becoming a champion, only to veer into drama when he is blinded by a punch to the head and washed up, while his manager is indifferent because he can always find another sucker. "Luna Park," which became one of Montand's all-time favorites, begins with a serious social theme but turns lighthearted with its description of a young buck on his day off. It tells of a factory worker who turns "the same damn little screw" all year long in a job that's dirty and soul numbing but who has his fun dancing and singing with the merry crowds at an amusement park when he gets his paycheck at the end of the month.

As Montand explained to a Paris newspaper that fall, "I believe very strongly that popular songs have to embody their times. That's why I try, with whatever talent nature has given me, to be the expression of the joys and sorrows of our times and touch the listener in his heart." The secret to getting this across was rehearsing so much that every note, every gesture, every dance step appeared relaxed and effortless, "giving the audience the impression that it hasn't seen everything."[12] The critics responded. *Le Monde,* for one, decided that he had found his style and deserved a place among stars such as Trenet and Chevalier. It loved his voice, "warm as velvet, clear and sharp on the final, lingering notes," and the way his "sure, feline" movements accompanied and underlined the rhythm and intention of his songs. It all showed "the intelligence of an authentic entertainer with exceptional gifts."[13]

It was around this time, in the fall of 1946, that Montand made the acquaintance of three like-minded musicians who would enrich his repertory and style and, in some respects, his life.

Francis Lemarque was a thirty-year-old singer and songwriter when he heard Montand sing at a Montmartre cabaret called Club des Cinq in 1946. Born Nathan Korb, the son of Jewish immigrants to France from eastern Europe, Lemarque had had some success singing in nightclubs, but felt he was going nowhere. When he heard Montand, he suddenly realized that this was what he had been trying to do, unsuccessfully. "What a revelation, what a shock," he recalled. "When he sang, it wasn't just ordinary songs. He sang about the pleasures, the hopes, the struggles and the revolts of a whole generation. Every member of the audience recognized himself in the characters that his songs brought alive. They flowed, limpid, with words and music that were so easy to assimilate that you remembered them immediately."[14] He decided on the spot that he would write for Montand, and he did. He was a communist sympathizer, like Montand, and politically they were very much on the same wavelength. Lemarque wrote dozens of songs for Montand over the years. Among the hundreds of songs he wrote during his career was

"Marjolaine," used by Stanley Kubrick in his antimilitarist film *The Paths of Glory* (1957).

Shortly thereafter, Montand met a musician of Italian origin, a pianist who would accompany him, in every sense of the word, for the rest of his career. Their connection came about when Montand had an engagement at a nightclub in Deauville, but his usual accompanist was unavailable. A friend suggested he try a certain Bob Castella, a virtuoso pianist who could play jazz and classical with equal ease. Montand invited Castella for a tryout; he played a few bars of "Rhapsody in Blue" and then some jazz. Montand took him on not only for the Deauville gig but as his permanent accompanist, orchestrator, and rehearsal partner. As time went on, he leaned increasingly on Castella, ten years older, to serve as secretary and confidant and to manage much of his life behind the scenes. Castella knew everything there was to know about Montand, including his complex finances. If there was a problem, professional or personal, it was Castella who fixed it. Eventually, the symbiosis was so complete that they couldn't get along without each other, despite Montand's monumental temper tantrums during rehearsals, with Castella willingly serving as whipping boy; he just hunkered down patiently at the piano until the storm passed. Their relationship lasted nearly forty-five years until Montand's death.

After meeting Castella, Montand came across Henri Crolla, a jazz guitarist who had played with Django Reinhardt and who was, many thought, as good as the great Django. The son of itinerant Roma musicians from Naples, Crolla immigrated with them to France in 1922 to escape fascism, much as the Livis had. He lived in a Paris slum like La Cabucelle of Marseilles, quit school at an early age, and played banjo and guitar in the street before going on to play jazz guitar by ear in night clubs. With such similar origins, he and Montand struck up a tight personal and professional relationship that lasted until Crolla's premature death of lung cancer at forty. Montand, who always had trouble with tempo during his numbers, owed much of his musical sense to Crolla's innate feeling for rhythm and improvisation. Crolla, with Castella, did musical arrangements for Montand's songs and formed the core of his orchestra for years. Montand also enjoyed Crolla's deadpan, irreverent sense of humor, which reminded him of Chico Marx. On one occasion, Crolla wanted to cross the Champs-Élysées on foot, but thick, stalled traffic blocked his way. He simply opened the rear door of a car, clambered through it while apologizing elaborately, and got out the other side.

⊙ ⊙ ⊙

It was while Montand was performing back at the ABC in January 1947 that he received an unexpected visitor in his dressing room. With little in the way of preliminaries, Jack Warner brashly informed him that Montand was going to Hollywood with a seven-year contract at a minimum of $700 a week. All he had to do was to remain at the studio's disposal and wait to be assigned a part. If he got homesick, he had the option of taking a six-month vacation in Europe after eighteen months. Warner, then the studio's vice president in charge of production, including the search for acting talent, laid it on thick: this was the first time since 1928, when he hired Al Jolson, that he would be signing a contract in person. Moreover, this was only the second time that a French music hall entertainer had been offered a contract, the first being Maurice Chevalier. Montand could expect to be used for many films. The full Hollywood treatment started with a first-class cabin reserved in his name on an ocean liner sailing for New York on July 16.[15]

At this distance, it is difficult to imagine why Jack Warner had suddenly seized on Montand as a hot prospect. Montand's experience on a movie set was minimal, and it had generally received lukewarm reviews at best, devastating at worst. His English was rudimentary despite his poring over *English without Tears*. Maybe it was a strategic move to keep the competition from getting to Montand first—Warner had recently committed the studio to boosting its star power. This coincided with the period when Warner had begun vacationing regularly in France and would eventually purchase a home there. It seems likely that Montand had come to his attention during a visit, and he decided on the spur of the moment to make some headlines by signing a big French entertainment name.

However that may be, it's easier to surmise what was going through Montand's mind. To the kid from La Cabucelle who played hooky to devour American films, this must have seemed like the realization of his dreams at the age of twenty-six. Here was Warner Bros., the studio of the stars he had admired, from Gary Cooper to James Cagney, Errol Flynn and Humphrey Bogart, asking him to become one of its own. Choosing between that and staying in dismal postwar Paris, living in an anonymous hotel room, and still feeling disconsolate after the breakup with Piaf, was a no-brainer. It looked like the chance of a lifetime, and he jumped at it. He signed the English-language contract, and by the end of January Warners had introduced its "French Danny Kaye" to a Paris press conference attended by Joseph Hummel, the studio's international vice president and European supervisor.[16]

But before sailing for America, Montand had a French film contract to honor. In *L'idole* (1948), directed by the Hungarian-born Alexander Esway, Montand had a role that suited his size and athleticism. He was Luc Fenton, a lumberjack that a boxing manager decides to turn into a heavyweight champion. He wins enough fights to earn a shot at the title, becomes the idol of the boxing world, then learns that the bouts were rigged, his opponents paid to throw them. His pride stung, he insists on a clean fight and is kayoed in the last round. Montand prepared for his part with what was becoming his usual meticulous approach. He went into training for six weeks at a Montmartre gym, lifting weights, skipping rope, hitting the heavy and speed bags, and sparring with Victor Buttin, a professional who was the only French boxer to have beaten Marcel Cerdan before Cerdan went on to become world middleweight champion. During the filming of the final championship bout sequence with another pro, Stéphan Olek, as his opponent, Montand was caught off guard and floored by a real, unplanned uppercut that put him out for twenty minutes.

He was lucky to have Esway, an old motion-picture hand with more than twenty films to his credit, as his director, and not only on the set. Esway had been a screenwriter and director in Germany and Great Britain in the 1920s and then in France in the early 1930s and after the war. His Atlantic Film Productions studio had notably produced *Thunder in the City* (1937) with Edward G. Robinson. When Montand told him of his contract with Warners, he took the young actor aside and explained the facts of Hollywood life to him. Signing with Warners did not necessarily mean that he would get a part right away or even ever. He would be one of many aspiring actors on call in a pool. From time to time, the studio would cull one from the herd for a screen test that might or might not result in a part. Meanwhile, he would be twiddling his thumbs. Even with the sun and palm trees as consolation, it could be a long seven years.

Esway's conviction that the contract was a mistake shook Montand enough that he finally got around to obtaining a French translation of it. In the fine print, he discovered that he was committed to being studio chattel with little say in essential matters such as his stage name and choice of scripts, that he was obliged to participate in promotional events so that he would no longer be master of his social life in the evenings, that his name could be stuck on advertising for whatever products the studio chose. For an entertainer accustomed to being his own man, running the show in the preparation and execution of his performances right down to the last detail, this was just not on. He cabled Warners that he was canceling the contract. The studio replied with a breach-of-contract suit and demanded 20,000 francs (about $170) a day in damages for as long as he refused to honor his commitment.

While lawyers argued, something was happening in world geopolitics that would unexpectedly help resolve the question. The United States, increasingly concerned about the perceived Red Menace from the Soviet Union and its communist satellites, began tightening its requirements for entry visas, paying special attention to anyone suspected of being a communist sympathizer. As the dispute with Warners dragged on, the window for visas was virtually closed by the US Immigration and Naturalization Service. Seeing the futility of litigating against a foreign actor who was unlikely to be able to enter the country, the studio cut a deal with Montand: he would pay it 100,000 francs (about $840), and it would drop its case against him. Still, Montand's reputation in American show business circles took a hit. At David O. Selznick Productions, for example, its foreign-production assistant and talent scout in London, Jenia Reissar, wrote an unflattering thumbnail profile of him, typing the note in red, as if in warning: "Yves Montand (French). Broke a seven-year contract with Warners. Had a lawsuit settled out of court."[17] It would be a dozen years before he would set foot on American soil.

6

Simone

His film career was on hold. Montand had suffered the slings and arrows of the critics long enough. He had made several attempts at acting and had virtually nothing to show for it but pride-wounding scorn. Clearly, there was more to acting before a camera than just showing up. It was a real métier, and he had to admit that he had not paid his dues by learning the trade in drama school and working for years under the orders of demanding directors. Perhaps worse, he felt he had been abused by a big Hollywood studio that had taken advantage of his inexperience and naivete. Maybe it was time to set aside those youthful dreams born at the Star theater in Marseilles. Except for a token part as a street singer in one of the four sketches in a fluffy, forgettable effort called *Souvenirs perdus* (1950), he now would go for five years without trying another movie part.

Yet he was undeniably a success when he was in control of his own show. Everybody loved him as a singer. Here was where his talent as a switch hitter served him well. Without missing a beat, he returned to his music hall and cabaret shows. He even had the payback pleasure of replacing Piaf at the ABC when she had a problem with her voice. He made important additions to his repertory, such as "C'est si bon," the worldwide favorite that he made his own in the spring of 1948. Dressed in his trademark plain brown slacks and open-neck shirt, he was a refreshing change from the usual artificial glitter of show business. His on-stage apparel was, wrote one Paris paper, "almost a factory uniform. . . . He steps before us as the representative of democracy."[1] With his poetic *chansons à textes* by Francis Lemarque, Henri Contet, and others who now competed to provide him with new material, the press dubbed him the "singing prole," the "working man's troubadour." Thus, it was only appropriate that he be selected to play Tom Joad, the impoverished Okie in John Steinbeck's *The Grapes of Wrath* in a French radio adaptation of the book. In his spare time, he continued to work on his accent to scrub out the last traces of Marseilles.

In the spring of 1948, Henri Crolla took him south to visit Saint Paul de Vence, about fifteen miles west of Nice. One of the oldest medieval villages on the Riviera, its vine-covered buildings with red-tile roofs and narrow, steep streets perched atop a thousand-foot hill fairly reek of local Provençal color. Today it is a popular tourist attraction known for the Maeght Foundation's collection of modern art, but in those days it still retained much of its local character—if that can include a small, exclusive, luxury hotel where Winston Churchill and Charlie Chaplin had stayed and where Marc Chagall, Pablo Picasso, Georges Braque, Alberto Giacometti, and other artists had sought refuge.

The hotel, La Colombe d'Or, was where Crolla and Montand put up—and where Montand soon would experience a life-changing encounter. While there, Crolla took his friend to meet Jacques Prévert, one of the first of the writers and artists to take up residence in the village after the war—whom Montand had apparently not met on the set of *Les portes de la nuit* in 1946. The entertainer and the poet immediately became friends, despite the cultural gulf between them; Montand later said that his relationship with Prévert was even more important to his development than his relationship with Piaf. Through Prévert, he became part of the village's transient community, engaging with writers, intellectuals, and artists whom he never would have met otherwise. In years to come, he returned frequently when between engagements or on tour in the South.

It was also during this cinematically fallow period that the singing prole sang for royalty. Prince Aly Khan was to marry his second wife, Rita Hayworth, in Cannes on May 29. He thought it would be amusing if Montand sang at the wedding party at his Riviera villa, the nearby Château de l'Horizon. Montand, then singing in Paris at the Club des Champs-Élysées, was tempted. The fee offered was, of course, substantial, but he didn't want to break his engagement at the nightclub. A trifling problem, responded the prince: he would send a private aircraft to pick up Montand and his accompanists at Le Bourget on the morning of May 29, fly them to Cannes, and return them to Paris in time for the show. The deal was done. Montand sang seven songs, one in phonetically learned English, in a room at the seaside villa converted into a cabaret. Present were not only the briefly happy couple—Hayworth would file for a Nevada divorce two years later—but also the prince's father, the Aga Khan, the begum (his wife), and the Hollywood columnist Louella Parsons.

In mid-August, Montand had an engagement in Nice and was staying again at the Colombe d'Or. As with his first meeting with Edith Piaf, he gives two versions of what happened there at that time. In his first autobiography, *Du soleil plein la tête,* published in 1955, he recalled: "In the middle of the courtyard, surrounded by innumerable doves, there is a young woman. Her hair is terrifically blonde. She is wearing blue pants, an open-neck blouse. She smiles like the young girls in old Italian paintings. I know her name is Simone Signoret. I have never seen her films, I don't know her, but I know that I am going to walk toward her, trying not to disturb the doves, and say two or three things, anything at all, so she will turn toward me."[2]

He later debunked that version. Calling it a fairy tale for public consumption, he said the truth was simpler.

> I was at my table in the dining room with Bob and Henri when Jacques Prévert came in with a woman. She was barefoot and dressed gypsy-style, with a rustling flowered skirt and a blouse knotted around her waist. She was outrageously made up, the way women made themselves up in those days, with far too much lipstick; I thought it was a pity to paint such a mouth. They came over. She and Crolla had been friends for years. He introduced us. . . . [The next day] we drank white wine. Looked at one another. Picked up the nonconversation of the day before. I "carelessly" took hold of her arm: "You have very slender wrists."[3]

In his memoir *You See, I Haven't Forgotten* (1992, in French 1990), he states that he was surprised by the casual way she ordered her wine, asking for "un coup de blanc" (a shot of white), as if she were in a working-class bar. After more small talk, he rose and excused himself, explaining that he was performing in Nice that evening and needed to take a nap. She suggested that he could rest at her house if he liked. He accepted. It became a nap *à deux.* Shortly afterward, he said, "I had to admit to myself that I had fallen deeply in love. You don't go looking for that kind of thing, it hits you right in the heart."[4]

Interestingly, Signoret's description of what those days in Saint Paul meant to her is much more succinct—and far less sentimental. She says simply that she accompanied him to his recital in Nice and that "in those four days we had been struck by lightning, and something indiscreet and irreversible had happened."[5] A very cool, impersonal account, with no mention of her feelings for Montand. And no mention of the famous nap at her house.

She had recently bought the house with the proceeds from her hit film *Dédé d'Anvers / Dédée,* alternatively *Woman of Antwerp* (1948, US 1949).

With her were her daughter, Catherine, then three, and stepson, Gilles, fourteen. Her husband, the film director Yves Allégret, was detained in Paris but planning to join them. Wanting to avoid his learning secondhand about Montand—gossip travels fast in a village—she waited for Allégret's arrival on the main road into Saint Paul and waved his car to a stop. There she told him the whole story. He slapped her hard twice, then calmed down, and they spent a few days of vacation in Saint Paul before returning to Paris together.[6] The reconciliation was short-lived. Montand finished his tour of Provence, returned to Paris, and he and Signoret began seeing each other secretly. For him, their trysts were "intense, violent, a joy, a celebration. And then, at seven, she would go 'home'—in other words, to someone else's home."[7] She was, like Montand, twenty-eight. It was clear to her that her marriage to Allégret, sixteen years her senior, was over. "I was ready," she recalled, "for a big passion."[8]

That big passion was to have its costs, both emotionally and professionally. Leaving Allégret was a wrenching decision, but, as she put it later, "I knew that something irreversible had happened. . . . The person who did the crying was mostly me. Nothing in the world is sadder than to cause hurt to someone for whom one wants only good, and to be incapable of doing the only thing that would fix everything, which is to stop loving the other."[9] As to her career, she was already France's new movie star, an established actress with nineteen films to her credit. Her most recent was the film noir *Dédée d'Anvers* directed by her husband, in which she played convincingly a restless, rebellious prostitute in a portside bar who wants to start a new life. Like Montand, she had been scouted by the Hollywood studios. Unlike him, she could read English and was well aware of the seven years of servitude such contracts involved. However, Howard Hughes had made a better proposition in the spring of 1949: a well-paid four-year deal for four films of her choice. She accepted and was due to leave for the United States for the final negotiations in the autumn.

That was before she met Montand. (She never called him anything else, avoiding "Yves" because it was also Allégret's first name.) Now, with her life in disarray, she had to make some hard decisions. He was becoming increasingly dissatisfied with their situation and accused her of dithering. To get far away and try to clear his thinking, he scheduled a tour in the Maghreb, with stops in Casablanca, Tunis, and Algiers. On his return, he gave her an ultimatum: leave Allégret, or they would have to break up. Within a week, she packed up and left husband and children and began divorce proceedings. She moved in with Montand at his apartment on rue de Longchamp in suburban Neuilly-sur-Seine. As for Howard Hughes, the deal was off. To friends who said she was crazy to sacrifice her career like that, she replied, "I was sacrificing nothing. I was simply clever enough not to sacrifice my life."[10]

To be sure, Signoret would still go on to have a long career, acting in some sixty films, including the British *Room at the Top* (1959), for which she won a Best Actress Oscar. But Montand was to be her life from now on, despite the great disparity in their backgrounds. They were, after all, exact opposites. She was a well-educated, intellectual young woman from one of the best residential neighborhoods around Paris, who frequented the smoke-filled cafés of Saint Germain des Près to argue politics all night and settle the world's problems. He was up from being a gritty slum kid who couldn't stand school, hardly wrote correct French, and seldom read a book. Yet somehow the inexplicable alchemy of the human heart made them perfectly complementary. Their friend Jacques Prévert saw this clearly: "Love for them was like discovering a new country; there was so much to learn, but they were never bored. Simone gave him culture, depth. He gave her an earthy sense of reality."[11]

⊙ ⊙ ⊙

Simone Henriette Charlotte Kaminker was eight months older than Montand, born on March 25, 1921, in the spa town of Wiesbaden, Germany. Her father, André, was a French army officer serving as part of the Allied occupation of the Rhineland after the defeat of Germany in 1918. Her mother, Georgette Signoret, was also with the army, serving as a secretary with the rank of sergeant. They had met and married in 1920, to the disappointment of both their families: André's Polish-Austrian Jewish parents because he was marrying a Catholic, Georgette's because André was nine years older and a Jew. That didn't worry the young couple, who moved to the handsome Paris suburb of Neuilly-sur-Seine when André was discharged in 1923. He found a job with a Paris advertising agency, where, as fate would have it, two of his creative colleagues were Marcel Carné and Jacques Prévert, both of whom would play important roles in Signoret's adult life.

She was a model little girl raised in the finest traditions of the French bourgeoisie. Georgette closely oversaw her social and intellectual development, enrolling her in the exclusive preschool program at the Cours Lafayette, where she mixed with the offspring of ambassadors and members of

Parliament, some of whom arrived in the morning by chauffeured limousine. André told her the stories of Wagnerian operas and Greek myths, took her on Sunday strolls of Neuilly's most fashionable streets, and brought her with him to visit his wealthy uncle Marcel and aunt Irène, who lived in an opulent apartment on the elegant square Lamartine near the Bois de Boulogne. Summer vacations were spent at a resort on the Atlantic Coast. At the dinner table, conversation was likely as not to turn to the latest volume of Marcel Proust's novel *À la recherche du temps perdu*. As an adolescent, she attended the girls' section of the prestigious Lycée Pasteur. Among its teachers was an unconventional, turtle-necked young philosophy professor named Jean-Paul Sartre, who lent his books to the students, introduced them to modern foreign authors such as Hemingway and Faulkner, and met them for discussions at local cafés. All the while, she was reading all the movie magazines she could find and dreaming of becoming a Hollywood actress after being discovered by a talent scout.

That idyll was shattered when she was nineteen. With the German army at the gates of Paris, André fled to London in May 1940 to join the Free French. His relations with Georgette had been strained for years, and the family was never reunited after the war, when André served as an interpreter with the United Nations. Someone had to provide an income, but Georgette felt incapable of returning to secretarial work. This meant responsibility for the finances fell to Simone as de facto head of the family. She found a job as a typist and gofer at a collaborationist newspaper called *Les nouveaux temps*. It was run by Jean Luchaire, who enjoyed and profited from close friendly relations with top Nazis such as Otto Abetz, Hitler's high commissioner and ambassador to the Vichy government.

Thus, Simone was working for a paper that regularly published virulent anti-Semitic and anti-British articles and had ties to the Nazis. This could hardly be more paradoxical, not to say compromising, in view of her later political positions as a pillar of left-wing causes and ardent communist fellow traveler. "I had no conscience then," she later explained, and her family needed the money, about $100 a month.[12] However that may be, at the same age, nineteen, Yves Montand and Simone Signoret unwittingly had this in common, though they were five hundred miles apart: neither did anything for the wartime defense of their country or to oppose its occupation by the enemy. On the contrary, Simone actually aided and abetted the Nazis by working for a paper that spewed their propaganda. Later she admitted that this period was a blot on her life.

Her epiphany occurred in the spring of 1941 when a date took her to have coffee at the Café de Flore in Saint Germain des Prés. To her wonderment, she entered a world totally different from the one she had known, full of people who, more often than not, were unemployed and seemed to live on ideas and endless febrile conversation. Sartre and his companion Simone de Beauvoir wrote and officiated there, holding sway over an assortment of aspiring writers, artists, and actors, with the occasional clandestine Resistance member mixed in. Signoret's conversion was complete and immediate: "The person I am today was born one evening in March 1941 on a banquette in the Café de Flore, Boulevard St. Germain, Paris, sixth arrondissement," she wrote in her memoir *La nostalgie n'est plus ce qu'elle était* (1977, published in English as *Nostalgia Isn't What It Used to Be* in 1978), "where at last I would find the world to which I belonged."[13]

Beyond discovering herself, her immersion in this brave new world had two concrete results. Her new companions, who now included people such as Henri Crolla, Sartre, Picasso, and Jacques Prévert, convinced her of the obvious: she had to stop working for a collaborationist paper. That autumn Simone Signoret—she had replaced her father's name "Kaminker" with her mother's maiden name, less risky under Nazi occupation—strode into Luchair's office and told him not only that she was quitting but that he would likely end up before a firing squad. The second important event brought about by her assiduous attendance at the Flore bull sessions was her meeting with Yves Allégret in January 1943.

Then thirty-eight, Allégret had been in films since the early 1930s, beginning as assistant to Jean Renoir, among other directors, and had done a half-dozen minor movies. She was flattered that an older man, a movie director, was interested in her. Soon they were living together, he having been separated from his wife for two years. They had two children, one dying in infancy, before they married in 1948. He directed her in four films, the best being *Dedée* and *Manèges / The Wanton* (1949, US 1950), in which she was, respectively, a prostitute and an unfaithful, exploitative wife. It was just as well that Montand had never seen those films. He always said that if he had, he wouldn't have fallen in love with her.

⊙ ⊙ ⊙

Signoret knew about the movie business, but music hall was a foreign country to her. She found it fascinating. "All of a sudden I was living with someone who knew something I didn't know, something I would never know how to do. I was curious, impressed, and, yes, intimidated." She discovered a side to Montand that wasn't on view during vacation in Saint Paul: he was wholly involved in his craft, and that meant devoting most of his time to readying his performances, rehearsing for them, and planning them with precision, almost obsessively.[14]

She accepted a supporting role graciously. She attended his rehearsals religiously, paying attention to every detail so she could discuss how it went with him afterward, running errands, leaving him alone when he needed complete privacy to concentrate in a bubble before a show, standing in the wings to hand him a towel when he finally came off the stage depleted, his face dripping with sweat. When she was doing a film on location, she looked forward to getting back to their routine: "And everything will be the way it was, with storms and rainbows, great times and little arguments."[15] She managed his mail and discovered, with a pang of jealousy, the effect his singing voice had on the female population. Many correspondents included crudely explicit photos, which, she noticed, often interested him. There were also his media relations to be organized, occasionally correcting a misstep. Claude Gauteur, one of France's premier film historians, covered Montand as a young reporter for *Le film français,* a weekly magazine for movie professionals. "He used to call me before a film was released and try to tell me what to say about it," he recalled. "Then Simone, whom I knew well, would call and ask, 'What kind of nonsense has he told you now? He's got no business calling up reporters to ask for special treatment.' She was really the brains in the family."[16]

She was the brains, he was the brawn. That's what was often said. To a large extent, it was true. He couldn't help feeling that his lack of education made him intellectually inferior to her, however much he read. The feeling was magnified in a country where being "covered with diplomas" is one of the most flattering compliments, and the self-educated person, the autodidact, is inevitably referred to with a hint of condescension. The undeniable fact was that he really did not share her love of books, which left him at a social disadvantage when they were with her bookish friends, and he had trouble following the conversation. That position was frustrating and galling for a man of his prickly macho pride. Attempting to compensate for his educational deficit, he never missed the chance to learn something new, peppering everyone he knew with questions and slogging laboriously through books looking for nuggets of information and knowledge he could use.

There was, however, something he could teach Signoret. Despite her evenings spent theorizing about the coming revolution of the working class, when everything, according to Karl Marx, would be distributed from each according to their ability, to each according to their needs, in her head she had never really left Neuilly and her middle-class upbringing. She and her café conversation partners were many things—writers, actors, artists, wannabees of every sort—but downtrodden members of the working class they were not.

Montand gave her a taste of how the other half lived when he took her to meet his family in La Cabucelle. As she admitted later, "Beginning with my time at the Flore, I had been living in a left milieu and feeling very much at home there, but I had never had any contact with what is called the working class. I really knew it only through what I had read and what people had told me. I was absolutely typical of what is called a 'left intellectual,' with all that includes of the ridiculous, but also of the generous. Oddly enough, my first meeting with Montand was also my first incursion into the workingman's world, the proletariat, if not the subproletariat. . . . I began to see things in a different light."[17]

Amid the odors of the slaughterhouse and the wail of the gasworks siren calling men to work, for the first time in her life she sat at a table with people who had actually toiled in factories for most of their lives. A bit like Edith Piaf, Signoret at first felt out of place amid the rapid-fire conversation in a mix of French and Tuscan patois but covered it up by questioning everyone about themselves. The Livis warmed to this Parisienne who ate her chicken with her little finger daintily raised. By the end of the family meal, they had adopted each other. She even undertook with Lydia to find a little house in the Marseilles suburbs that Montand gave to his parents.

The time had come to consider their own living arrangements. The apartment in Neuilly was comfortable but filled with the memories of Montand's numerous exes, some of whom continued to call him there. While looking for an alternative, they learned from Henri Crolla that the bookshop next door to the hotel where he and his wife, Colette, were living was for rent. It was on place Dauphine, a tree-lined sandy square at the western tip of the Ile de la Cité, the island in the middle of the Seine where Paris had originated nearly two thousand years earlier.

The shop was in a seventeenth-century building between the city's oldest bridge, perversely named the Pont Neuf, and the wondrous stained-glass windows of the Sainte Chapelle. A little farther on to the east loomed the twin towers of the cathedral Notre-Dame de Paris. It's hard to imagine more history, beauty, and charm all grouped in one place, and Montand and Signoret decided on the spot that they would transform the bookshop into their home. The fact that it was one of the more elegant, expensive, and sought-after addresses in Paris did not seem to trouble the leftist intellectual of the Café de Flore. Nor, for that matter, did it bother Montand, who habitually carried plenty of cash on him and owned at one time or another and sometimes simultaneously a Packard, a Bentley, and a red Ferrari, among other cars.

The storefront, on the side that opened onto the Quai des Orfèvres, became the apartment's cramped living room, with a ceiling barely two inches above Montand's head and just enough space for his piano and a few chairs. Their bedroom was upstairs with a window giving onto the river; Catherine would sleep on a folding cot in what had been the office. There was a small kitchen, which was used only by their cook, Marcelle Mirtilon (Signoret was known to have prepared dinner only once during their marriage, and that was overdone spaghetti). The apartment, which they later purchased and nicknamed "the Caravan," also became home to brother Julien, his wife, Elvire, and their son, Jean-Louis, who moved in when more rooms on upper floors were added. The Montand–Signoret clan also included actors such as Bernard Blier, Serge Reggiani, and François Périer as well as Henri Crolla and others, who often crammed into the Caravan for parties.

Their domestic details settled, the couple's thoughts turned to marriage. True, it was a bourgeois institution, and they were opposed to it in principle, but Catherine was starting school, and they didn't want her to be taunted by schoolmates and teachers with less liberal ideas. Thus it was that they were at the town hall in Saint Paul de Vence at 11:00 a.m. on December 22, 1951, for a civil wedding. (Signoret always liked to backdate their married life to August 19, 1949.) Jacques Prévert gave away the bride, who wore a gold-and-diamond necklace and a cream-colored silk Balmain suit under a mink coat. Picasso couldn't make it, but his chauffeur delivered a felt-pen drawing of a dove dedicated to them. Reporters and photographers jockeyed for position, the local hunters' association shot off a salvo. The wedding dinner was at La Colombe d'Or, complete with a fluttering flight of doves, one of which, as if on cue, landed on Signoret's head and folded its wings. Everyone found that it looked just like Picasso's drawing. "It's exactly the village wedding I wanted," Signoret said.[18] The local communist paper reported, without apparent irony, "It was the great friend of the workingman who walked with springy stride down the narrow streets of Saint Paul de Vence." They were "a wholesome couple marching into the future."[19] It didn't mention the necklace or mink coat.

For the next thirty-four years, they would be France's most famous pair, stars of the celebrity press, asked their opinions on everything from freedom to feminism. Interviewed for a television documentary in the 1960s, Signoret revealed that she no longer wore makeup because Montand didn't like it. Asked if she always did as he said, she replied, "I generally do as he says, and I like it that way." So she wasn't a liberated woman? "I'm free exactly the way I want to be. As little, and as much as I want."[20] For an alumna of the Café de Flore, her attitude toward marriage was distinctly old-fashioned, believing, as she said, that it had to be built on a solid base where each partner knew his or her place: "It's a law of nature, the man dominates, the woman submits. I've never been anything but his groupie. And I'm proud of it."[21]

It was to be anything but an easy marriage. Both had the temperaments of show business performers, with all that implies of egocentric edginess. In France, they were known as *monstres sacrés,* "sacred monsters," a frequent description of stars. Besides that, they were from very different worlds, and although they generally appreciated and reveled in their differences, the gulf between their social and educational backgrounds sometimes grated. She could be assertive and directive and could not always conceal a basic feeling of intellectual superiority, correcting his pronunciation or vocabulary when he made a mistake. It annoyed him, too, when she critiqued a song or dance move in front of friends. As for Montand, his explosive outbursts over a disagreement or an imagined slight—even the clicking of needles as she knitted in the evening—could go on for hours. "We have quarreled a lot," she once admitted, managing to put a positive spin on it. "But that is good. Otherwise things would have been very sad."[22]

Then there was the problematic question of fidelity. Montand exuded virility across the footlights, leading to crowds of stage-door Janes to whom he was not always indifferent. Signoret could try to manage that, stationing herself backstage after a show to guard the dressing-room door. "Occasionally, when it gets too boring and a woman won't leave the dressing room," she said, "I put on my prostitute face and just tell her to scram."[23] But she could not change his very Mediterranean view that faithfulness was for wives.

Since adolescence, Montand had always had an outsize sexual appetite. Not to put too fine a point on it, he wanted relations frequently, casually, and in variety, and everyone—Signoret, friends, other actors on the set of his movies, the public—knew it. With a shrug and a giggle, the French called him a *quétard,* a slang expression derived from the word for the male sex organ. In his view, his affairs didn't matter to their marriage as long as they were merely, as he called them, "little adventures."[24] Signoret apparently made her peace with that on the condition that he leave her friends, such as the actresses Danièle Delorme and Jeanne Moreau, alone. No moral judgment is made or implied here; his infidelity was a fact of life for Montand and Signoret. It was an arrangement that functioned more or less to both partners' satisfaction for ten years. Until he went to Hollywood.

7

Political Activist

It was Simone Signoret who made Yves Montand a political activist. Before he met her, there is no sign that he ever gave political questions a moment's serious consideration, despite the fact that his father, who was one of the main influences in his life, was a militant communist who had to leave his home country because of his political beliefs and even though his brother, Julien, to whom he was very close, held increasingly important positions in the Confederation générale du travail (CGT), France's aggressive communist labor union that, in those days, took its orders from Moscow.

Montand gives the impression in his memoirs that his political conscience was awakened when he felt the human solidarity of the working class in the factories and on the docks of Marseilles. But those books were written in hindsight well after Signoret had steeped him in the ideas she had picked up at the Café de Flore and must be taken with a grain of salt. The fact is that he never even joined the show business chapter of a labor union, which was done routinely by most professional entertainers in France.

Once she began to serve as his *maître à penser,* however, the socialist/communist ideals he had picked up by osmosis from his father and brother began to crystallize. Politics, in particular devotion to the communist ideal, quickly became a virtual obsession with him. At the parties in the Caravan on place Dauphine, he talked about nothing else, sometimes to the annoyance of his friends. When invited out to dinner parties, he and Simone would get up and storm out if anyone suggested there were political prisoners in the Soviet Union. If they saw one of the mediocre Russian films of that period, full of praise for the worker's paradise, they would find something to like, if only the technical quality of the film used. He would tolerate no criticism of Stalin, who had defeated the German fascists on the battlefield and who, Montand believed, was building a new, more just world. If communism was the new secular religion, Stalin was its infallible pope. One day when

Montand was at the movies, the audience jeered at a newsreel showing a military parade on Red Square. Furious, he stood up and shouted, "Stalingrad!," as if that settled all arguments about Soviet communism.

The couple attended peace rallies organized by the French Communist Party. They signed petitions, lots of them, calling for peace and disarmament and promoting the class struggle to build socialism, unwittingly supporting themes promoted by Soviet agitprop and front organizations such as the World Peace Council to weaken the West while the Soviet Union rebuilt its army. From January 1951 to June 1953, for example, they signed sixteen such appeals and joined fellow travelers such as Pablo Picasso to aid party recruitment. They preached the good word to all and sundry.

When the impressionable twenty-six-year-old Jane Fonda was in Paris in the fall of 1963 to be in René Clément's film *Joy House* (1964) with Alain Delon as male lead, she looked up Montand and Signoret. She had met them in 1959 when they were in New York for his first show there. She particularly admired Signoret, "with her charming lisp, sensual bee-stung lips, and heavy-lidded blue eyes—tough, opinionated, always insisting on being a human first, a star second." Soon she was joining the evenings of passionate, endless political discussions at place Dauphine. It was there that the dormant activist was awakened in her: "All of them were *engagé,* committed to activism, and in sympathy with the French Communist Party."[1] She liked the way they agreed with the party on many issues without actually joining it, instead practicing communism with a small *c*, as she put it. In particular, Signoret taught Fonda about the history of French colonialism in Vietnam. That was a key factor in turning Fonda against US involvement there.

The party ballyhooed the event when Montand went to the big Renault automobile plant in the Paris suburb of Boulogne-Billancourt to sing for the workers, as he often did for protesters during strikes and at rallies. In April 1950, only eight months after meeting Signoret, he told the communist youth newspaper *L'avant-garde,* "The role of a singer is to reflect the life of all workers without exception."[2] Since he had begun singing in Marseilles ten years earlier and then in upscale Paris music halls and chic Champs-Élysées nightclubs, he had never considered that a singer's role was other than to entertain. Suddenly he was now singing regularly for workers on strike, at peace rallies, and at communist demonstrations.

However, Montand trod a fine line between being a fellow traveler and actually joining the French Communist Party. Although the press frequently called him a member and party leaders pressured him to join, neither he nor

Signoret ever took the proffered membership card. Their main reason was its position on culture, which they found suffocating for the arts. Artists and writers who were party members were expected to toe the party line in every respect, a virtual straitjacket. Party leader Maurice Thorez had laid out that line as early as 1947; the party was against "the decadent works of bourgeois aesthetes, partisans of art for art's sake, against the deep-rooted pessimism and backward-looking obscurantism of the existentialist philosophers," and in favor of "an art drawing its inspiration from socialist realism and comprehensible to the working class."[3] The couple also disagreed with communist censorship of Hollywood films. Thus, Montand kept a prudent public distance from official party functions to avoid being tagged as one of its artists. He refused repeated invitations to perform at the annual Fête de l'Humanité, a popular fair sponsored by the party newspaper and held on the outskirts of Paris.

Montand didn't pay membership dues, but he did contribute substantially to the party. On one occasion, he discreetly wrapped one million francs (about $285,700) in a newspaper and dropped it off at the offices of *L'humanité*, the party newspaper. On another, he had his sister-in-law, Elvire, take 600,000 francs (about $171,430) to the party offices.[4] He also engaged in some self-censorship to please the communists. "C'est si bon," for example, was too American—it had already been popularized in the United States, notably by Johnny Desmond and Louis Armstrong—so he stopped singing it for some time. Nor did the communist censors like "Luna Park" because it told of a factory worker out looking for weekend fun instead of devoting his spare time to the revolutionary struggle. Songs about pretty girls, such as "Une demoiselle sur une balençoire" (The Girl on a Swing), her legs visible beneath her petticoats as she swings to and fro, and "Sanguine," describing a woman whose amorous body was lovingly described in a poem by Jacques Prévert, were too frivolous and naughty for the New Man of the hard-working masses. He rejected the party's requests that he not sing these standards in his repertoire, but his new political scruples made him think twice before adopting a new song.

In May 1950, Montand and Signoret signed the Stockholm Appeal demanding a ban on all nuclear weapons and holding that any country that used them should be charged with crimes against humanity. They had plenty of company: 273,470,566 others, including the entire population of the Soviet Union, if we are to believe the official figures. Sponsored by a Soviet front organization, the World Peace Council, the appeal was initiated and given respectability by the French communist physicist Frédéric Joliot-Curie. It garnered the support of notables ranging from Louis Aragon, Marcel Carné, and Maurice Chevalier in France to Leonard Bernstein, Paul Robeson, Dashiell Hammett, and Charlie Parker in the United States, along with clergymen, educators, and ordinary citizens. The vast majority of the signatories undoubtedly signed in good faith, yet the appeal was a clever, simple-minded hoax designed to make the world's public believe that the Soviets stood for peace and the United States for war. It easily attracted mass participation because who, after all, could be against peace?[5]

Montand—who had added a line to his signature saying, "I sign so that I may continue to sing for a long time"—came to see the light much later. "We were manipulated," he said in a French television interview in the 1980s. "But I don't regret signing the Stockholm Appeal. In the context of the time, of the Cold War and the threat of war, fighting for peace seemed all-important. . . . We went along wholeheartedly. It wasn't until much later that we realized the whole campaign was intended to gain time until the Russians, too, acquired the bomb."[6] He later explained more fully his pro-Soviet positions in the 1950s:

> How could we have swallowed such horrors? It must seem strange indeed to the youth of today. How could eminent scientists have believed in "proletarian science"? How could brilliant writers and superior minds have given their blessing to such a system? If all those people with intelligence and knowledge were led astray in this way, how could I—uneducated, a product of La Cabucelle—have had doubts? If I wavered for a moment, I thought of the heroes of Stalingrad, of the 20 million Soviet citizens killed in the war against Hitlerism, of a country devastated by war. If I had known about the gulag during the war I would have been horrified, but I still would have been on the side of the Red Army. That kind of loyalty may be incomprehensible to those who have not lived through war, but for my generation it was an article of faith. Yet it was in the name of that loyalty that we accepted the unacceptable.[7]

The party spirit canceled out questions and criticism. Fear of giving ammunition to the enemy pushed aside all doubt.

The Stockholm Appeal branded Montand and Signoret as communist fellow travelers, with consequences in both France and the United States. The

French government opened a file on them at the police prefecture. The Renseignements généraux, a domestic spy agency, appointed an agent to keep Ivo Livi and Simone Kaminker under observation and file regular reports on them. The file eventually amounted to seventy pages, noting their every political move and even their sexual activities. Montand, one report noted, was a skirt chaser. Signoret, said another, was an easy woman.[8] In the United States, they were effectively personae non gratae: the State Department refused for years to issue them visas after they signed the petition. They shrugged it off as best they could. "Montand and I were dismayed by the idea that we would never set foot in America," Signoret remembered. "We'd say to ourselves: 'It's a pity. We'll never see Broadway; we'll never watch Fred Astaire dance or meet Henry Fonda; we'll never know what Hollywood is like, or the Golden Gate, or the Brooklyn Bridge; we'll never know all those things the American film world meant for all those people of our generation and profession."[9]

But in their circles, being banned by the US State Department was considered a badge of honor. It didn't blunt Montand's new political activism. On the contrary, it sharpened that activism, and he had the courage of his convictions. As time went on, France's prominent political couple would march in demonstrations, join left-wing peace movements, protest vocally against the French war in Indochina and later in Algeria, US troops in Vietnam, and Greek and South American dictatorships supported by Washington. Montand vowed never to set foot in Spain as long as Francisco Franco was in power. He demonstrated against McCarthyism as well as against the trial and execution of Julius and Ethel Rosenberg on charges of spying for the Soviet Union and providing it with secrets of the atomic bomb.

The first test of his mettle was his stance against the French war in Indochina in the early 1950s. France had been bogged down in anticolonial wars since the late 1940s, and public opinion was hardening on both sides. The Left condemned the French government's commitment to keeping its colonies and used its sway over labor to incite actions, such as dock workers refusing to load war materiel on ships bound for the region. The Right supported the war, often with strongarm tactics.

It was in this tense atmosphere that Francis Lemarque wrote an antiwar song for Montand entitled "Quand un soldat" (When a Soldier). Denouncing the stupidity and futility of war, it describes the typical soldier who goes off gaily to war with a flower in his rifle barrel as the heavens look down upon those about to die marching in step. If he's able to return home, he's not a hero; he's just a lucky guy with some dirty laundry in his duffel bag. Montand loved it and sang it so soon after it was written that he held the text in his hand because he hadn't taken the time to memorize it.

The song seems innocent enough, but in those fraught times reactions were on a hair trigger. The government banned broadcasting it on the radio, and Montand's mailbox was filled with death threats from right-wing groups. When he took it on tour, hostile crowds demonstrated outside theaters. Stink bombs were thrown in the auditorium in one city; his posters were smeared with tar in another. In Paris, a gang of right-wing activists bought up all the front-row seats at a performance, and when he came on stage, they ostentatiously opened wide their copies of *L'humanité* to unsettle him and block the audience's view. He stared them down and kept on singing, reassuring his orchestra that if anyone came on stage, he would beat that person's brains out. When invited to perform at a white-tie event at the Comédie-Française, where President Vincent Auriol was expected, the organizers asked him not to sing that controversial text. He did anyway. His refusal to back down was typical of the way he stuck with songs he believed in, imposing them on a reticent public. "Quand un soldat" eventually became one of his most popular pieces, and he kept it in his repertory for the rest of his career. As Bernard Kouchner, a communist turned socialist, founder of Médecins sans frontières (Doctors without Borders), and foreign minister under President Nicolas Sarkozy, told a French television interviewer after Montand died, "His songs became political tracts. For the Left, and I was on the Left, he was our hero."[10]

Given his lifestyle, however, it was easy to charge Montand with hypocrisy. The right called him *gauche caviar,* "left caviar," the French version of *limousine liberal.* During one of the frequent French public-transport strikes in 1952, a newspaper published a photo of him and the Bentley he had bought secondhand from Prince Rainier of Monaco, hoping its more sedate lines would attract less attention than the more spectacular Packard he had owned previously. "You might not be able to catch a bus," it headlined, "but Montand has his Bentley."[11] He retorted that he didn't see how it would make him any more on the left if he wore a worker's flat cap and rode a bicycle; he made money out of the capitalist system, he argued, but he worked for it. Signoret, too, came in for her share of mockery. The conservative press depicted her out selling *L'humanité-dimanche,* the Sunday edition of the party paper, in a mink coat or sending the maid out to sell it while she watched from a distance to be sure the maid did it right.

There is no doubt that Montand was sincere in his political activism once it had been stimulated and given an ideological basis by Signoret. He showed considerable courage in sticking with it in one form or another for the rest of his life, even though after he saw the reality of life under Soviet communism, individual freedom and human rights replaced the communist-capitalist dichotomy for him. In later life, he came to take a more tolerant, balanced view of right and wrong, of left and right, acknowledging that people of good faith could hold different political positions. "It's dangerous to push idealism too far," he reflected. "Because I'm a Latin, I had a tendency to replace God with Marx."[12]

⊙ ⊙ ⊙

Songs with a political slant were increasingly important as Montand returned to his favorite theater, the Étoile, in the spring of 1951 with a beefed-up repertory. The event marked a milestone in Montand's career, for this time he would be alone. He would not be an opening act warming up the audience for a star. There would be no contortionists, magicians, mimes, acrobats, or jugglers for variety. There would in fact be nothing but him, his small orchestra, and the songs. He felt he was ready to go solo, to be on stage for a two-hour recital without intermission. It would be the first one-person show in French entertainment history.

It was a daunting challenge, and he went about preparing with meticulous attention to detail. His "costume" of plain brown slacks and open-neck shirt were now a given, and he saw no reason to change that. However, he wanted more direct contact with the audience. He recalled the way Piaf had staged the orchestra behind her instead of in the pit at the Moulin Rouge. He adopted that idea and improved on it by placing a sea-green scrim as a backcloth between him and the orchestra. It was semitransparent, and he always introduced his musicians by name, but some cranks in the media complained that he was depriving them of their due. The musicians themselves never quibbled about it, and other performers soon followed suit.

He composed the program as a mix of song, dance, and short sketches, building and then relaxing in intensity, creating an alternating rhythm of music and action designed to keep the audience's attention. He liked to compare himself to an artisan who bult a mood the way a cabinetmaker fashions a table. For this show, he chose twenty-two songs varying in tone from the political to the dramatic, the humorous to the romantic, and two poems. Unlike Piaf, he didn't write any of his own material. He always considered himself an interpreter of the texts that others, with more writing skill, provided him. What set him apart was, first, his very personal, idiosyncratic choice of material according to what he felt was his style and, second, his well-honed performance of each number, in which every move and gesture was timed and burnished and rehearsed until he had it down pat. He regretted that there was no word in French equivalent to *entertainer.* The latter is a much more comprehensive and professional term than *amuseur* or *saltinbanque,* both of which carry connotations of amateurism.

His perfectionism was too pat for some critics, who found that it came at the cost of spontaneity. They accused him of working it all out in front of a mirror, of rehearsing everything—every riff by the orchestra, every stab of the following spot—even of moving his hands exactly the same way every time. To take one example: he worked for four months learning to do a cartwheel that he appeared to throw in on a sudden impulse during his number "Les saltimbanques" (The Entertainers). Such stunts were all part of his rapport with the audience. "It's like an 18-year-old that you're trying to please," he once explained. "If there's a spectator in the back of the theater who's not happy with the show, I feel it. You have to convince and seduce the first rows, then win over the rest bit by bit."[13] The effort cost him physically. He calculated that every recital was the equivalent of a marathon in which he lost several pounds and left him wrung out.

He developed a preshow routine that he would follow for the rest of his life. It began with arriving several hours early at the theater, which gave him plenty of time to detach himself from all quotidian worries and activities. In this bubble, he went into a trance of deep immersion in the show, a time when Signoret, the stage hands, and the musicians knew it was forbidden to speak to him. As she described this trance, "Wherever he may be, he isn't where he is. He's somewhere else, and already he's alone. At first that was quite hard to understand. It was as though he had suddenly left me. . . . It took a little while before I realized that from six o'clock on, I wasn't supposed to talk. I was supposed to be available, invisible, and especially I wasn't supposed to be elsewhere."[14] To parry the inevitable stage fright, he warmed up his voice with Henri Crolla; then when the curtain rose, he ritualistically patted Crolla on the head, removed his wedding ring—the show was to be between just him and the audience—and stepped onto the stage.

The political songs began with a poke at both capitalism and racism as imagined in America. "Les cireurs de souliers de Broadway" (The Broadway Shoeshine Boys) tells of wealthy white men of New York who contemptuously toss a few cents to the Black boy who has shined their shoes so well and conscientiously that they seem to capture the sun. Then they stroll away into the crowds of Broadway, indifferent to the luminous miracle the boy has worked on their shoes. In spite of the way he is treated, he goes on happily singing as he works, smiling and full of joie de vivre. Then, a few songs later, came "Actualités" (News), a parody of a news bulletin that begins on a light note and progressively gets darker and crueler. After hearing that the weather is fine and farmers are contentedly plowing their fields, we learn of two well-off men drinking a morning whiskey in a bar and talking about their hunting dogs, while elsewhere a blue baby closes its eyes and slowly dies. The Seine flows placidly, young lovers embrace, and somewhere under the earth a hundred trapped miners scream; only ten will survive. Montand sings the song lightly and without emphasis, accompanied only by Henri Crolla on guitar, seemingly not even noticing the tragedies he has just described, which adds to the pathos.

Then there was "Barbara," an antiwar poem by Jacques Prévert that Montand simply recited softly without musical accompaniment—something that performers occasionally did in the intimate atmosphere of a Paris nightclub but had never tried before a music hall audience of thousands. In it, an anonymous narrator recounts how he saw a young woman rush happily into the arms of a man who called her name, Barbara, in a rainy street in Brest. Then the text veers away from what appears to be a love song into a statement about the stupidity of war, rhetorically asking Barbara what became of her and her lover after it rained steel and fire and blood on Brest, a port city on France's Atlantic coast that served as a base for German U-boats during the war and was almost totally destroyed by Allied bombing. "Barbara" became one of Montand's most famous and popular numbers and won France's top prize for recordings, the Grand prix du disque.

Among the romantic songs was "Demoiselle sur une balençoire," which, thanks to the party censors, had also become political, an exercise in freedom of speech. In this bit of whimsy, the narrator not only glimpses the young lady's legs beneath her petticoats on the swing but proposes to her, and she accepts. But after a while she gets bored, thanks him, and goes back to the swing. Montand also retrieved Prévert's song "Les enfants qui s'aiment" (Young Lovers) from the film *Les portes de la nuit* and made it a music hall hit, portraying young lovers who kiss in public despite the mockery of adults who are secretly jealous; the youngsters notice nothing but each other in the dazzle of their first love. In Lemarque's bittersweet "Cornet de frites" (A Bag of French Fries), a man remembers how happy he had been when he and his girl munched a bag of them as they strolled beside the Seine. Now they are parted, and he is left with his memories of those days when a bag of fries was all they needed before rushing off to make love. In "Clémentine," a young swain tells of the first time he made love, at sixteen, to a beauty whose "nice little breasts" were just visible beneath her light blouse. Walking beside a river, she trips and falls in. He attempts to save her, forgetting in his passion that he can't swim. It is she who saves him and makes love to him on the moss of the riverbank.

The show began its run on March 5, 1951, and went on for four months, until June 27. The 1,700-seat Étoile was sold out for all 112 evenings. In the audience at one time or another—and in his dressing room to congratulate him after the show—were many of the French entertainment elite, from Edith Piaf to Charles Aznavour, Jean Gabin, Erich von Stroheim, Maurice Chevalier, and many others. Humphrey Bogart and Lauren Bacall took it in during a week-long vacation in Paris at the Ritz Hotel between Bogart's final takes for *The African Queen* (1951) in London; after the show, they dined with Montand and Signoret at Maxim's. The critics loved the show, calling Montand number one among popular singers. They approved of the way he blended song genres, switching smoothly from whimsical to serious, funny to dramatic. *Le Monde* consecrated him as simply prodigious: "Yves Montand can no longer be compared to any others," it proclaimed. "He is Yves Montand just as Chevalier is Chevalier and Edith Piaf is Edith Piaf."[15] Its only concern was whether he could stand up to the effort of performing for two hours every evening for months.

He could, he did. Given the continuing demand for tickets at the Étoile box office on June 27, he could have taken the show to another theater and continued for some time. It was the last great period to be a live performer in France, a country still rebuilding after the war with few other diversions: there were a total of 3,794 television sets and one channel. To his surprise, the audience got younger toward the end of the run, composed mainly of teenagers. That was good news because he was beginning to wonder whether young people might find his repertory old hat compared with that of new pop singers. He could have continued the show, but Henri-Georges Clouzot wanted him for a film, and he wouldn't take no for an answer.

8

Star

Henri-Georges Clouzot was depressed. At forty-four, he had had a checkered career as a director, screenwriter, and producer in wartime Germany and Vichy France. He had experienced the best and the worst of the cinema world and had acquired a scandal-tainted reputation to show for it.

In the 1930s, he had the luck to work as a screenwriter with the Russia-born director Anatole Litvak at the big Babelsberg studios of the major German film company Universum Film AG (UFA), where Litvak did his first films before moving to France after the rise of Adolf Hitler and later going to Hollywood. At UFA, Clouzot mixed with a small colony of French actors, from Jean Gabin to Arletty, Charles Vanel to Marcel Dalio, who acted in the French versions of German films. Through his work there as well as in Munich, Prague, Budapest, and Vienna, he developed a taste for the sort of tough-minded German expressionism and film noir he saw in classics such as F. W. Murnau's eerie vampire story *Nosferatu* (1922), Fritz Lang's science fiction *Metropolis* (1927), and Lang's uber-realist *M* (1932). "I owe my taste for film noir to the Germans," Clouzot said later.[1] He fell into disfavor with UFA, however, and was fired because of his friendships with Jewish producers.

After a five-year bout with tuberculosis, Clouzot returned to France during the war. He worked for the German-owned Continental Films and managed to offend just about everybody with his film *Le corbeau* (The Crow; 1943, US 1948). Continental, which answered to its Nazi masters, fired him for doing a work that it feared cast Vichy France in an unfavorable light. Rooted in the undeniable fact that French citizens sent an estimated 3 million letters to the German occupiers denouncing their neighbors for alleged offences, the film was a bleakly misanthropic, noirish look at the inhabitants of a small provincial town terrorized by poison-pen letters: *corbeau,* literally "crow" or "raven," can also refer to a writer of malicious anonymous letters. It simultaneously managed to offend the Catholic Church, the Resistance, and the postwar French government for its pitiless portrayal of the darker side of France under the Occupation. In 1944, France's witch-hunting Comité de libération du cinéma français (Committee for the Liberation of French Cinema) banned *Le corbeau* and forbade Clouzot to make films or even use a film camera until 1947.

By 1951, Clouzot had done five films, including the excellent *Quai des Orfèvres / Jenny Lamour* (1947, US 1948), a crime thriller with the great Louis Jouvet as a methodical detective unraveling a murder case; it won him a Best Director award at the 1947 Venice Film Festival and the Edgar Allan Poe Award as Best Foreign Film in 1949. He had also received praise for *Manon* (1949, US 1950), an adaptation of the nineteenth-century opera by Jules Massenet that Clouzot used to show what he considered the breakdown and corruption of French postwar society. But, moody and temperamental at best, he was now feeling frankly fed up with the whole business. "I'm sick and tired of working myself to death in this trade," he confided. "The anxiety, always being anxious, it's no way to live. One of these days I'm going to give it up. In fact, this will be my last film. When does the angst end? Never. And the more things you do, the more you're afraid. And after that? After that, you die."[2]

The film that he was convinced would be his last was based on a thriller novel that had caught his director's eye, *Le salaire de la peur* (*The Wages of Fear,* 1949) by Georges Arnaud. It was the story of four desperate men of different nationalities who had nothing in common but being stranded without work and without hope in a dusty, dead-end South American village. With no money to pay for a ticket out of there, they loiter all day at a ramshackle bar, arguing and ogling the waitress, Linda. Then an oil well in the region catches fire, and the callous American owner, the Southern Oil Company—any resemblance to the Standard Oil Company seems purely intentional—needs four expendable men to drive two trucks loaded with the nitroglycerin necessary to blow out the fire. The four seize the chance to make $2,000 each and begin a three-hundred-mile trek over perilous mountain roads where each bad jolt or mishap might set off the explosive load.

Arnaud, whose real name was Henri Girard, was, like Clouzot, a maverick. The son of a well-off family who grew up in their chateau in the Périgord region of southwestern France, he, too, had suffered from tuberculosis. He also had gotten on the wrong side of the establishment: he was accused, jailed, and acquitted of the brutal sickle murder of his father, an aunt, and their housemaid and later did more jail time for taking the side of the rebels in the Algerian war. He squandered his inheritance and headed to South America, where he knocked around for three years as a taxi driver, bar tender, gold prospector, and truck driver. The novel's jaundiced view of the human race as venal, cruel, and corrupt fit well with Clouzot's fundamental misanthropy. He bought the film rights and did the screenplay adaptation. Despite his lassitude, he wanted to do that film. It had the makings of the ultimate road movie, a guaranteed nail-biter with attitude.

And he wanted Yves Montand as the male lead, a cocky young Corsican named Mario who struts around the village and treats his girlfriend, the waitress, with contempt. Montand's status as a famous music hall star would pull audiences in. But, perversely, what really attracted Clouzot was Montand's pallid performances in his previous attempts at films. He thus incarnated nothing and had no established screen persona, but he had the former dock worker's muscular physique necessary to be credible for the role Clouzot had in mind. He would, in short, be putty in Clouzot's hands. First, however, he had to overcome Montand's reluctance to try another film.[3]

Montand had been stung by the reaction to his previous attempts at acting and was convinced that he would never be at ease on a set the way he was on a stage. Besides, more bad film reviews could tarnish his singing career. So when Clouzot approached him about *Salaire,* his answer was no, for many reasons. Not only was he riding high as a singer and had no motivation to do another film, but he also hadn't read the novel, and, besides, he didn't like what he saw as Clouzot's bilious, right-wing view of humanity as opposed to the optimistic communist theme of the perfectible New Man. Moreover, he was not attracted by the idea of working with a volatile, tyrannical director known for getting angry when a scene didn't go well—Clouzot had slapped the seasoned actors Bernard Blier and Suzy Delair while filming *Orfèvres.*[4]

Clouzot persisted. He and his Brazilian-born actress-wife, Vera, besieged the Caravan at place Dauphine and pressed their arguments: the film had a strong subject with anticapitalist overtones; it reflected the reality of life in South America; it was a man's film, with brutal masculine dialogue. Sensing that Montand was tempted but still apprehensive about his acting ability, Clouzot used his clinching argument: he proposed to work with Montand personally before filming began, coaching him to develop and refine his technique.

The final question remaining was where the shoot would take place. It was too expensive to go on location to South America, so Clouzot had decided to film in Spain. That was a red flag to Montand and Signoret, who told him flatly that they would never set foot there as long as Franco was in power. With Vera on their side, Clouzot gave in and chose the barren Camargue region of southwestern France to construct the fictional banana republic town of Las Piedras. That settled, Montand had one final demand: Clouzot would release him from his contract if the daily rushes showed that his part wasn't working out.[5]

The two couples took up residence at a country auberge called La Moutière in the fashionable village of Montfort L'Amaury, about thirty miles west of Paris. It was a country auberge in name only, being, like La Colombe d'Or, an exclusive hostel and restaurant frequented by visiting VIPs, including Grace Kelly, Ava Gardner, the shah of Iran, Orson Welles, and an aristocratic young English couple known by their first names only, Elizabeth and Philip. Doing it by the numbers, Clouzot gave Montand a one-on-one master class in in acting: diction, tempo, movement on the set, the blocking of actors in the frame, camera angles—it was like the course at drama school that Montand had never had, finally filling in the gaps in his acting skills. It was the first time that a director had coached him in the basics, especially in the art of forgetting himself and *becoming* someone else. Eschewing for the moment the *Salaire* script, Clouzot gave him one by the prolific playwright Jean Anouilh to work on and auditioned him every afternoon. Then, Montand's run at the Étoile not quite finished, he would leave for the theater and his two-hour performance.[6]

With Montand committed, Clouzot completed his casting. For the other main role, that of Jo, a former French gang boss, he wanted Jean Gabin. It was a strange choice because it is difficult to imagine the forty-seven-year-old Gabin, even though he was at the time going through a fallow period, playing second fiddle to Montand. In any case, he turned down the part, refusing to play a pathetic coward, Jo, who gets roughed up and ordered around by Mario when he loses his nerve during the drive.[7] Clouzot then turned to Charles Vanel, a veteran who by sixty had done more than a hundred films during his forty-year career—he would go on acting for years, having the longest screen career of any French actor—and whose next film would be Alfred Hitchcock's *To Catch a Thief* (1955). To play the other two drivers, Bimbi and Luigi, Clouzot chose respectively the German-born Peter van Eyck and the Italian Folco Lulli, both of whom had had busy and varied acting careers, though usually in secondary roles. Clouzot's wife, Vera, rounded out the principal cast by taking the film's single female part as the waitress.

Years before the Nouvelle Vague (French New Wave) revolutionized filmmaking, Clouzot decided to shoot *Salaire* almost entirely outdoors, shunning conventional studio sets. He also shunned mood music, the only melodies heard in the film coming from a radio sporadically turned on and off in the bar. The spot he chose near the village of Saint Gilles in the Camargue had been a Vichy internment camp for Roma from 1942 to 1944. Some seven hundred persons had been forcibly relocated there and put in cabins without electricity or running water and swarming with mosquitoes and rats; dozens had died. (Whether that history figured in Clouzot's decision to locate the film there is unclear.)[8] In this spot, he and his set designer, René Roux, created a destitute South American village complete with houses, church, bar, workshop, and cemetery. Cutouts stood in for tropical vegetation. Dark-skinned extras, some made up to resemble loin-clothed Indians, were brought in from Marseilles. The cast and crew were housed at a hotel in the former Roman city of Nîmes, twenty miles away.

Filming began on August 27, 1951, with everyone in high spirits. Signoret joined the group in Nîmes, where she and Vera went shopping. In the evenings, they sewed glass beads on espadrilles and laughed at the cast's off-set antics—on one occasion Montand and Vanel bought extra dinnerware and proceeded to break it during a violent argument as the distraught hotel owner watched what he thought was the destruction of his crockery. Clouzot enjoyed getting a predictably angry rise out of Signoret by praising the notorious anti-Semitic journalist and writer Robert Brasillach, who had served as editor in chief of the collaborationist paper *Je suis partout* during the war and was executed for treason after the liberation.[9] Then it began to look like the shoot was seriously jinxed.

The location had been chosen for its remoteness and desolation but also for its sunny climate. With autumn, however, came atypical torrential rain that went on for more than a month, making on-location filming impossible and slowly degrading the newly built décor. Then Clouzot broke an ankle, and Vera fell ill. November came, daylight grew short, the rain continued. Only thirty-five minutes of footage had been shot for a film due to run for nearly two and a half hours. With the production already over budget, the initial producer, Raymond Borderie, went bust. Clouzot had no choice but to abandon the shoot. It took him seven months to find a new injection of funds from the producer Georges Lourau and the Italian production company Fono Roma. Meanwhile, Montand and Signoret took off and got married in Saint Paul. Filming resumed in June 1952.

The film, done in harsh black-and-white, is a nihilistic shocker from start to finish, especially for the early 1950s. Clouzot's opening shot set the tone: a village toddler is playing with several writhing cockroaches that have been tied together with string. It's like something straight out of Luis Buñuel, a telling image of the human race as helpless vermin toyed with by the gods. The film begins slowly, with the first half hour spent setting the scene in Las Piedras. But once the two dilapidated trucks without shock absorbers begin their nitro-laden trip over rocky, unpaved roads, the tension builds as Clouzot, often called the French Hitchcock, bores in on three bravura scenes of suspense.

First, the four drivers encounter a large boulder that blocks the mountain road and has to be blown up delicately using drops of nitro. Then they have to negotiate a tight turn that requires them to back their trucks onto a rickety platform of rotting wood overhanging a canyon—a film crew member backed the truck to within one foot of the edge, while the planks began to give. After the first truck, driven by Luigi and Bimba, hits a bump and blows up, Mario and Jo arrive at the spot to find the road blocked by a crater filling with oil from a ruptured pipeline. Jo gets out to lead the way through the oil pool but falls and is run over by Mario, who won't stop for fear of getting stuck. He gets through to the blazing well head, receives his check (in an insider joke, a close-up reveals it's made out to Mario *Livi*), and joyfully begins the drive back to Las Piedras, only to lose control and veer over a cliff.

Salaire opened the Cannes Film Festival of 1953, where Vanel won a Special Mention, and the film won the Palme d'Or and drew raves from the critics. The usually reserved *Le Monde* called it "the most violent, the most passionate work imaginable. Clouzot is a realist the way Hugo and Balzac are realists in certain of their works, a hallucinating realism that pulls us into its universe . . . a coup de foudre."[10] For *Le Figaro,* it was "a cinema monument"; for the influential film magazine *Cahiers du cinéma,* "an unforgettable image of the atrocity of the world."[11] At its US release in 1955 as *The Wages of Fear,* it was as a shorter, bowdlerized version cut by forty-three minutes because distributors were afraid that Clouzot's pessimism and "anti-American" sequences—for example, a woman haranguing a crowd in protest at the oil company's treatment of the natives, "who are always the ones who suffer," while "the foreigners never die"—would alienate Eisenhower-era audiences. The critics loved it anyway. Even many years later, *Esquire* thought Montand looked like a young, Gallic Humphrey Bogart and found it "the most suspenseful movie ever made. . . . Clouzot slowly twists the knife of fear into these characters, and the audience. . . . You'll never look at a pothole the same way again."[12] When the complete version was finally released in the United States in 1991, the *New York Times*'s longtime critic Vincent Canby praised it as "one of the most remarkable examples of nonstop movie wizardry ever seen. . . . Like Hitchcock at his best, Clouzot manages to keep topping himself until the film's very last frame." As for Montand, he was "splendid. . . all swagger and self-assurance, though still not fully formed."[13]

Salaire went on to win the Golden Bear award at the Berlin Film Festival, becoming one of the very few French films to win at both Cannes and Berlin the same year. Later it sparked two American remakes. Howard W. Koch did *Violent Road* in 1958, substituting rocket fuel for the nitroglycerin. In 1977, William Friedkin did *Sorcerer,* with dangerously aging dynamite replacing the nitro; Montand told a French biographer that Friedkin asked him to take on the same role again, but he refused.[14] Both remakes, lacking Clouzot's corrosive contempt for the human race, appeared insipid compared with the original.

This was the film that made Montand a movie star. For the first time, he had top billing, as he would for the rest of his career. His acting is solid if lacking in depth or character development. He manages to express convincingly the nerve-stretching tension of the sequences when he is at the wheel of an ancient rolling bomb. But it's clear that, once again, a director has chosen him as much for his working-class style and muscular physicality—he wears a singlet for most of the film—as for his acting ability. During the filming, Clouzot had to do multiple takes of scenes with Montand but never more than two with Vanel. *Salaire* was the beginning of movie stardom for him, but it would take a while for that star to reach its full magnitude. At Cannes, it was the film that won the Palme d'Or, and Charles Vanel, not Montand, who received a Special Mention.

⊙ ⊙ ⊙

Salaire had just been released when Montand began preparing his next show at the Étoile, due to begin October 5, 1953. Although similar in style and content to his performance there in 1951, this one would mark a turning point and confirm beyond a doubt his standing as France's premier music hall star. It was also the first of his recitals to be recorded live. With twenty-three songs and two spoken poems, it was scheduled for three weeks but ran on and on for six months and nearly 200 two-hour shows before ending in April 1954.

It could no doubt have continued still longer, for the audiences had never been so enthusiastic. At the end of each performance, they called him back for more, although he never liked or encouraged encores, believing that they detracted from the emotion of the high note on which he always ended. When he took his final bow after giving in and singing "C'est si bon," cheers turned to good-natured boos of disappointment that it was over. Many had braved a Paris public-transport strike and littered the lobby with dozens of bicycles. It was an exceptionally cold winter in Paris, and for five days the theater's heating system was out of order, but the show went on, spectators wearing overcoats and gloves. Congratulatory visitors to his dressing room ranged from Romy Schneider, Alain Delon, Sophia Loren, and Gérard Philippe to Kirk Douglas, Gary Cooper, and Maurice Chevalier. Montand himself later considered it one of the most accomplished recitals he ever gave.

Some of his old familiar songs, such as "Dans les plaines du Far West" and "Luna Park" were discarded. This time he divided the program into four main parts. One quarter was composed of popular themes, such as the new, show-opening "La ballade de Paris," a love letter to the city by Francis Lemarque praising its beauty, history, and monuments, and another new song, "Faubourg Saint Martin," about a Paris neighborhood whose old houses speak of the happiness of life and love. One-quarter was poetry, including Jacques Prévert's bit of whimsy "Le peintre, la pomme et Picasso," about two artists' different reactions to a still life with apple, and Guillaume Apollinaire's ode to traveling troupes of entertainers, "Les saltimbanques." Another quarter was comic sketches, such as "Le chef d'orchestre est amoureux," the story of a conductor who falls in love with a beautiful girl in the audience. The last quarter was composed of songs with a social/political aspect, including "C'est à l'aube," describing the different dawns when convicts are executed and lovers part but also when the hope of a better tomorrow is born, and his perennial antiwar song "Quand un soldat."

As always, his performance was physical. Sensing that the audience would get bored if he just stood at the mike and belted out a song, he moved around the stage constantly, sculpting the air with his large hands, miming and mugging, dancing and prancing, sometimes acting out a number, as in "Le chef d'orchestre est amoureux." His material was always idiosyncratic *chansons à textes,* where the important things were the language and its subtle poetic potency to convey emotion. He sang what he liked, even if it didn't always go over well with audiences and critics; he sang "Les feuilles mortes" for years before it really took. He didn't do popular standards, generally shunning songs that he considered merely "commercial." While he was triumphing at the Étoile with controversial numbers such as "Un soldat" and the frankly erotic "Sanguine"—banned on French radio for being too lubricious—top-forty charts in the United States in 1953 were being led by Patti Page's "How Much Is That Doggie in the Window?" and Joni James's "Your Cheatin' Heart."[15]

Many considered Montand's material too intellectual or engagé. It's true that many of his songs are difficult to understand the first time. Like all genuine poetry, they are marked by indirection, obscurity, unexpected allusions. Also, they often treat subjects that the public, in particular a music hall public, would rather not think about: loss, death, unrequited love, senseless combat. When Montand introduced "Mon frère" by the activist Turkish poet Nazim Hikmet in his recital in 1968, he spoke softly into the microphone without accompaniment about humans' universal egotism, their cowardice, their tendency to follow the crowd passively rather than revolt against injustice and tyranny, making all of us responsible for much of the misery in the world.

The press often referred to Montand as a troubadour. In fact, he was indeed following in the footsteps of the Provençal troubadours of the twelfth and thirteenth centuries, such as Folquet De Marseille, who performed love lyrics, crusading songs, and religious poems at the courts of Provence and Aragon. Their designation derived from the Occitan word *trobar,* meaning "to find" or "invent," the troubadours of the High Middle Ages wrote and performed the first lyric poetry in a European language, "finding" poetic and musical expression for the topics of the day, ranging from chivalry and courtly love to politics and scatology. Often from the nobility, such as the duke of Aquitaine, they enjoyed considerable freedom of speech and came to have important social influence all over cultivated Europe.[16]

In the 1910s, the young modernist poet Ezra Pound was fascinated by medieval Provençal poetry, which influenced his epic *Cantos,* and spent months touring the South of France to discover its essence. "We are perhaps too apt to think of the troubadour as a person in mediaeval clothing," he concluded in the notebooks that later became *A Walking Tour in Southern France,* "walking about on air to find sea-coasts in Bohemia or princesses in Tripoli, or suffering amorous mishap and ending, with his heart in my lady's pastry, as did literally poor Guillaume de Cabestang." Actually, he noted, they had a more down-to-earth function: "There was unspeakable boredom in the castles. The chivalric singing was devised to lighten the boredom."[17]

As indicated previously, Montand did not compose his own material, technically making him a medieval Occitan *joglar,* literally a juggler, who sang and danced at the chateau to ease the ennui. He couldn't read a musical score and had trouble keeping time with the orchestra. His success was due to his hard work, innate showmanship, and rich baritone voice, which he trained and developed professionally in his early Paris period with Piaf's encouragement and guidance. Ana Guigui, an associate professor of voice at the Berklee College of Music in Boston and a professional performer, gave her evaluation of his voice:

> When I hear Yves Montand sing, I hear an ease and a versatility that comes from a singer understanding their voice and how it works. Montand makes conscious interpretation choices depending on the style/genre of the song, the text, melody, the accompaniment, instrumentation, and so on. He chooses when and how he applies certain expressive devices (like vibrato or legato/staccato) in his singing and in his speaking voice. His is a naturally produced technique, creating a light, flexible, and graceful tone quality in his medium and high registers. His singing never sounds forced or strained. His vocal timbre is warm, mellow, and sensual, like a masculine, musk-infused pipe tobacco scent that lingers in the air long after the pipe smoker has left the room.[18]

⊙ ⊙ ⊙

Montand and Signoret were now established stars and ready to enjoy the financial rewards that went with it. *Salaire,* his show at the Étoile, and newly booming record sales had been immense sources of revenue, as had been Signoret's film *Casque d'or / Golden Marie* (France and US 1952), which won her a British Academy of Film and Television Arts (BAFTA) award in 1953 as Best Foreign Actress. Communist sympathizers or not, Frenchmen of all stripes traditionally long for a place in the country. The couple began to scour Normandy, that fashionable Parisian playground between the city and the chic seaside resort of Deauville, for a house. What they chose was a palatial eighteenth-century mansion near the village of Autheuil-Authouillet, sixty-five miles west of Paris, known locally as the *château blanc* due to its imposing white facade.

Access was by a long entrance road lined with double rows of century-old linden trees. Beneath its black-slate mansard roof were twenty-four rooms on two floors, large fireplaces, beamed ceilings, tile floors, an expansive living room, and a grand staircase leading to the bedrooms upstairs. Situated on seventeen acres of meadowland, it came with outbuildings and an adjacent farm with ten cows and fifteen sheep, the latter branded with a large M, which allowed Montand to play the role of weekend gentleman farmer. A barn was transformed into a small theater with a projection room and a stage where he could rehearse. They added a swimming pool. The house was furnished with what Signoret termed "good stuff" that she liked shopping for in flea markets, as opposed to more expensive "really good stuff."[19] It was decorated with a Giacometti painting, a Picasso ceramic, an Aubusson tapestry by Jean Lurçat, and sculptures by the modern artist César. It was looked after by Marcelle Mirtilon, the cook at place Dauphine, and her husband, Georges, both originally from Normandy.

Fully aware of the glaring gap between their communist convictions and their lavish lifestyle, both Signoret and Montand did a certain amount of defensive explaining about their country estate. "Money came to me all at once and I was able to buy that house," he said. "When wealth comes to a man, it can change where he lives, but not necessarily the man himself. . . . Having a compact house [*sic*] at your back is not just idyllic. It becomes a fortress, a safe haven for those bad times that can hit you by surprise."[20] In other words, he was just a poor boy at heart, trying to put aside a little for a rainy day. In her autobiography, Signoret performed verbal acrobatics to argue that the mansion was not really what could be called luxury. "The place symbolizes luxury for us, but not in the usual sense of the word as applied to a house. It symbolizes the luxury of being able to buy something with the fruit of one's labor, rather than to labor in order to buy something. . . . Autheuil was bought with the *sous* earned by an artisan who exploits himself only by producing the things he likes."[21]

Complicated Marxist reasoning aside, the house became a joyful weekend retreat for the couple and their clan, including François Périer, Serge Reggiani, Bernard Blier, Claude Brasseur, Costa-Gavras, Alain Resnais, and many other show business friends who had their own rooms there and came and went as they liked. Sometimes there were more than twenty guests, along with their children and dogs. Périer, a mainstay of the weekend frolics who acted with Montand in several films, said it was like a summer camp, except that there was plenty of whiskey and poker, and bedtime was rarely before dawn. Reggiani scotched the idea that it was a forum for heated political argument. "What I remember most," he recalled, "is how much we laughed."[22]

On Sundays, all gathered around the dinner table for *spaghetti al ragù* with meat sauce, prepared by Montand. Just the way Giovanni used to do it back in La Cabucelle.

9

Salem

Yves Montand and Simone Signoret were so excited about the new script a friend sent them in late 1953 that they couldn't sleep. They spent the night sitting in bed reading and discussing it, passing the pages of a rough translation from the English between them. By morning, they agreed that they had to perform that play, *The Crucible.* It was written by a playwright named Arthur Miller, whose name they knew only from conversations with their friends John Berry and Jules Dassin, American film directors who self-exiled to France after being blacklisted in Hollywood as communists. They didn't know that Miller was the author of some of the most important and enduring theatrical works of twentieth-century American theater, including *All My Sons* (1946) and *Death of a Salesman* (1949). Nor did they know anything about a seventeenth-century Puritan community called Salem in the Massachusetts Bay Colony.

But they knew about the anticommunist campaign and ruthless persecution by both the House Un-American Activities Committee (HUAC) and Senator Joseph McCarthy's Permanent Subcommittee on Investigations. "McCarthyism," as the Red Scare came to be known, was a notorious bête noire among French artists and intellectuals. They detested its bullying smear tactics that gave the accused the choice between losing their jobs and/or going to jail or confessing their own guilt and denouncing colleagues as communists. Montand and Signoret admired American democracy despite their communist sympathies. They had refused to join the Communist Party because of its treatment of cultural figures, so in the late 1940s and early 1950s they had watched with dismay as Washington's zealous antisubversives, often in search of publicity, ruined the careers of many Hollywood directors, actors, and writers whom the couple admired, including Jules Dassin, Joseph Losey, Charlie Chaplin, John Garfield, Dalton Trumbo, Nelson Algren, and dozens of others. The American public, alarmed by a threatening

Soviet Union, Mao Zedong's communist takeover of China, large communist parties in western Europe, and the Alger Hiss case, which gave the impression that the federal government was infiltrated by communists, mostly supported the investigations.

Montand and Signoret could see analogies between the Red Scare in America in the 1940s and 1950s and the hounding of innocent people there as witches 250 years earlier. More important to them, they also saw Miller's play as a thinly veiled portrayal of the recent trial and execution of Julius and Ethel Rosenberg in 1953 on charges of espionage for the Soviet Union—they, like many in France and elsewhere, had signed petitions and participated in demonstrations and fundraisers in favor of the couple, whose guilt, they felt, had not been established. For them, the play stood as an indictment of intolerance in general, with its protagonists John and Elizabeth Proctor, like the Rosenbergs, victims of repression by the powers that be. Reading the play was, Signoret said later, "a shattering experience."[1] It would be an ideal vehicle for the expression of their political convictions.

Miller had written *The Crucible* as a way of exposing the dangers of individuals denying their own consciences in the face of hostile public opinion and demands by the state. This denial, he felt, was due to a deep feeling of guilt, spurred on by mass hysteria, that could be assuaged only by confession, even if it meant confessing to crimes they had not in fact committed. "When I began to think of writing about the hunt for Reds in America," he later explained, "I was motivated in some great part by the paralysis that had set in among many liberals who, despite their discomfort with the inquisitors' violations of civil rights, were fearful, and with good reason, of being identified as covert communists if they should protest too strongly."[2] He didn't know quite how to tackle the subject in the form of a play until he came across a two-volume, thousand-page account of the witchcraft trials written in 1867 by Charles W. Upham, then mayor of Salem. The study revealed the details of the personal relationships of those involved in the trials. That was enough to convince Miller that he had the necessary dramatis personae for a play. He gathered the necessary details during a visit to the Salem courthouse, where he read the actual transcripts of the trials in 1692, which resulted in nineteen adults and two dogs being hanged as witches and one man being pressed to death for refusing to confess.

Miller, who would be questioned by the HUAC in 1956 and convicted of contempt of Congress for declining to reveal the names of persons in certain communist meetings he had attended, agreed to having the play adapted for the French stage if it were done by either Jean-Paul Sartre or the novelist and playwright Marcel Aymé. When it was offered to Sartre, his secretary turned it down without even showing it to him. Aymé, who couldn't read a word of English and, like many Frenchmen of the day, was proud of it, initially wasn't interested in the play. He finally accepted the job on condition that an actress of whom he was fond be given a part.[3] He worked from a rough translation, which had the advantage that he didn't try to tamper with the wording.

Montand and Signoret asked that the director be the old theater hand Raymond Rouleau, a fifty-year-old Belgian actor and director and a meticulous, demanding product of the Royal Conservatory of Brussels, who was familiar with the play and had met Miller in New York. They renamed it *Les sorcières de Salem* (The Witches of Salem). It was to be staged ambitiously at the grand old Théâtre Sarah Bernhardt, built originally by Baron Georges-Eugène Haussmann during his mid-nineteenth-century renovation of Paris. The theater had long been an elaborate showplace for opera, with elaborate red-and-gold décor and four balconies.

The only remaining problem: the male and female leads had virtually no experience acting in legitimate theater. Doing this play looked like an enormous risk for them. Could a music hall singer and a movie actress convincingly play tragedy on stage? In his early Paris period, Montand had tried acting in a silly operetta, *Le chevalier Bayard,* in 1948, which was a resounding flop. Signoret was beset by doubt. Accustomed to underacting for the camera, she was afraid that neither her presence nor her voice would project in an immense theater like the Sarah Bernhardt. Actor friends tried to dissuade her from such folly, emphasizing the technical differences between a movie set and the stage. Besides, she was then busy with a starring part in Henri-Georges Clouzot's thriller *Les diaboliques / Diabolique* (1955, France and United States), which he had begun following *Le salaire de la peur;* he had beat Alfred Hitchcock by only a few hours to acquire the screenplay rights. That meant she had to be on his set all day and then try to rehearse for the play at home in the evening without the benefit of either working with the other actors or getting used to the theater's stage.

In his role as John Proctor, Montand had to play for the first time a man whose struggles are not physical but interior as his soul is tested and purified in a crucible of collective hysteria. Denounced vindictively as a witch by Abigail Williams, a former servant with whom he had an affair, Proctor must decide whether to confess falsely that he has made a pact with the devil and thereby save his neck or stick to proclaiming his innocence and be hanged along with other innocent Salem inhabitants. Plagued by self-doubt, he weakens for a moment and signs a confession, but when the judges demand that it be made public, his courage returns, and he refuses in order to obey his conscience. Abigail also accuses his wife, Elizabeth, of witchcraft. Elizabeth has been cold to John after learning of his affair, but as her character develops during the play's action, she comes to recognize that despite a flaw in his character that led him to sin, he is basically a good man. She tries to lie to save him, but he won't have it and insists on the truth. Both difficult, complex roles called for Montand and Signoret to express moral conflict and project it across the footlights.

To get his stage acting up to speed, Montand, still doing his successful show every evening at the Étoile, crammed drama lessons during the day from experienced actor friends. François Périer and Serge Reggiani had him recite passages from classical dramatists such as Racine and Molière. He was trying to learn in two months of rehearsals what they had acquired from years at Paris's famous Cours Simon, a school for the dramatic arts, where they had been trained, along with Michèle Morgan, Gérard Philippe, and many other stars of stage and screen. He also asked Raymond Rouleau frankly what he needed to do to prepare for the part. The director responded by going to Montand and Signoret's house in Autheuil, script in hand, and drilling him for hours. It was also at Autheuil, where most of the cast had come to spend a weekend, that Rouleau wrote the first stage draft of the play.[4]

Signoret, too, had extra work to do. She recognized that she was not as at ease on stage as the other actors, which meant she had to prepare harder. Her profound conviction that the Rosenbergs were innocent was a well of emotion into which she dipped to become Elizabeth Proctor. To reach the necessary pitch of emotion for the farewell scene with John in act 4, when he embraces her with fettered hands—a deliberate replica of the photo of the condemned Rosenbergs seen around the world—she read and reread the recently published book *Death House Letters of Ethel and Julius Rosenberg* and transferred the overwhelming emotion they provoked to that scene.[5]

The different fates of the play after opening in New York and Paris provide a revealing look at the profound disparities in political attitude between the American and French publics in the early 1950s. *The Crucible* premiered in New York at the Martin Beck Theater in January 1953 and ran for 197 performances. Although it won the Tony and Donaldson Awards as the Best American Drama of the year in 1953, its run was short, and both audiences and critics were lukewarm. The *New York Herald Tribune* said that "Arthur

Miller is a problem playwright in both senses of the word" and called the play "a step backward into mechanical parable."[6] The *New York Times* dismissed it as "too much excitement and not enough emotion."[7]

A year later a new production in New York would be better received, and the play would eventually become an international classic. But for the moment Miller himself was resigned. "I knew that the atmosphere would be pretty hostile," he said. "The coldness of the crowd was not a surprise; Broadway audiences were not famous for loving history lessons, which is what they made of the play. It seems to me entirely appropriate that on the day the play opened, a newspaper headline read '*all thirteen reds guilty*'—a story about American Communists who faced prison for 'conspiring to teach and advocate the duty and necessity of forcible overthrow of government.'"[8] The tepid reaction of American audiences to plays like *The Crucible* might be explained by their general aversion to plays with political themes.

However, in France, a country where politics is a favorite, not to say obsessive, conversational topic, the interest in political plays such as *Sorcières* was high. After a triumphal opening at the Sarah Bernhardt in mid-1954, its run was prolonged for 365 standing-room-only performances divided over two six-month periods, extending into the first half of 1955. It was hoped that Arthur Miller would attend the opening, but he was unable to leave the United States, his passport having been revoked for refusing to name names before the HUAC. French audiences had no trouble seeing the metaphorical relation between the events in Salem and those in Washington. More than that, they appreciated the universality of Miller's depiction of human credulity and cruelty, the desire for the safety of conformity.

The play was a personal success for Montand and Signoret. He had made the perilous jump from music hall to legitimate theater, and the critics applauded. "As for Yves Montand, he is overwhelming," wrote *L'humanité dimanche*. "He is a great actor because he has thrown onto the scales his pound of flesh, his heart, along with his conviction and his convictions. We were expecting an actor. We were given a man."[9] *Le Monde* praised his presence, his voice, and his authority on stage, which its critic found "not so bad, for a beginner."[10] Signoret, too, made an important transition from film to stage. Her Elizabeth was lauded for its dignity, telling silences, and rendering of a woman with an incurable wound. "All our friends took a deep breath," she recalled. "They had worried incessantly from the moment we had decided to play together in this difficult, sober and politically engaged play. They believed that had it failed, we wouldn't have come out of the wreckage alive."[11]

Jean-Paul Sartre's reaction was a heady mixture of enthusiasm and indignation. Charging into Montand's dressing room after the third performance, he demanded, "This play was for me. Why didn't you ask me to do the adaptation?" He calmed down after the secretarial mix-up was explained. He didn't know it then, but he was going to get his chance.[12]

Only a few months after *Sorcières* had finished its run, Raymond Rouleau decided that the keen public reaction to the stage play warranted a film version. He set up a coproduction with financing from a French consortium and East Germany's state-owned production company Deutsch Film AG (DEFA), the puppet of a German Democratic Republic no doubt eager to score points with Moscow by showing the oppression and exploitation of American "peasants." Filming was to be done mainly in the vast Babelsberg studios in Berlin, with exteriors in the nearby village of Trebbin and finishing touches in Paris. The screenplay was assigned to Sartre. The shoot began in July 1956 and was due to end in October. Montand insisted that the film be finished by then because he had something important on his agenda. No one foresaw that the complicated logistics of working in several locations would mean his deadline could not be respected, and Montand grew increasingly upset about the production's impact on a prior commitment.

Sartre went to work on the adaptation. He corresponded with Miller by mail because he wouldn't go to the United States, and Miller, still without a passport, couldn't for the moment leave there. (Later he would be able to travel, and while seeing his wife, Marilyn Monroe, in London, where she was filming *The Prince and the Showgirl* [1957] with Laurence Olivier, he crossed the Channel to visit the *Crucible* set in November 1956, his first meeting with Montand and Signoret.) As a loyal disciple of Marxism, Sartre gave Miller's story a leftist twist, turning it into more of a tale of class struggle than the original intended.

In Sartre's reading of the play, the poor are helpless in the face of the wealthy landowners; John Proctor is hanged because he opposes them. In one sequence, Elizabeth does some shopping, and during their talk about the witchcraft trials, the storekeeper notes that none of the accused is wealthy: "There are no witches among the rich." The gallows have to be constructed behind the prison walls because the authorities are afraid the people will revolt and prevent the execution. In the end, a crowd of armed citizens does breach the walls in rebellion, but too late to save Proctor. As Miller notes in his memoir, "Jean-Paul Sartre's screenplay . . . seemed to me to toss an arbitrary Marxist mesh over the story that led to a few absurdities. Sartre laid the witchcraft outbreak to a struggle between rich and poor peasants, but in reality victims like Rebecca Nurse were of the class of relatively large landowners, and the Proctors and their like were by no means poor. . . . Nonetheless, Simone Signoret was immensely moving, and the film had a noble grandeur, Salem and the Proctors sharing a wonderfully French sort of sensuality whose repression trembled with imminent disaster."[13]

Les sorcières de Salem / The Crucible (1957, US 1958) is a powerful film that shows Montand had become a first-rate movie actor, thanks in good part to the one-on-one schooling he received from Clouzot and Rouleau. His performance of John's relation with Elizabeth is marked by a complex mixture of guilt, yearning, and reproach that he embodies with moving pathos. The sequence in jail where he writhes with self-loathing at his own weakness as he struggles to decide whether to confess falsely or obey his conscience is painful to watch. Sometimes it was Rouleau's demanding direction that generated Montand's emotion on the set; for one key scene, Montand had to do thirteen takes until his eyes were burning with genuine anger.

For the first time in his acting career, Montand received the official recognition of his peers. The Karlovy Vary International Film Festival in what was then Czechoslovakia, the most important festival in central and eastern Europe, awarded the Best Actor prize to him in 1957; Signoret and Mylène Demongeot, who played the mischievous Abigail, also received awards. In Britain, Signoret also won a BAFTA for Best Foreign Actress. The *New York Times* raved, "Out of Arthur Miller's explicitly American play, *The Crucible,* which had to do with the witch trials in Salem, Mass., in 1692, Jean-Paul Sartre and Raymond Rouleau have got a powerful and compelling French film. . . . Perhaps the outstanding performance is that of Yves Montand as the weak Puritan husband who succumbs to the lusts of the flesh and then struggles through a tormenting succession of vacillations until he goes to a heroic death. . . . [T]his is a persistently absorbing film."[14] In France, *Le Monde* found that Montand was "torn between his faith, his passions, and the solidarity that unites him with his brothers, the poor. He lives the character intensely."[15]

Although there would be a made-for-television movie of *The Crucible* in 1967 with George C. Scott as John Proctor and Colleen Dewhurst as Elizabeth, nearly forty years would pass before Hollywood producers would feel comfortable enough with the political climate for big-screen treatment of *The Crucible.* Directed by Nicholas Hytner in 1996 and starring Daniel Day-Lewis as John and Joan Allen as Elizabeth, it had a screenplay by Miller himself. But the subject's moment had passed, along with the Red Scare, and the

American public didn't relate to it anymore. Although the adaptation won Miller an Academy Award nomination for Best Screenplay Based on Material Previously Produced or Published, it was a flop at the box office, grossing only a bit more than $7 million on an estimated budget of $25 million. Its main value was to Day-Lewis, who met Rebecca Miller, the daughter of the author, during the shoot and later married her.

10

Moscow

If Montand was becoming more and more nervous as the filming of *Les sorcières* dragged on into November, it was because eighteen months earlier he had agreed to go on a months-long tour in the Soviet Union and its satellites in eastern Europe.

The tour was brought up when Sergei Obraztsov, People's Artist of the Soviet Union, hero of socialist labor, and director of the renowned Moscow Puppet Theater, attended Montand's show at the Étoile during a Paris visit in 1954. He contacted Montand and suggested that he come and sing in the "homeland of socialism." His songs were known there from radio broadcasts, and he was something of a cult figure among the young. At the time, reaching out to the Soviet Union this way seemed a perfect fit with Montand's admiration for everything Soviet and his desire to advance the peace movement.

It also fit well with Nikita Khrushchev's new policy of peaceful coexistence with the West that he had begun to follow gradually after Stalin's death in 1953. This thaw in the Cold War resulted in reduced political repression in the Soviet Union and an attempted opening to the world, in particular Europe. Key to this strategy were cultural and intellectual exchanges and increased possibilities for interaction with foreign peoples and ideas. The policy became known as "cultural diplomacy." The Kremlin saw Montand's visit to the Soviet Union and the Eastern Bloc countries as a great opportunity to highlight the bloc's new, friendlier attitude and to show the world that it was not an isolated, hostile enclave. The fact that this visit would certainly garner much media attention was an added advantage.

Montand agreed to the tour, beginning with Moscow in early December 1956. But for the Soviet Union, its satellites, and communist parties everywhere, 1956 would be a very different geopolitical year from 1954. In February 1956, Khrushchev delivered a historic speech behind closed doors to the

Twentieth Congress of the Communist Party of the Soviet Union. To the surprise and consternation of the high-level comrades present, he denounced the personality cult and terrorist methods of the deceased Joseph Stalin. When contents of the speech leaked out, the ensuing move toward de-Stalinization sent shockwaves throughout the self-styled people's democracies of the Eastern Bloc and, more generally, through world communism itself.

Uprisings in Poznań, Poland, the following June were put down with military force, killing dozens of protesters and wounding hundreds, but they resulted in a new reformist regime headed by Władysław Gomułka. Then came the October revolt in Hungary, with its demands for free elections and withdrawal of Russian forces. It was ruthlessly repressed in November by Soviet tanks and troops firing on freedom fighters in Budapest as the Western powers and United Nations stood by. Some 20,000 civilians were wounded, and 2,500 killed.

In a state of initial disbelief, then horror, then anguish, Montand and Signoret followed these events in the media as they unfolded. How could this be happening? The Soviet Union, the beacon of a communist ideology that preached the equality of all people, sending tanks to kill comrades demanding free elections and other basic human rights? These moments were the beginning of a painful crise de conscience for both of them. Their secular faith in communism as the answer to the problems of the human condition was shaken. "For Montand and me," Signoret recalled in her memoir in 1976, "November 1956 was the most absurd, the most cruel, the saddest and most destructive month of our 27 years of life together[;] . . . we were sad and upset, and upset and sad, but most of all we were in a mess."[1]

Montand was due to make his big tour of the East in a month, but how could he do it without appearing to sanction the repression that put Budapest in flames? Signoret, always intellectually a step ahead of him, was first to grasp the significance of the events. She realized that she, Montand, and all fellow travelers of communism had been misled and wanted him to accept that the ideals of his youth were founded on lies. He wasn't ready for that. It would mean a wrenching break with the communism of his adored father, his polestar and the single individual who, since his infancy, had had the most important influence on him, including on his political convictions.

Besides, his professional conscience dictated that he had to honor his contract. It was an excruciating dilemma that talks with friends and relatives did nothing to solve. He changed his mind daily, almost hourly. One day when he was supportive of the freedom fighters, he had an argument with his brother, Julien, who hewed to the party line come what may against the "counterrevolutionaries." They almost came to blows in the apartment at place Dauphine. Another time, when he was taking the other side of the argument, he reacted in confused, angry frustration when friends who had been fellow travelers condemned the party.

> I knew that my friends were saying fair and true things, but at the same time I didn't want to hear them, I didn't want to accept them. It wasn't clear in my mind—it took me years to get to the bottom of my hesitations, to understand that accepting their remarks meant rejecting my father's ideas, the ideas of the world I was born into. . . . I went off like a bomb.
>
> "Stop! I don't want to hear any more. None of you sitting around this table can hope to understand the Russian Revolution; it wasn't made for people like you. It was made for the workers and peasants. It isn't our revolution. It's theirs."
>
> I was yelling, and all the angrier because I knew even as I spoke that my argument was falling flat, which just made me sadder. My words were like a cold shower. People stopped talking. They looked at me, and I could see a gleam of pity in their eyes.[2]

He decided to buy time. Signoret helped him draft a carefully worded statement explaining why he could not leave France for the moment: "My orchestra and I have jointly decided to postpone our tour of the USSR and the people's democracies. World events, and France's internal situation, make it impossible for us at this time to leave our wives and families and travel to any country whatsoever."[3] The statement neatly avoided taking sides on the tumult in eastern Europe. But the dilemma and the arguments continued. Signoret strongly opposed his going, often weeping as she did so. She told him that if he did, he would never be able to sing in France again. Jean-Paul Sartre talked it over with Montand, but he declined to advise him one way or the other. He simply summed up the dilemma clearly: if Montand went, he would be seen as backing the Soviets; if he did not, he would be seen as backing the reactionaries. Damned if he did, damned if he didn't.

Some made light of the dilemma. *Le Figaro* published a front-page cartoon with Khrushchev giving orders on the telephone: "Send the tanks to Paris if necessary, but Yves Montand must sing." But the threats against Montand from both sides of the political spectrum were real. Anonymous phone calls and letters were full of insults and menace. Some people went to place Dauphine to shout abuse and knock on the windows. Although Montand was due to do a radio broadcast of his final rehearsal from the Olympia in early December, that broadcast was canceled after the music hall management received warnings of violence. Finally, there was one threat too many. The German producer of a film Montand was due to make the next year called to say that the deal was off if Montand went because he couldn't sell a film whose male lead supported the Soviet bloodbath in Budapest. That ultimatum crystallized the issue for him: he would not yield to that sort of blackmail. He attempted to explain his decision to go by publishing an open letter in the press, saying he hoped the tour would contribute to cultural exchanges and peace.[4]

⊙ ⊙ ⊙

It was the middle of the night on December 17, 1956, when the Aeroflot Ilyushin airliner landed at Vnukovo Airport outside Moscow, but hundreds of fans and journalists were still waiting in the cold to welcome Montand and Signoret. When the plane's door opened, Montand appeared, waved, and shouted, "Bonjour, les amis." He was greeted with bits of French: "Bravo d'être venu! C'est si bon, Montand!" He made a brief speech emphasizing that he wasn't a politician, only a singer who came in the interest of peace. Then he and Signoret were hustled into a black ZIM-12 limousine with curtained windows and whisked through the eight-lane avenues of a sleeping Moscow to the Sovietsky Hotel, a luxurious Stalin-era marble pile on Leningradsky Prospekt. They were given head-of-state treatment with an apartment including living room, dining room, bedroom, and, in case Montand wanted to rehearse, a grand piano. Their four young interpreters, who would accompany them for the entire month, were waiting for them.

His first recital at the 1,500-seat Tchaikovsky Concert Hall on December 19 was attended by Moscow's high society: members of the nomenklatura—state officials, many top officers of the Red Army, and representatives of nearly all the foreign embassies in the capital, with the notable exception of the French ambassador and his wife, who were afraid of taking sides in the debate over whether Montand should have come. The rest of the audience was made up of Muscovites who had waited for hours in lines curling around the block to buy tickets in advance.

Montand overcame his usual stage fright and boldly launched into the antimilitaristic song "Quand un soldat," disregarding the presence of gold-braided officers, who consulted the translation in the program with surprise. The remainder of the show was his standard Paris material, from "Une demoiselle sur une balençoire" to "Les grands boulevards" and "Battling Joe." Few could understand all the words, but they knew "C'est si bon," and when he did "Les feuilles mortes," it was in an almost religious silence, with many in tears. Seeing the public demand for the event, the Ministry of Culture shifted the venue for four evenings to the enormous, newly built Luzhniki Stadium, where 20,000 indoor seats were made available, the largest live audience he would ever have. He ended the show with a resounding "Long live friendship between the peoples, long live peace!"

Those shows still weren't enough to satisfy the demand to hear and see Yves Montand, the famous singer, and his glamorous wife, the messengers of peace, in the Soviet Union. Officials, exhibiting them like a trophy—his presence there showed the world that the Soviet Union was not a pariah; after all, it was admired by a famous couple from the West—arranged what they called singing visits to factories, where he often clambered atop a flatbed truck to perform on an improvised stage. Other visits were to schools, universities, and kolkhozes (collective farms), all of which expected songs. All these visits were grist for Moscow's propaganda mill, getting heavy coverage in both the Russian and the international media.

Moreover, from the moment Montand and Signoret stepped out of the plane at Vnukovo Airport, their every movement, from concerts to attendance at the Bolshoi to racing across snowy fields in a three-horse troika, was filmed. At the conclusion of their stay, the screenwriter and director Mikhail Slutsky put together a slick documentary, *Yves Montand Is Singing*, which was produced by the Moscow-based Central Studio for Documentary Film and distributed widely.[5] It showed the Soviet Union at its best, with happy youngsters doing folk dances, the streets of a prosperous Moscow full of automobiles, and the illustrious visitors full of wonder at it all.

Montand was performing constantly: two hours in the evening plus the obligatory visits. It was exhausting, but seldom had he experienced such overwhelming popularity, such genuine warmth. Letters, poems, telegrams poured into his hotel room. Some informed him that children born as far away as Siberia were being named "Yvesmontand"; one set of twins, a boy and girl, were named "Yves" and "Simone."[6]

Their minders kept them on a short leash during the tightly organized visits, making sure they had little chance to engage in conversation. They tried to ensure that the visitors saw only what they wanted them to see, which was mostly the equivalent of Potemkin villages. But the visitors weren't fooled. As they were driven through the streets in the limousine, they saw the long lines at food stores, old women sweeping streets in the bitter cold and stepping aside obediently to let the official car arrogantly sweep by, restaurants and stores reserved for the party elite only. Montand was annoyed when Signoret called these things to his attention; he was still clinging to his faith in the New Soviet Man, hoping that now that Khrushchev was being more open about past mistakes, the party would right itself in time.[7]

But even with the blinders on, he couldn't help noticing how during his visits to factories, workers turned away when he approached. He could see in their eyes a silent reproof for letting himself be used that way as they equated him with the apparatchiks who were showing him around selectively. He heard that satirical pamphlets were being circulated secretly, mocking him as a toady for the authorities. One evening just before the show, a man got past security and reached Montand's dressing room to beg for help in fleeing the Soviet Union; Montand shrugged him off, irritated as he tried to concentrate on the show. Still, he was shaken to see that the real Soviet Union was far from the workers' paradise he had imagined.[8]

On the fourth evening of his five performances at the Tchaikovsky Music Hall, December 24, he recognized the occupants of an official box that had been empty before: Nikita Khrushchev and the leading members of the regime. After the show, a flunky came to his dressing room and announced that members of the Supreme Soviet were expecting him and his wife for a little supper in an improvised dining room behind the official box. When they entered, they were greeted by Khrushchev and leading members of the Politburo: Anastas Mikoyan, Vyacheslav Molotov, Nikolai Bulganin, and Georgy Malenkov. Khrushchev broke the ice by praising the performance, and then Molotov, well briefed, toasted Montand's family, complimenting his father for his lifelong opposition to fascism. Then the gloves were off.

First Deputy Premier Mikoyan asked, "So, Monsieur Montand, the Fascists allowed you to leave?" Taken aback, it took Montand a few seconds to react before responding, "It wasn't the Fascists who delayed me, it was what happened in Budapest. It was unspeakable, we were stunned, how could you have done it?" He and Signoret described the events in Paris, from the demonstrations and counterdemonstrations to the disarray among party members and doubts in the peace movements. Khrushchev, on the defensive and surprised that it was not only fascists who opposed the Red Army invasion of Hungary, answered by repeating his attack on Stalin's crimes, explaining that he and the others were too afraid of Stalin to do anything about the trials, executions, and deportations.[9]

The back-and-forth continued for three hours, Montand's tone polite but firm, Khrushchev alternately pounding on the table for emphasis and smiling at such unaccustomed candor from a visitor. "I was horrified, frightened," Montand recalled. "He was looking me straight in the eye and talking about Stalin's crimes. So it was true! Words poured out of him, he played whole scenes, he mimicked famous people. He was a fantastic actor, but I sensed the accents of truth. He seemed relieved to talk, to justify, to explain before his colleagues."[10] Montand ended the discussion by underlining that his decision to honor his commitment to tour the Soviet Union must not be interpreted as approbation of its actions in Hungary.

It was an astonishing, little-noticed moment in the depth of the Cold War: a no-holds-barred debate between two visiting show business people, mere *amuseurs*, and one of the most powerful and autocratic men in the world. And the visitors were getting the best of it. As Signoret later summed up that encounter, "Here we were, telling the representatives of the biggest Communist Party in the world to their faces just those things we had tried to say to militant French communists. It gave us the most extraordinary feeling of relief."[11]

Khrushchev relaxed, thanked Montand for his frankness, and drank to their friendly expression of opposing opinions. Montand countered with a toast of his own, thanking Khrushchev for letting him speak truth to power and concluding by raising his glass to the people of the Soviet Union and to peace. He knew that, back in France, the arguments for and against his making the trip would continue. "Now nobody likes us," he said to Signoret at the hotel. "But don't we feel good about ourselves!"[12]

They felt good about having been faithful to their convictions, but they would never again know the reassuring comfort of belonging to a group of like-minded believers in a better tomorrow thanks to the coming revolution. They suffered long after, both from what they observed during that trip to "the socialist homeland" and from the hostile way their former fellow travelers in France treated them for daring to relate on their return the truth of what they saw. As José Artur, a popular radio broadcaster and close friend of the couple, said, "They went hoping to see God. They met the devil."[13]

11

New York

Montand and Signoret spent New Year's Eve 1956 as special guests at a Kremlin party in the enormous, vaulted Saint George's Hall along with about 3,000 others, mainly ranking party members, the diplomatic corps, Red Army officers, and a smattering of artists and war heroes. The French couple kissed as the lights went out at midnight. When the lights went back on, the first secretary of the Communist Party of the Soviet Union pulled Signoret out of her chair and kissed her on the mouth, Russian style. Then Nikita Khrushchev shook both of Montand's hands before hurrying off to do traditional dances with Nikolai Bulganin, squatting on their haunches and kicking their legs.

After Montand's final performances in Russia at Leningrad, they moved on to the Eastern Bloc countries for three months, with shows in Poland, East Germany, Czechoslovakia, Romania, Bulgaria, Yugoslavia, and Hungary. It was a grueling tour, with few breaks for time off. But at each stop Montand looked, listened, and learned more, often painfully, about the god that had failed.

> It opened my eyes. I learned, on the spot, many things they didn't know in Paris. I had believed in the possibility of a better world and had met fine men and women with the same dream. For me it was a true and fundamental belief. In the name of that belief I condoned crimes and horrors through my own ignorance. What that tour of 1957 allowed me to do was to reclaim myself. I stopped being a faithful follower. From that point on, I formed my own judgment of things. I never again said a cat was black when it was gray. The events of 1956 and 1957 meant the loss of faith for me. I began a long march within myself. I continued to hope; I ceased to believe.[1]

Their trip from Leningrad to Warsaw was in a specially equipped plane provided by Khrushchev. Used by high-level Kremlin officials, it boasted plump armchairs, areas for reading and card playing, and a samovar with hostess for the inevitable tea. It had one major inconvenience, however. To the Poles who came to welcome the couple, an aircraft emblazoned with the letters CCCP gave the impression that they were cozy with the Kremlin—not the sort of impression to make on people who only months earlier had staged a revolt against the Soviet stranglehold on them that was brutally put down by Red Army tanks.

There were other sour notes. The rumor was spread that Montand insisted on being paid in gold dollars, which explained the high prices for tickets that made it difficult for many to attend his recitals; on the first day of his stay, he had to call a press conference and explain that he was in fact being paid in złotys, even though that money could not be exchanged for hard currencies and was useless outside Poland. With those matters cleared up, Montand's show at the 3,500-seat Palace of Culture was so popular that four additional performances were added, two of them televised.

In Prague, Montand's handlers kept him so busy with official receptions, dinners, and interviews that he and Signoret saw little of the city that has the largest medieval town square in Europe. The visit was marked by two events—one annoying, the other premonitory. The local organizers made a last-minute request that he sing at a special concert for the Czech police and army. Checking his exasperation, he explained patiently that as a matter of principle he never sang especially for the police and/or army in any country. Then there was the visit of Lise London, the wife of Artur London, a former Czech deputy foreign minister who had been arrested in 1952 on trumped-up charges of being a Zionist, Trotskyite, and Titoist. He was tortured until he confessed and then sentenced to life in prison. His sentence was commuted, and he had been released only a year before his wife visited Montand in his hotel room. "Montand, who did not know I was London's wife, told me about his talk with Khrushchev," she recalled, "but I sensed that he was most disturbed by the Hungarian events. He needed to talk; he was a man in pain."[2] Twelve years later, Montand would play one of his finest roles in a film based on London's case.

The Yugoslav leg of the tour, beginning March 4, 1957, was one of the most enjoyable. Not only did Montand and Signoret have the pleasure of seeing *The Crucible* played with an all-Croatian cast in Belgrade, but they were also invited to tea by Mr. and Mrs. Josip Broz, also known as Marshal Tito and his wife, Jovanka, who welcomed them cordially enough at their country villa. But it quickly became obvious that the marshal thought he was dealing with hostile members of the French Communist Party. The FCP, like other Moscow-leaning parties, had criticized him severely as a traitor for distancing himself from Stalin over policy differences in order to pursue a course of non-alignment between the two superpowers.

Once Montand made it clear that he was just as independent-minded and had never been a card-carrying member of the FCP, the tone of their conversation changed, and the former partisan fighter replaced the tea with chilled champagne in bottles labeled "Reserved for Marshal Tito." Natty in English flannels and a diamond stickpin in his tie—Signoret remembered it as being a pearl—for two hours Tito regaled his visitors with tales of his clandestine days in Paris when he recruited volunteers for the International Brigades fighting for the Republicans in the Spanish Civil War. Before parting, a starstruck Jovanka held both their hands and said, "I feel as though I were at the movies." "We do too," replied Signoret. "A newsreel."[3]

Hungary was the last stop and something of an anticlimax. Four months after Budapest had been in flames, everything was calm, the people were resigned. They had seen generations of political activists come and go during the first half of the twentieth century—fascists, then Stalinists, then revolutionaries—and nothing seemed to change. Now they had opted to live for the present and to shun ideology. Nobody wanted to talk about "the events of November," as they were euphemistically called. The gutted buildings the visitors saw were explained as the result of an accidental fire; they had nothing to do with shelling by Soviet tanks. Montand met with the minister of culture and asked about the dozen writers he knew to be in prison because their ideas offended the regime. The minister was shocked at how misinformed he was; there was not a single intellectual of any sort in Hungarian prisons, he dutifully insisted.

The people were obviously glad of the opportunity for some diversion: Montand's recitals, which he did despite threats of tear gas bombs and a boycott by some hard-line freedom fighters outraged by his meeting with Khrushchev, were as successful in Hungary as elsewhere on the tour. He and the musicians donated their fee to the Hungarian Red Cross to help those still suffering from the merciless Soviet put-down of the revolt. Signoret couldn't help noticing that the girls were particularly excited. "They loved the music and adored the musicians. They also adored the singer, but unfortunately for them, and perhaps for him, the ancestral groupie was always there, planted in his dressing room, just as she was at the Étoile."[4] Montand could only agree and regret. "I saw the most sublime girls in Budapest," he sighed. "Twenty-year-olds, girls you could die for. And yet, not a single one. . . ."[5]

⊙ ⊙ ⊙

Montand returned to Paris in March 1957 a sadder, wiser man after being mugged by the reality of life under communism. "I don't want to be anybody's spokesman," he said while resting up at Saint Paul. "I say it openly. I admit publicly that I realize that a man who thinks the opposite of me isn't automatically an enemy." He added: "It's largely out of respect for my father that I did what I did. But today I have the distinct impression that I was exploited, used exactly like an ad for a shampoo or a drink. I still believe in goodness and fraternity, but no longer as a one-way street."[6] Philosophically, he adopted as his new motto a phrase he had come across in F. Scott Fitzgerald's novel *The Crack-Up:* "One should be able to see that things are hopeless and yet be determined to make them otherwise."[7]

Now he faced criticism from both sides, as he had predicted to Signoret in Moscow. The French Left turned on him as an apostate; the Right panned him for singing in Moscow and meeting Khrushchev. As *Le Figaro* put it, "It took courage on Montand's part, for the communists will never forgive the ex-comrade's lifting the iron curtain."[8] These responses frightened off French film producers, for whom he was now toxic. He would not do another purely French-produced film from 1956 to 1964. During that time, he did ten foreign or coproductions: five Italian, one East German, four American.

The first of those films, thanks to Jules Dassin, was a Franco-Italian production filmed in the spring of 1958. As Montand explained the genesis, "It was a year after our trip to the USSR, Simone and I, and we were still boycotted. So Dassin, who had suffered from McCarthyism, told the producer, 'Either you take Montand, or I don't do the film.'"[9] For *La loi / La legge / The Law,* also called *Where the Hot Wind Blows* (France and Italy 1959, US 1960), Dassin cast Montand as Matteo Brigante, a mustachioed, scar-faced gang boss. The rest of the impressive cast included Gina Lollobrigida, Marcello Mastroianni, and Pierre Brasseur.

Based on the prize-winning novel of the same title published in 1957 by the versatile French novelist, screenwriter, and journalist Roger Vailland, *La loi* recounts the competition for power and love in a sun-blasted Adriatic port town in Puglia, a poverty-stricken region in the heel of the Italian boot.

Montand carries his part off well, but the film was too plagued by contradictions to achieve the necessary coherence. The Italian government, unhappy with the film's depiction of life in southern Italy, refused to allow the Italian coproducer, Cinematografica Titanus, to be the majority partner. The financing was reversed, with the French producer Jacques Bar assuming the lead and the studio takes being done in France. The Italians also insisted that the setting for the Italian version be described as "Corsican" to avoid offending Puglia; the French version showed it as "southern Italy," but without the depiction of poverty Vailland had described. In both versions, the jumble of actors' accents further blurred the film's identity. The result was a predictable flop despite excellent performances by Lollobrigida, Mastroianni, and Montand.

Montand was scarcely through with the film before he was back rehearsing for his third major solo recital at the Étoile, due to open on October 8, 1958, with twenty-four songs, including sixteen new numbers. Always liking to keep audiences off-balance, he avoided the somber political tone many might have expected after his eastern tour and opted for a lighter, more amusing evening. That meant eliminating "C'est à l'aube" (It's at Dawn) with its promise of communist-style "marvelous tomorrows" that Khrushchev had admired.

Among the new songs were some that would become his standards, such as the whimsical "Le chat de la voisine" (The Neighbor's Cat), which ironically praises the cat next door that does nothing useful, such as catching rats, but spends its time eating chicken and foie gras and sleeping on a comfortable eiderdown. With "Sir Godfrey," he had fun gently mocking the English. This caricature of the perfect gentleman prefers horses to pretty girls, plays golf or goes duck hunting on weekends, and of course wears a bowler and carries a furled brolly. But he's actually a con man whose real name is "Smith" and who turns gangster at night. The song touches all the bases of the French prejudices about the British as ignoring the pleasures of *l'amour,* preferring snobbish sports such as golf and hunting, and isn't really about an aristocrat at all but about a cheap crook. Sympathy for the working man still figures in the program, but that man is in South America rather than in France. "Planter café" (Planting Coffee) is the plaint of a plantation worker who spends his days stooping to plant coffee beans beneath a torrid sun—"it's no job for weaklings." The song ends with the spotlight focused tightly on Montand, who stands limply, a tattered straw hat tipped down over his eyes.

He was aware that sometimes his songs were over the heads of the audience or treated subjects that were less than amusing. For example, "Soleil d'acier" (Steel Sun) and "La grande cité" (The Big City) described a hard, mechanized, dehumanized world where the only thing that makes a man want to live is his love for his woman. But he insisted on continually trying new themes, even if not popular at first, and bearing witness to his times. "You have to understand," he once explained, "that a song is like a compressed stage play, a play that lasts only two and a half minutes; that's not long to present the actors, the story, the dénouement, whereas a playwright would have three long acts. A listener has to hear a new song two or three times to assimilate it and own it. It's like a little objet d'art."[10]

The show ran for five months, with 160 performances and 200,000 tickets sold. The critics were again won over, *Le Monde* praising "his beautiful, warm, supple voice" and his professionalism: "Put together with all the attention of a careful craftsman, his show reaches a point of technical perfection that is beyond belief."[11] The audience on a glitzy opening night included many show business stars, from his *Salaire* colleagues Charles Vanel and Henri-Georges Clouzot to Michèle Morgan and Sophia Loren. Also present was a certain American impresario named Norman Granz, who had big plans for Montand in New York.

While Montand was doing *La loi* and then rehearsing for his new show, Signoret was also busy. She had been offered the female lead as Alice Aisgill in the film version of the 1957 best-selling British novel *Room at the Top* by John Braine, the story of an ambitious young social-climbing cad played by Laurence Harvey who loves Alice but marries another woman for money. Alice, an unhappily married middle-aged woman who offers him good conversation and great sex, was the part of a lifetime. With Jack Clayton in his directorial debut, Signoret spent three months on the shoot in the North of England and in London.

When the film was released in early 1959, it was an immediate hit, dominating the BAFTA Awards that spring as Best British Film and Best Film from Any Source, and Signoret was named Best Foreign Actress. She also won the Palme d'Or as Best Actress at Cannes. The film was just as popular in the United States, the *New York Times* hailing her performance as a "woman clutching at her last chance at happiness,"[12] and the *Saturday Review* raving, "Adult! A whole new chapter is about to be written in motion picture history!"[13] (The film was less successful in France, where explicit references to sex were ho-hum.) Signoret was walking on air when she returned to Paris and her backstage routine at Montand's show: "He had no idea that it was Greta Garbo handing him his Turkish towel," she joked later.[14]

⊙ ⊙ ⊙

Montand had dreamed of going to America since those early days in La Cabucelle. Once he had become a star, he had been approached by New York nightclubs for singing gigs and by Gene Kelly for work in films. But his honestly affirmative answer to the question on the US visa application, "Are you now or have you ever been a member of the Communist Party or an organization affiliated with or having common activities with the Communist Party?," resulted in an inevitable refusal of entry by the US Immigration and Naturalization Service. He tried explaining this to Norman Granz when Granz visited him in his dressing room in December 1958.

But Granz wanted Montand for a one-man show he had in mind. It would be called *An Evening with Yves Montand,* and it would be not in a nightclub but at a Broadway theater. Granz was the most successful concert promoter and jazz record producer in the United States—he had created Verve Records two years earlier—with clients such as Ella Fitzgerald, Oscar Peterson, Stan Getz, and Billie Holiday. He had founded and toured the world with the all-star Jazz at the Philharmonic concerts. He assured Montand that he would take care of the visa problem.

He did, but it took longer than he expected. When Montand and Signoret sent their first request for visas, it was routinely turned down. The news was delivered to them personally and regretfully by a cultural attaché from the US embassy in Paris who visited them at place Dauphine. Granz went back to work on the problem, and by January Mr. and Mrs. Livi had their visas, albeit on a special waiver: they were allowed one entry only and could remain only from July 15 to December 15, 1959. Montand had little time to celebrate. After the last curtain fell on his show at the Étoile in March, he took the show on a lengthy tour of England, Belgium, Holland, Sweden, West Germany, and Israel, followed by several stops in the French provinces.

On his return to Paris, Montand had time to realize what he had committed himself to in the United States. He was assailed by doubt. Except for "Autumn Leaves" and the handful of American cinephiles who had seen *The Wages of Fear,* he was an unknown there. This was the country where they loved home-grown megastars, the land of Frank Sinatra, Sammy Davis Jr., Dean Martin, and Ray Charles, while he was a mere French music hall singer who had done a few films. No French singer had attempted an American show since Maurice Chevalier years ago. Americans were not known for their prowess in foreign languages, and he would be trying to win over audiences with a program entirely in French.

He wasn't the only one who considered spectacular failure a real possibility in a city where shows closed fast if the newspapers panned them after opening night. His contract stipulated that his show would last only as long as more than half of the chosen theater's 1,000 seats were filled. The theater's owner further hedged his bets and booked a different show after three weeks. Montand and Signoret also prepared for possible disaster: they would leave fourteen-year-old Catherine behind in Paris. She would join them only if the show was a success. If not, they would be back home within days. Except for Signoret's encouragement, Montand was getting precious little moral support. "When our friends heard about the offer," he remembered, "they all warned me that I'd fall flat on my face. Everything was against me: my reputation as an Iron Curtain star, my alleged political beliefs, my total ignorance of the English language."[15]

Montand's first few days after landing in New York on September 10 were inauspicious. After spending the night at the Algonquin Hotel, where Granz had reserved the couple a room, he woke up with terrible pain in his jaw. A dentist diagnosed an impacted wisdom tooth. With only ten days to prepare his show, there was no question of oral surgery. So every morning he began with palliative treatment to reduce the pain so he could sing. Then he learned that the New York musicians' union would allow only one member of his own orchestra, Bob Castella, to play; Granz found six others that Montand had to integrate into his tightly timed recital, where every note, every drumbeat had to be coordinated with his movements onstage.

And there was the language problem, which he tried to alleviate, if not solve, by taking Berlitz lessons three times a week. That wasn't enough for the brief, twenty-second introduction in English to each song that he planned to do. The screenwriter Michael Wilson, who had been blacklisted by Hollywood as a communist and whose most recent but uncredited script was for the Academy Award–winning film *The Bridge on the River Kwai* (1957), was engaged to write them; Montand then laboriously memorized each one phonetically with Signoret's help. The linguistic culture shock was brought home to him one day when he overheard someone ask, "What's Eve Montand like? Is she exciting or dull?"[16] Still, it was the New York of their dreams: photos in the French press showed them, hand in hand, touring a garish Times Square at night, happy as kids in a candy store.

Signoret had her own private worries that she kept to herself for fear of adding to Montand's. She came to understand that most shows were not opened on Broadway first. The usual routine was to take a show on the road to Boston or Philadelphia or Hackensack, New Jersey, on a shakedown cruise, where it would be honed and polished, mistakes corrected, audience reaction measured. Montand's cold-turkey Broadway opening was a high-wire act without a net. She had a recurring nightmare that they would have to slink out of town in disgrace if it flopped.

Then, too, the fact that "Yves Montand" was hardly a household name even in New York concerned her. *Room at the Top* was still playing at movie theaters; everyone from taxi drivers to restaurant waiters recognized her, occasionally greeting her with "Hi, Alice." She was afraid of upstaging him, or as she put it later, "My greatest worry was that they would see Montand as an actress's husband."[17] But she couldn't do much about that—although she had briefly considered delaying her arrival by a week to avoid having the spotlight on her instead of on him—or about the fact that he noticed it and didn't like it.

Opening night was September 21, 1959, at Henry Miller's Theater on West Forty-Third Street. On hand, besides members of New York's considerable French colony, were many of the show business glitterati, from Ingrid Bergman and Lauren Bacall to screenwriter Sidney Green, director Sidney Lumet, Marlene Dietrich, Paulette Goddard, and lyricist Frank Loesser. Montgomery Clift escorted Marilyn Monroe because Arthur Miller was busy with the screenplay of *The Misfits.* To be sure of making the premiere, Monroe had just flown back to New York the previous day from Hollywood, where she had met with producer Jerry Wald, director George Cukor, and writer Norman Krasna to discuss her upcoming film, a mistaken-identity comedy called *The Billionaire.* It would be her first look at Yves Montand.

Along with the rest of the audience, these celebrities gave him such a thunderous welcome that he had trouble with his memorized introduction to his leadoff song, "À Paris." For the next two hours, he would give them a good whiff of Paris with twenty-four songs, including "Les grands boulevards," "C'est si bon," "Luna Park," and, of course, "Les feuilles mortes." He generally shunned political songs, the only one being the short "Flamenco de Paris" about a Spanish Republican exile. As it was, the American press showed very little interest in his politics, a pleasant change from Paris.

Back at the Algonquin afterward with friends, there was champagne and much congratulatory kissing on both cheeks, but he was in a trance of anxiety. He knew as well as anyone that nothing was won until the first editions came out with the critics' verdict. It was nice that Ingrid Bergman had shown up in his dressing room with hearty congratulations, as had Marlene Dietrich, who gave him a big hug. It also helped when Richard Maney, his New York press agent, told him Marilyn Monroe's reaction: "He's so wonderful, he sings with his body!"[18]

He need not have worried. When Maney triumphantly brought in an armful of early editions, it was clear that the city's hard-nosed critics were bowled over. "Yves Montand is wonderful, superb," said the *New York Post.* "All our singers, including the great Mr. Sinatra, could sit at his feet and take a lesson from him. I could have listened to him all night."[19] *Variety* said he had "such extraordinary versatility that he seems like a combination Danny Kaye, Ray Bolger and Maurice Chevalier . . . a standout in every department."[20] The weeklies were even more dithyrambic. *Time* called him "the hottest music hall performer to hit the scene since World War II. . . .Yves Montand has an air of casual virility that can curl the hair of every properly nourished female in the house[;] . . . his simplest movements are vibrant with innuendo."[21] The *New York Times,* noting his proletarian origins and his appeal to both the working class and intellectuals, listed everything it liked about him: "Skill, personality and showmanship. . . . He was subtle and he was funny. . . . His voice had a fine, throaty resonance. . . . He was intensely simple and direct. . . . He even managed to look like [Fred] Astaire."[22] In *The New Yorker,* the brilliant, biting British theater critic Kenneth Tynan uncharacteristically gushed over the show's star. Although he found that Montand, dressed in his simple brown slacks and open-neck shirt, looked like a taxi driver or the theater electrician when he appeared on stage, he wrote that when Montand began singing, he was "the prince of the *trottoir* troubadours, and the natural successor to Trenet and Chevalier." He loved his charm and exuberance and even a certain naive innocence "that makes most criticism seem snide and sniping." As to his voice, "He lets [it] creep up to the important notes, sliding from baritone to tenor, at which point it idles, producing a careless, caressing vibrato. The touch is light, the tone pervasively dark."[23]

Montand and Signoret didn't have to worry about slinking out of town as failures. They even enjoyed their new American stardom, venturing so far as to dine regularly at Sardi's restaurant, a popular hangout for Broadway actors—many hoping to see their caricature on its walls along with those of hundreds of others—where they had felt intimidated the first time they went. They sent for Catherine, who quickly knew New York better than they did, lunching at drugstores and sleeping over with her new friends at the home of the French consul. They enrolled her in the Lycée Français de New York so she could keep up with her studies.

After three weeks of a packed house, the Henry Miller's owner regretfully had to honor his contract with the following show and close the money-making *Evening with Yves Montand.* Norman Granz had prepared for this event, though, and easily moved the show to the Longacre Theater on West Forty-Eighth Street, where it ran for another five weeks. In all, Montand gave forty-two standing-room-only performances, including a special on October 25 with proceeds to go to the Actors Fund. He was in any case popular with the New York actor community. They often came to greet him in his dressing room. To their surprise, he recognized many who were not especially well known, calling them by name and sometimes mentioning their best roles and even miming certain scenes. One who needed no introduction was a tall, mild-mannered man who entered almost timidly and announced, "My name is Henry Fonda." Montand and Signoret answered in unison, "We know," and they hugged.[24]

Marilyn Monroe, who had been so impressed on opening night by the way Montand sang with his body, also attended the second night, this time with her husband. Arthur Miller, who had met Montand three years earlier on the set of *Sorcières,* greeted him in his dressing room after the show and invited him and Signoret to his apartment on East Fifty-Seventh Street for dinner. There they met Marilyn for the first time and were pleasantly surprised to find her an unaffected woman who enjoyed playing hostess and called Miller "Poppy."

Over Italian wine and a dinner prepared by the Millers' Naples-born maid, Lena Pepitone, Miller and Signoret talked politics—her first opportunity to do so with a left-wing intellectual since leaving Paris—while Montand and Marilyn worked to overcome the language barrier. Asked about their tour of Moscow and the Eastern Bloc, the Montands admitted that it had altered their views of communism. Miller indicated that he understood and tended to agree with their position. The seeds of a new friendship had been sown. It did not have enough time to grow, however, for Norman Granz had arranged for Montand to sing in Montreal, Toronto, Los Angeles, and San Francisco, before going on to Japan, immediately after the show closed at the Longacre.

After Canada, they arrived in Los Angeles on November 4. As their plane descended over the city, Signoret couldn't help feeling a thrill when she saw the famous sign spread over the hills—HOLLYWOOD—the mecca that she dreamed of as a girl playing actress at home in Neuilly. "I was eating one of Proust's memory madeleines, as big as a donut," she recalled. She knew that the city was founded on an often-meretricious myth composed of sun, palms, flashy cars, swimming pools, famous studios, and instant fame: "You had to have your head screwed on not to go completely crazy in Hollywood."[25] She spoke truer than she knew.

12

Hollywood

Montand had only four days to prepare for his Los Angeles concert. Besides setting up the stage to his taste at the recently modernized, 1,000-seat Huntington Hartford Theater at Hollywood and Vine, he again had to recruit several new musicians for his orchestra to comply with the state's union rules. But with curiosity running high about the French stars who had conquered New York, he and Signoret had to take time for the Hollywood social scene. Kirk Douglas's German-born wife, Anne (née Hannelore Marx), had called when they were still in Manhattan to invite them to a party when they arrived on the West Coast. It so happened that on the same day, November 7, 1959, the Republican Party was sponsoring an event to honor California's favorite son, Richard Nixon, who was running against John Kennedy in the 1960 presidential election. *Le tout* Hollywood thus had to choose between the two events; many decided to shuttle between them.

At the Douglas party, the new arrivals were introduced to the sort of party guests that only Hollywood could bring together. Judy Garland was there to sing, while Gary Cooper, George Cukor, Gene Kelly, Gregory Peck, Dean Martin, and director Henry Hathaway, who had directed Marilyn Monroe in her breakthrough film *Niagara* (1953), bid them welcome. Walt Disney was there too, which gave Montand the opportunity to ask why Disney had not answered the fan letter he had sent to him when he was a thirteen-year-old devouring American films in La Cabucelle. France was represented by the novelist Romain Gary, then serving as consul general in Los Angeles and looking bored. Jack Warner took time out from attending the Nixon gala to drop by and shake the hand of the actor who had broken a contract with him years earlier.

Montand's week-long show was the now predictable success, with reviewers echoing the raves of their New York counterparts. What was not predictable was the surprise invitation by Dinah Shore to appear on her

Sunday evening prime-time program, *The Dinah Shore Chevy Show,* then one of the most popular television programs in America. On November 15 "in living color" on NBC, she introduced him as "the idol of France" to her tens of millions of viewers. He did three songs in French, then engaged in some well-rehearsed patter with her in his memorized English. He next did a comic number about learning English at Berlitz, where they taught him to improve his *h*'s by holding a piece of paper in front of his mouth and saying, "How, where, when," exhaling enough air with each word to make the paper wave. Then they sang together "Ain't We Got Fun" while doing a perfectly timed dance routine—he appreciated that Shore's professionalism was as painstaking as his—wearing bowler hats like the one he wore for his "Sir Godfrey" song. He came across as funny, relaxed, the perfect showman.[1]

After *The Dinah Shore Chevy Show,* Montand and Signoret went to San Francisco on November 16 for the last leg of his American tour before returning to France for Christmas. Then he was supposed to tour Japan, where two large theaters in Tokyo were booked solid, plus the Olympic stadium in Osaka with 50,000 seats. That plan was upended when the Twentieth Century–Fox casting department called Montand at his hotel. They wanted him to return post haste to Hollywood to be Marilyn Monroe's leading man in her next film. Signoret, who took the call because of her fluent English, explained that his schedule was already full, but she was willing to read the screenplay.

Casting rushed the script to San Francisco, she read it rapidly, they talked it over. Montand hesitated, worried about whether his approximate English would be adequate to act in an American film. Signoret, however, was excited about this opportunity to break into American movies; with a cast including Monroe and Tony Randall, it was certain to do well at the box office. After all, it was only a musical comedy, and he was a singer. Besides, Arthur Miller, whom they had met and liked, had worked on the screenplay. Montand decided to go for it. As he explained later when asked during an interview about the time he felt he had become an international star, "The minute they said to me, 'Monsieur, do you want to make a movie with Marilyn Monroe?' Can you imagine, this kid from Marseilles and Les Crottes ending up in the Hollywood he'd been dreaming about all his life?"[2] Arthur Miller understood. As he said afterward, "I'm sure he accepted for one good reason. It meant he was breaking into movies as a leading man opposite Marilyn Monroe."[3]

It was early December when they returned to Los Angeles. Fox had reserved a suite for them in Bungalow 20 at the sprawling pink-and-ochre complex of the Beverly Hills Hotel, where the motto was "the best of everything, regardless of cost." Their bungalow was nestled amid twelve acres of tropical gardens, manicured lawns, and exotic flowers. Bungalow 20, with living room, bedroom, kitchen, and bath, was on the second floor of a two-story building. Bungalow 21, on the same floor and across the hall, was where Monroe and Miller were conveniently lodged. The ground floor, where the curtains were always drawn, was occupied by Howard Hughes and his wife, actress Jean Peters. Signoret, with nothing else to do, enjoyed shopping, sunning, and leisurely lunches in the hotel's Polo Lounge while waiting for Montand to return from the studio.

The Montands and the Millers picked up their friendship where they had left off in New York. Signoret and Monroe went shopping together, tried different recipes for pasta—a bit of Livi sauce, a pinch of DiMaggio seasoning—in the kitchen, and had their hair color touched up by a hairdresser who had once done the same for Jean Harlow. They exchanged stories about their professional lives. Signoret was struck by the fact that Monroe didn't seem happy and that she really found little personal satisfaction in acting. Friendship developed. She referred to Monroe simply as her pal, a neighbor across the hall of whom she was fond, who looked, when in her blue polka-dot rayon dressing gown, with no false eyelashes or makeup, barefoot in the bungalow, "like the most beautiful peasant girl imaginable from the Île-de-France, as the type has been celebrated for centuries."[4]

Meanwhile, Montand and Miller enjoyed strolling together around the antiseptic streets of Beverly Hills to the amazement of neighbors who wondered why they were walking instead of driving—once a motorcycle policeman found that suspicious enough to stop them for an identity check. Montand, having agreed to Fox's impromptu proposition but not yet having a contract, was unaware for the moment that when that call came in San Francisco, he had been last on a long Fox list of potential candidates to play opposite Monroe.

The role was that of a wealthy, well-known playboy who hears that an off-Broadway cabaret is rehearsing a musical that satirizes him. He visits a rehearsal, notices its attractive star, Amanda Dell, and decides that the best way to see more of her is to join the cast under a pseudonym—playing himself. Basic to the comic idea behind Academy Award–winning writer Norman Krasna's screenplay for *The Billionaire* was that the part would be played by an actor whose audience image was that of a bumbling stuffed shirt with no notion of how to sing and dance. Krasna, one of the highest-salaried screenwriters in Hollywood, was an old hand at plots whose mainspring was mistaken identity or impersonation. His first was *The Richest Girl in the World* (1934), in which an heiress changes places with her secretary in her effort to find a man who will love her for herself instead of for her money.

The Billionaire (under the changed title *Let's Make Love*) had that tried-and-true plot. In this case, a wealthy playboy, Jean-Marc Clément, struggles to shed himself of his billionaire persona—he takes the name "Alexander Dumas"—and be loved for himself, not for his money. In one of the film's few really amusing sequences, he hires a comedian, a dancer, and a singer (Milton Berle, Gene Kelly, and Bing Crosby) to teach him how to tell jokes, dance, and sing. Kelly, who has only a few minutes of on-screen time, was in Paris working on a jazz ballet number for the Paris Opera when he got the call. He flew to Hollywood, spent two hours on the set, and returned to Paris the next day. Berle's cameo, in which he tries to get Montand to do a comic turn walking on his ankles, learn original jokes, and improve his diction, all to no avail, is one of the best things in the movie.

Although *Variety* said Montand gave "a sock performance, full of both heart and humor,"[5] and the critics generally praised Monroe's rendition of "My Heart Belongs to Daddy," the verdict on *Let's Make Love* was mostly thumbs down. The *New York Times* found "a strange heaviness in Montand," due perhaps to an accent that made him hard to understand, and thought Monroe's usual dynamism lacking, while the script was full of clichés.[6] Back in France, *Le Monde* liked the musical sequences but thought the film lacked warmth and charm, while Montand did well enough in a part obviously designed for another actor.[7] Montand himself said later that "it was a part that could have shot me down in flames for the rest of my career . . . a part that just didn't hold up. It hammered me into the ground. There are movies where you need to be Einstein, but you're only a human being."[8]

⊙ ⊙ ⊙

Putting the project together was more difficult and complicated than anyone imagined. The ebullient, energetic screenwriter and producer Jerry Wald, son of a dry-goods salesman from Brooklyn, had a long career as screenwriter and producer for Warner Bros. before leaving that studio and creating Jerry Wald Productions, releasing through Fox, in 1956. Since then, he had had hits with the weepy romance *An Affair to Remember* with Cary Grant and Deborah Kerr and the Oscar-winning melodrama *Peyton Place* with Lana

Turner (both 1957). He was looking for a new vehicle for Gregory Peck. It was decided that Peck, with his stolid persona, would be ideal as the awkward, smitten playboy trying to dance his way into Amanda's favor. He was signed with a $100,000 advance. George Cukor agreed to direct on September 16, 1959. Then there remained the question of who would be the female lead.

Buddy Adler wanted to get Marilyn Monroe back to work. He had produced the Academy Award–winning film *From Here to Eternity* (1953) at Columbia Pictures before joining Twentieth Century–Fox and replacing Darryl F. Zanuck as Fox's head of production in 1956, when he had produced *Bus Stop* (1956) with Monroe. Her performance in that film prompted the *New York Times* to proclaim that "Marilyn Monroe has finally proved herself an actress."[9] However, her contract called for her to do seven films for Fox by 1962, and so far she had done only *Bus Stop.* Adler sent Krasna, working from his first draft, to give her an oral presentation of *Billionaire.*

She liked it, and she also liked the idea of working with Cukor, known for his skill at dealing with difficult actresses. Her contract provided that she could choose her own directors, and he was on her list. She signed on September 30 for the part of the chorine Amanda Dell without thoroughly reading the script. "It's wonderful," she said at the time. "I'm so enthusiastic. I can't wait to get started."[10] She would be back in the fold of Fox president Spyros Skouras—the man who had first signed Norma Jean Baker to Fox and made her Marilyn Monroe, the man she called "Papa Skouras." According to Arthur Miller, she had agreed to do "a stupefying comedy that Fox had forced upon her."[11]

Skouras's first job for her after she signed with Fox was to entertain Nikita Khrushchev on the Hollywood leg of his thirteen-day state visit to the United States in September. The visit was at the invitation of President Dwight Eisenhower, who hoped to promote the new East–West policy of peaceful coexistence. Skouras, as Fox president, hosted a luncheon for Khrushchev at the studio's luxurious commissary, the Café de Paris—making it, some wags said, the greatest spectacle ever staged in a motion picture studio.[12] America's film industry turned out in force for the event, with executives from the major studios, journalists, and stars attending, including Elizabeth Taylor, Debbie Reynolds, Kim Novak, and Judy Garland, along with directors Billy Wilder, Joshua Logan, and William Wyler. Monroe arrived escorted by Cukor and was introduced to the head of the Soviet Communist Party, who shook her hand so hard it hurt for days afterward. "He looked at me the way a man looks on a woman [with desire]," she said.[13]

Skouras, the boy from Skourochori, son of a Greek sheep herder who immigrated to the United States in 1910, couldn't resist teasing Khrushchev. "I was just a poor boy, and now I'm head of a studio," he said in his thick Greek accent. To which Khrushchev shot back via an interpreter, "I was just a poor boy and now I'm head of Russia."[14] Afterward Fox pretended to let Khrushchev watch a soundstage take of its upcoming musical *Can Can* (1960) with Frank Sinatra, Shirley MacLaine, and Maurice Chevalier—without film in the camera.

In October, Monroe began working with Cukor and *Love*'s choreographer, Jack Cole, with whom she had done *Gentlemen Prefer Blondes* (1953) and, most recently, Billy Wilder's very successful *Some Like It Hot* (1959). Color tests—*The Billionaire* was to be shot in CinemaScope and Deluxe Color—wardrobe fittings, and rehearsals got underway. Monroe seemed happy, and her attitude professional. She recorded a breathy, faux-naïf version of Cole Porter's song "My Heart Belongs to Daddy" (1938) for later lip-synching into her big opening scene. Her habitual problems with lateness and absences for rehearsals were in abeyance. The project seemed well and truly on the rails.

It was derailed in November. When Monroe and Arthur Miller got around to reading the script thoroughly, they demanded that her role be beefed up. "There was no script, really," she said. "There was nothing for the girl to *do*."[15] Fox had no choice but to go along with their demand. A new writer, Hal Kanter, also a producer and director, was called on for two rewrites. When the Millers still found them unsatisfactory, Wald assigned Miller himself, for a $15,000 fee, to develop her part. Though the solemn, humorless intellectual was the last writer one would associate with musical comedy, he would do two more uncredited revisions, stopping his work on the screenplay for John Huston's *The Misfits*. One was done in December for $5,000, followed by still another for $7,500. By then, the screenplay had been through one original version and four rewrites. Krasna's sure comic touch was lost. A script written by a committee, it had all the defects and compromises that implies. It was a botch, with jokes that fell flat, wooden dialogue, predictable situations.

Seeing that the film was in trouble, the studio tried perking it up by changing the name to *Let's Make Love*. When Peck read the revised script, he was so appalled by the way Monroe now dominated the film to his detriment that he asked Fox to cancel his contract. He returned the $100,000 advance to get out of it. Fox reluctantly agreed. The casting department went into frantic high gear to find a replacement: the film was already in rehearsal, running behind schedule, and there was no male lead.

Casting tried everyone they could think of for the role. Urgent calls were reportedly made to Charlton Heston, James Stewart, Kirk Douglas, Cary Grant, Yul Brynner, Peter Lawford, Tony Curtis, Rock Hudson. All refused for various reasons. That was when Arthur Miller, possibly at the suggestion of Monroe, reminded Fox executives of Montand's sensational reception in New York and recommended they try him. Dinah Shore confirmed to Wald how smoothly he had handled his guest-star routine on her show, how it had generated an avalanche of fan mail.

The clincher came when Monroe herself weighed in: she made it clear that Montand was the one she wanted. Wald, ready to do practically anything to keep his erratic star happy, motivated, and, above all, stable, decided that Montand was the answer to his problems. No matter that it was a spectacular, risky, case of casting against type—one of the best song-and-dance men of the day chosen to play a clumsy, tone-deaf character who could do neither. But the press loved the choice. "Powerful Stars Meet to Play-Act Romance," headlined *Life* later in 1960, which had a cover showing Montand nuzzling an ecstatic Monroe's neck.[16]

There was as yet no contract, but the Montands had something special to celebrate on New Year's Eve 1959. They splurged on dinner at the clubby Romanoff's restaurant on Rodeo Drive in Beverly Hills, a popular, expensive watering hole for the Hollywood elite where they could dine on noodles Romanoff and frog legs. The lights went out at midnight, they kissed, and when the lights went back on, a tall gentleman with a slight limp said, "Happy New Year." Gary Cooper then asked Montand's permission to dance with his wife. Permission granted, Signoret, who couldn't dance well, managed a slow fox trot with this handsome man. The evening was an uncanny mirror image of their New Year's Eve in the Kremlin. They had gone, in twelve months, from the severe citadel of communism to the capitalist glamor of palmy Tinseltown.

Contract negotiations began in earnest in early January 1960, with the Screen Actors Guild providing an agent to deal with Fox on Montand's behalf. During the first round, the studio offered $50,000, to which the agent merely laughed. Montand was alarmed. That sounded like plenty to him, so why refuse? The agent told him to stay calm; this was how these things were done in Hollywood. Fox got back and said maybe they could go as high as $75,000; the agent replied that they must be joking. Now Montand began to panic, fearing that his great opportunity might fall through because of this ego game of bluff and counterbluff. "These Americans are crazy," he whispered to Signoret. Finally, there was one more negotiation. It was a done deal for $100,000 per film.[17]

Fox contracted Montand for not one but three films. Suddenly, nothing was too good for its new star. Changes were made in the script to accommodate his accent, transforming the male lead into a French playboy named Jean-Marc Clément—the film's first minutes are spent laboriously describing in what is supposed to be a jocular way how his family became wealthy over the centuries. The studio used its influence to obtain a work permit for him. It leaned on the State Department to have Montand's and Signoret's visas extended. As for the canceled tour of Japan and the $120,000 that organizers demanded for breach of contract, Skouras offered to cover that in return for Montand's accepting to do a fourth movie. He was now officially a Hollywood actor. The Fox Employee Personnel Statement showed that Yves (no middle name) Montand (Livi), address 15, place Dauphine, Paris, France, occupation actor, a married white male, had been assigned Social Security Number 554-60-0448.[18]

Then he began to wonder whether he should not have been more careful about what he had wished for. "The celebrations were short-lived. Once everything was signed and sealed I said to Simone, 'Well, now I have to make this movie!' I dived right in; it was sink or swim, so I swam. The old fears returned. . . . I struggled to get out words like 'I shouldn't, I couldn't.' They came out something like 'I shouduhuh.' I felt as if I were back in *Les Portes de la Nuit* all over again."[19] Or, as Signoret later summed up his dilemma with her usual lucidity, "It would have been crazy to say no to Cukor. It was also crazy to have said yes. Montand was crazy. But he was right."[20]

Skyros Skouras was delighted with his new talent. He had, in effect, gotten a twofer when signing Montand because with him came a glamorous French actress who could only add to the publicity for *Let's Make Love*. As a sendoff to the studio's publicity campaign, Skouras hosted a press party for Montand in mid-January 1960. Canapés were nibbled, champagne and scotch flowed, shots of vodka followed bites of zakuski. Dozens of photographers jockeyed for the best angles on the costars and their spouses. An obviously pleased Marilyn, smiling and exuberant, was on hand. Asked about Montand, she said with a verbal wink, "I *like* him. Next to my husband and Marlon Brando, I think Yves Montand is the most attractive man I've ever met." Whether she also liked him because he reminded her of her exhusband, Joe DiMaggio, as rumor had it, is uncertain. In response to a similar question, Montand read a prepared statement that revealed the current state of his English: "Everything she do is original, even when she stand and talk to you. I never see anybody who concentrate so hard. She work hard, she do scene over and over and over but is not happy until perfect. She help me, I try to help her."[21]

Skouras would take any publicity for the film he could get. He was desperate to lure audiences away from their television sets and back into movie theaters as the new medium began seriously to affect the movie business's bottom line. Writing in the studio magazine *Fox Dynamo* in February 1960, he said, "Twentieth Century-Fox has launched the new decade with a necessary and intensive drive, backed by all of its resources and facilities, to restore motion picture patronage to its pre-television proportions. Obviously that, in light of the diminished patronage sustained during the previous decade, is no small undertaking in these times. . . . There is no alternative, for unless we work together as a team we will needlessly, but seriously, jeopardize the future of our industry."[22]

As to *Let's Make Love,* it was to be produced on an even more lavish scale than *Gentlemen Prefer Blondes* and *How to Marry a Millionaire.* In addition to Monroe, the magazine added in a separate article, the film would feature Yves Montand, "the greatest all-around European performer to come to this country, the performer who can do everything[;] . . . he's sensational—and Marilyn's got him!" It quoted from an article in *Variety:* "Yves Montand is one of those performers whom audiences can't resist. Little known in the US, but a great favorite in Europe, he's a charming, relaxed and immensely talented Frenchman. . . . There's plenty of room at the top of the entertainment ladder and Yves Montand's got all it takes to get there."[23]

Fox's press department arranged interviews with Montand for gossip columnists such as Louella Parsons, who had heard him sing at Prince Aly Khan's wedding on the Riviera in 1948. She spoke with him at her house in Los Angeles one morning shortly after the press party and gushed as only she could gush. For her, he was "the fascinating Frenchman with the overabundance of sex-appeal, the man for whom 'all' women fall with a more resounding crash than for any male since Rudolph Valentino held sway with his animal-masculinity . . . the complete charmer . . . all-male virility." She also got to Monroe, who echoed the sex angle the studio was promoting: "Yves is the most exciting male star in years," Monroe said. "He's all *male,* too, a cross between Clark Gable and Marlon Brando. He's going to be a big success in American movies, watch and see."[24] As in France, Montand's looks and physicality were still appreciated more than his acting.

He became aware that he had not been the first choice for the role. He didn't like it, but he wasn't going to let vanity spoil his budding Hollywood career. He plunged into the grind of learning his lines by rote, lines in a foreign language that he would have to repeat under Cukor's direction on the set as naturally as possible. He wrote the most important ones on bits of color-coded paper and taped them to the walls of their bungalow. Signoret drilled him for a while before a studio-appointed tutor took over and worked with him every morning. Spencer Tracy once said that the most important thing about acting was "learning the blasted lines."[25] And he didn't have to do it in a foreign language.

Principal photography began in late January. The first day of the shoot, Monroe called in sick, returning to the pattern of capricious absences that had driven directors crazy in the making of previous films. Cukor called Montand and told him to be ready for scenes that did not require her presence, sending him scrambling to learn new lines in a few hours. That went on time and again, with everyone on the set becoming increasingly exasperated. Cukor, to calm his frustration, began tearing off pieces of the script and chewing them, gulping them down when she finally showed up.[26]

When she did arrive for her first scene with Montand, he found her a nervous wreck, trembling, edgy, drinking cup after cup of coffee in an effort to overcome the effect of the cocktail of sleeping pills and tranquillizers—sodium pentothal, Demerol, phenobarbital, Amytal—she took habitually. "You're going to see what it means to shoot with the worst actress in the world," she warned. "So you're scared," he replied gently, trying to think of English words that would reassure her. "Think of me a little bit. I'm lost."[27]

13

Marilyn

That was the moment when an unexpected bond developed between Yves Montand and Marilyn Monroe. It was an unlikely pairing. He was a Parisian, moved in sophisticated intellectual and artistic circles thanks to Signoret, barely spoke or comprehended English, and found himself on the set of *Let's Make Love* by sheer chance. She was the product of Los Angeles, had spent her life being exploited as a sex symbol in the shallows of the show business/cinema world, had no notion of French or any other foreign language, and was selected for this film simply due to a contract obligation.

Strange as it may seem, at the time he knew very little about her. He had never seen her films—not Wilder's *Seven Year Itch* (1955), with its iconic image of Monroe standing on a sidewalk with her dress blown up by a subway vent, not Joshua Logan's *Bus Stop,* in which she used her Actors Studio training to give a performance with real depth. Nor did he know the backstory of her unhappy childhood, the foster homes and orphanages, her struggle to make it in Hollywood despite the abusive studio system and the toll it took on her. As he discovered these things, he began to feel if not love, then at least compassion.

As for Monroe, for the first time she had met a leading man who admitted that he too was grappling with his role, who lacked confidence that he could meet the director's expectations, that he was afraid. Instead of the intellectual inferiority she felt with Miller, unlike the contempt she saw in the eyes of many in Hollywood who considered her not a real actress but only another studio bimbo, she felt understood by this man who was the toast of Paris and New York and yet was as vulnerable as she was. They found that they had much in common, even if it was only their self-doubt and anxiety, their humble origins. They were, they both realized, cast in roles they despised: she because once again she was the ditzy blonde, he because his abilities as a singer and dancer were largely unused—he did only two songs, including their duet in the title song, one mime number, and one humiliating imitation of a crowing rooster—while serving simply as a foil in a vehicle tailor-made for his costar.

To calm their fears, they decided to help each other by rehearsing together in the bungalow, she correcting his English, he encouraging her to trust her acting talent. Every evening on returning from the studio, they worked for a couple of hours on particular points that were troubling them and then had dinner. For a week after the shoot began, these informal therapy sessions appeared to have their effect on Monroe. She worked steadily, and her mood improved. She arrived on the set on time, joked with crew members, had lunch in the commissary instead of in her dressing room with her guru and Method acting coach, Paula Strasberg.

Then she swung back to the old bad habits. She would arrive around noon for an eight o'clock call, obsessively ask to redo numbers (sometimes Cukor, to placate her, would simply do them without film in the camera), find reasons to procrastinate. As Jack Cole analyzed her state of mind in *Life* in August 1960, "She is a great star without the background or experience. She is afraid and insecure. That's why she is late. That's why she stalls . . . anything to stall facing the specter, the terrible thing of doing something for which she feels inadequate."[1] Physically, too, she was a mess. Cukor had to find unusual camera angles to film her face, avoiding profiles because she looked unattractive, and that took extra time. When producer Buddy Adler saw the rushes, he was aghast. Nothing looked right; she was not like the Marilyn Monroe of *The Seven Year Itch* and *Some Like It Hot*. He thought she looked fat and frumpy, especially in the dance numbers, where she almost looked pregnant. The stunning star quality was gone.[2]

Montand was becoming increasingly fed up with his partner, however much he sympathized with her. Not only did he have to put up with frequent changes in the shooting schedule to accommodate Monroe's lateness and absences, not only did he have to mouth lines that often meant nothing to him, but he also had to wait on the set or in the bungalow for hours not knowing whether she would show up. Then came the day when she failed to respond at all—not to the chauffeur who came every morning to pick her up, not to the studio's repeated phone calls, not to Signoret's banging on her door. The hotel switchboard said Monroe had made one call, so they knew she was in there.

Exasperated, Montand wrote a note with Signoret's help to let her know how he felt and slipped it under her door:

> You can do whatever you like to Spyros Skouras and the Fox studio and all the producers in town, if that's what you want. But next time you decide to hang around too late listening to my wife tell you stories instead of going to bed, because you've already decided not to get up the next morning and go to the studio, please tell me! Don't leave me to work for hours on end on a scene you've already decided not to do the next day. I'm not the enemy, I'm your pal. And capricious little girls have never amused me.[3]

Her reply came via Dublin. Miller, who had gone there to discuss *The Misfits* script with Huston, called in the middle of the night to announce that Monroe had contacted him to say she was ashamed and didn't know what to do. Would they please go knock on her door one more time? When they did, she came out and fell weeping into Signoret's arms, saying, "I'm bad, I'm bad, I'm bad. I won't do it again, I promise."[4] Montand patted her head and said it was all right, but he also told her to try to be on time. To no avail. By the end of the shoot, her tardiness and neurotic insistence on redoing scenes multiple times would cost Fox twenty-eight extra days of filming and almost $1 million in added costs. In fact, the filming took so long that Montand's English, difficult to understand in some of the early takes, actually improved in the final shots to the point where earlier scenes had to be redubbed.[5]

Production was further slowed, indeed stopped completely, by the joint strike of the Writers Guild of America and Screen Actors Guild in March and April. That didn't inhibit the thirty-second Academy Awards ceremony, however, which was held on April 4, 1960, in the RKO Pantages Theater. Montand, invited to perform, did the same two songs he had done on *The Dinah Shore Chevy Show* and went backstage, where he predicted to everyone within hearing that his wife was going to win an Oscar for Best Actress. He watched from the wings as Rock Hudson announced the nominees: Doris Day for *Pillow Talk*, Audrey Hepburn for *The Nun's Story*, Signoret for *Room at the Top*, Katharine Hepburn for *Suddenly, Last Summer*, Elizabeth Taylor also for *Suddenly, Last Summer.*

Signoret leaped from her seat when her name was called, nervously pulling up the shoulder straps of her low-cut black gown as she rushed to the stage as the first French citizen to win the Best Actress Academy Award. Her emotional acceptance speech was mercifully brief as she grasped the statuette to her breast. Hurrying backstage, she found Montand weeping with joy. At the celebration banquet afterward at the Beverly Wilshire Hotel, her main concern was trying to ensure that her sudden glory didn't overshadow Montand and make him feel like "Monsieur Signoret"—he assured her that he didn't.[6]

Five days later Signoret left for Rome, where she was to act in *Adua e le compagne / Adua and Her Friends* (1960, US 1965). Miller was in New York, leaving Montand and Monroe to continue their evening rehearsals. One evening she didn't show up, and Paula Strasberg called him to suggest that he check in on her. When he visited her, she was in bed, but he noticed that room service had delivered caviar and pink champagne. They made small talk as he sat on the edge of her bed and held her hand. Reassured that she was all right despite a light fever, he bent to give her a goodnight kiss on her cheek before returning to work on his lines for the next day. "Her head turned, and my lips went wild," he remembered. "It was a wonderful, tender kiss. I was half stunned, stammering. I straightened up, already flooded with guilt, wondering what was happening to me. . . . It was a forest fire, a hurricane, I didn't even try to calm myself down."[7]

What was happening to Montand was the beginning of his only real extramarital affair, the only instance of what he and Signoret considered infidelity, as opposed to his "little adventures," during their marriage. This was no one-night stand. It was based on a feeling that had grown slowly as he got to know what he called a woman with the heart of a child. "I was a million miles from thinking that anything whatsoever could happen between Marilyn and me," he said later. "What contributed enormously to bringing us together was, first, that we both came from poor backgrounds and, second, Marilyn's behavior during the witch hunt, when she wholeheartedly supported Miller, to the fury of the studios. My affection for her grew once I realized her vulnerability, her lucidity, her true sadness at not being given a real part to play in our movie."[8]

This man notoriously susceptible to feminine allure was of course not immune to what the film critic Pauline Kael later called Monroe's "mixture of wide-eyed wonder and cuddly drugged sexiness [that] seemed to get to just about every male."[9] But for him, she was more than just an alluring movie star. He saw her as "a being apart, in the sense that it was her own inner light that drove her into the spotlight. If you believed in God you'd say that God alone could generate such a light."[10] For him, the attraction was considerably deeper than merely carnal.

Neither he nor Monroe made any serious attempt to hide their affair. They dined out together frequently in full view, attended cocktail parties and film screenings. When she spent the night in his bungalow with him, she was still there when housekeeping arrived in the morning. One time she was spotted hurrying to his room dressed only in a fur coat. Reporters smelled a big scandal story and staked out the bungalow, paying housemaids and messengers for tidbits. The columnist Dorothy Kilgallen broke the story, with all due innuendo, in June. "An actress nominated for an Academy Award is sweating out a domestic crisis far more important than Oscar voting," she reported. "Her husband—also famous—has fallen in love with a beautiful lady also married to a big name."[11] *Life* leered that a love scene that took a whole day to shoot "evidently left them unwearied by their jobs."[12] *Modern Screen* screamed the headline "The Man Who Almost Destroyed Marilyn Monroe's Marriage."[13]

Montand must have known that he was being reckless, that an affair with Monroe was not like one of his dalliances with a French starlet, that the hurtful news would quickly get back to Signoret in Rome. The affair was a huge lapse of judgment on his part that can't be explained simply by attributing it to his passionate, impetuous nature. Although he did feel something for Monroe, he was trapped in a situation that she had created. All his life, it was the women who took the initiative in his important affairs of the heart: Piaf, Signoret, and now Monroe. With her, the relationship was complicated by the fact that keeping her happy was key to getting the film—his first, critical attempt at a Hollywood movie—done. Without saying so, Jerry Wald and George Cukor were counting on him to stabilize her sufficiently to get to the final take.

Montand did not take this first infidelity lightly, but he saw nothing sordid in this relationship. Did he love Monroe? He never said so publicly or in his memoirs. What he did feel, certainly, was friendship, kinship, and genuine admiration. "On the outside she played at being Marilyn," he reflected later. "Inside I encountered a woman who was strong, full of good sense, with the vitality of a peasant. . . . She had a kind of innocence; and the less she tried, the more attractive she was."[14] How far could their affair have gone? "Not for a moment did I think of breaking with my wife, not for a moment; but if she had slammed the door on me, I would probably have made my life with Marilyn. Or tried to. That was the direction we were moving in. Maybe it would have lasted only two or three years. I didn't have too many illusions. Still, what years they would have been!"[15]

In an interview in mid-2021, Montand's nephew Jean-Louis Livi, who served as his agent and confidant for many years, said, "He had a real love affair with Marilyn based on mutual attraction. It wasn't just about sex, and he was very affected by it. He often talked to me about it. She wrote magnificent letters to him. It's a very beautiful story, even if it doesn't square with conventional morality. But his life was in France, his life was with Signoret."[16]

It has been suggested that Monroe did not really love Montand, that she was using him to test and provoke Miller, to make Miller come down from his intellectual high horse and take her seriously. But her actions belie that theory, and in any case their marriage had been disintegrating rapidly all year; they agreed to divorce in October 1961, and the dissolution of their marriage became official in November.

She clung to the relationship with Montand for months after their last scenes were filmed on June 16, 1960, and she returned to New York. He stayed in Los Angeles to dub some scenes—to Cukor's amusement, he pronounced it "dumbing"—before leaving on June 30 for Paris. Monroe had learned of his stopover in New York to change planes. To his surprise, her press secretary met him in the arrival lounge and took him in tow through a gang of reporters to a rented limousine. Inside, Monroe was waiting for him with chilled champagne and caviar. She had rented a hotel room under a false name and implored him to go there with her. He refused as gently as he could, explaining that he was returning to Signoret but that he hoped they could remain friends; maybe the Millers could visit them in France. His flight to Paris was delayed by a bomb scare. They sat in the car for a couple of hours sipping the champagne before he kissed her goodbye.[17]

Later, during the filming of *The Misfits* in Reno, she left the set and went to Los Angeles to try to see Montand, but they didn't meet. At one point during the shoot in Reno, she was so exhausted and drugged that she had to be flown to Good Samaritan Hospital in Los Angeles for treatment; from her sickbed, she repeatedly tried to phone him. The pursuit went on relentlessly, with Monroe attempting to contact him with letters and telegrams. In her affectionate letters, she addressed him as "Monsieur." One postcard said simply, "I love you." In late December, she found out that he was planning to stop off in New York on his way to Tokyo to film *My Geisha* with Shirley MacLaine. After she let him know she hoped to see him there, he changed plans and stayed a few extra days in Paris to avoid her.

Montand might have felt momentarily that he could remake his life with Monroe, but by midsummer 1960 he had come back down to earth and realized, as Jean-Louis Livi said, that the only life for him was with Signoret in France. He began to make it clear publicly that there was no question of divorce, as he had to Monroe when they sat in the limousine at the airport drinking champagne. When Hedda Hopper called him on August 21 at the Beverly Hills Hotel, where he had returned to begin work on *Sanctuary* with Lee Remick and director Tony Richardson, he surprised her by agreeing to an interview. There was no love lost between the Montands and Hopper, who disliked them for their leftist politics. Indeed, she had attempted to smear them as communists, going to Washington in March to ask the FBI in person for any information they could give her that would prevent Signoret from winning an Oscar for *Room at the Top*. Her request was refused, but her enmity toward the Montands continued. If he received her for an interview in his room at the hotel, it was to seize the opportunity to get the word out, including to Signoret, that his affair with Monroe was over.[18]

Hopper asked him if it was right to have an affair with Monroe when he knew she wasn't as sophisticated as he was. "I think she is an enchanting child," he replied, "a simple girl without any guile. Perhaps I was too tender and thought maybe she was sophisticated, like some of the other ladies I have known. I did everything I could to make things easier for her when I realized that mine was a very small part [in the film]. The only thing that could stand out in my performance was my love scenes, so naturally I did everything I could to make them realistic. Perhaps she had a schoolgirl crush. If she did, I'm sorry. But nothing will break up my marriage."[19]

Fox had already decided that *Let's Make Love* was a problematic film and needed all the publicity it could get. An illegitimate affair between its costars was made to order, and its media-relations department began leaking information about it to gossip columnists and made Montand available for interviews. After Hedda Hopper, it was Louella Parsons's turn to publish a one-on-one with Montand. Again, he accepted these interviews as part of his effort to cool things down and reassure Signoret. *Modern Screen* called the affair "The Love Scandal of the Decade," promising on its cover "the unvarnished truth straight from the lips of 'the other man.'" When Parsons probed him about his feelings for Monroe, he replied with what was likely a well-rehearsed answer: "I more than 'like' Marilyn. I tell you this because I trust you, Madame. She is an enchanting child. And I won't say that if I had been free, I wouldn't have fallen in love with her. But for eleven years I have been married to a wonderful, understanding woman. Simone and I have been very happy. There will be no divorce."[20] This was the second time that he had called Monroe a child, a schoolgirl, compared with the sophisticated ladies he had known and the real woman to whom he was married.

Signoret had learned of the affair on a fine Roman spring day in June. She had been enjoying her time there, exploring the shops and finding new trattorias for dinner with the film crew of *Adua e le compagne,* in which she played, once again, a prostitute. One day, as she had time off from the shoot and was walking through the city, a headline at a newspaper kiosk caught her eye: "Schiaffi a Hollywood" (Slaps in Hollywood). Assuming it was the usual amusing Hollywood gossip, she bought a copy, only to learn that the slaps in question were aimed at her. According to the totally fabricated story, Montand, true to his Italian ancestry, had hit her a couple of times during a domestic spat over his affair with Monroe—despite the fact that they were at the time on different continents. Suddenly one of the best years of her life—an Oscar, the good times in Hollywood with new friends—became one of the worst as she read with increasing alarm the headlines about her husband's infidelity across the Atlantic.

She wasn't the only family member to see the headlines. As her teenage daughter, Catherine Allégret, recalled, "I was with friends on the beach in St Jean de Luz and a guy went by selling newspapers. He was yelling, 'Will Montand leave Signoret for Marilyn Monroe? Will he leave France to live with Marilyn?' It was one of the worst moments of my life."[21] Montand, trying to keep the family together when it was in real danger, sent her a telegram that summer telling her not to believe what she read in the papers and reassuring her that he wasn't leaving anybody—except Monroe.[22]

Montand also sent an uncomfortable cable to Simone in Rome to try to defuse things. She decided not to reply by cable or telephone but to clip all the gossip columns she could find and include them with a carefully understated letter in which she told him coolly, without reproach, that she was trying to understand how this could happen. She also instructed him how to handle the immediate situation: when he returned to France, he was to go straight to Autheuil, stay there, and avoid the press. She would not be at Orly airport to meet his plane on June 30 and confront the press alone, playing the role of the wronged wife as she waited for him to arrive. On the contrary, he was to meet her plane from Rome a few days later, putting him in the inferior position. Guiltily, he complied.[23] Then there was the inevitable confrontation. Montand remembered:

> On my return, of course we had a fight, but just one, and we didn't mention it again for three months. At first our feelings were terrifying, violent; then things calmed down, peace returned—or seemed to. She said, "Tell me everything, and I'll understand

> everything." I told her everything, or everything I could tell her without kindling the retrospective jealousy that is the worst of all. It was at Autheuil. There she was—beaten, sad, wounded at the thought that the fantastic ten years we had shared had been tarnished in this way. I was sorry to have inflicted pain on her. That was what I was sorry for—only that. Wherever I went and however I lived, she would be there. And I didn't want to drive her away. When I tried, when I succeeded a little it was because I, too, was fighting to survive. . . .
>
> Our life started up again—wobbly at first, but it started up. We were able to get the engine going. And Simone made a mighty effort not to use the episode to fuel her anger during those husband-and-wife arguments in which everything just comes tumbling out. She behaved like a real grownup. Which I was not, and still am not.[24]

He was right about that last point. Signoret, the most painfully afflicted by the affair, was the one who kept a level head, at least in public, and handled the situation adroitly and with the most dignity. When a British television channel sent a journalist to interview her, ostensibly about her Oscar for *Room at the Top,* he couldn't resist asking her about what had happened in Hollywood. She shrugged it off. "Do you know many men who would sit still with Marilyn Monroe in their arms?" Again, when Montand was about to begin the shoot of *Goodbye Again* with Ingrid Bergman, Signoret was asked by a journalist whether she planned to be with him during the filming. "Do you think I'm crazy," she joked, "leaving him first with Marilyn, then with Ingrid?"[25] She also tried to deny the authenticity of Hedda Hopper's interview with Montand, insisting that the grammar and wording in it could not have come from him, given his difficulty with the language.

Although she could have overlooked the affair if it had been another of Montand's reasonably discreet little adventures, being held up in the international press as the scorned woman hurt deeply and permanently. Following the lead of its American media *confrères,* the French press couldn't get enough of it. "Marilyn a-t-elle seduit Yves Montand?" (Has Marilyn Seduced Yves Montand?), asked *Jours de France* in a headline, calling them the new enfants terribles.[26] "Marilyn Monroe divorce-t-elle pour Yves Montand?" (Is Marilyn Monroe divorcing for Yves Montand?), wondered *Noir et blanc.*[27] Not only did Signoret have to put up with such headlines, but there was also the unwanted commiseration of everyone from fellow sufferers who sent well-meaning letters of comfort ("My rival was as blonde as she is") to shopkeepers who offered hope ("He'll come back, you'll see") while wrapping a package.[28] As she told their mutual friend, the journalist Ivan Levaï, a regular at the Autheuil get-togethers, "I'm not the only woman to have an unfaithful husband, but I'm the only one whose case is known to the whole world."[29]

After the affair was over, both Montand and Monroe tried to minimize the gravity of what had happened. She had her agent issue a bland statement from New York saying that most of her costars had said unpleasant things about her after they worked together, "but is that any reason for me to marry him?"[30] He downplayed the damage to his marriage because of the affair, for which he never apologized beyond saying he regretted that it hurt Signoret.[31] For example, years later, in 1988, he told *People* magazine that Signoret's anger lasted for a while, and he just hunkered down, waiting for it to pass. He claimed that he finally put an end to that one day by threatening to write about the affair in all its details and publish it. "And it was over. Finito."[32]

Well, not quite. The fact is that although their marriage officially survived, their relations would never be the same. From then on, there would be "before Monroe" and "after Monroe," ten years of marital happiness followed by more than two decades of hurt pride, simmering anger, and increasingly violent fights. Benjamin Castaldi, Catherine's son and Signoret's grandson, recalled one quarrel at Autheuil that began as a routine spat and quickly escalated to uncontrollable rage as Montand grabbed Signoret by the hair and dragged her, howling, nearly twenty feet down a hallway.[33] On another occasion there, Catherine witnessed Montand locking himself in the little theater next to the main house and Signoret hammering on the door yelling for him to open up because she knew he was in there. According to Catherine, "They played *Who's Afraid of Virginia Woolf* twenty-four hours a day." Despite it all, Signoret's daughter felt that "Montand came back [to Mama] because he wanted to. It certainly wasn't his first slip. It's not his fault—he can't help paying court to women, he doesn't know how to form friendships with them. But Mama always stayed his wife, as he wanted."[34]

They stopped sharing the same bedroom, often communicated by notes they slipped under one another's door. She began drinking heavily, a bottle of alcohol a day, and neglected her appearance as she began what Catherine called her "slow descent into hell."[35] Revenge is a dish best served cold, and she would make him pay in her own way. They still had the complicity born of ten good years, and they would make the effort to stay together, but the old passion was gone. She told him frankly but wearily, "I love you, but I am no longer in love with you."[36] At one point, she suggested that the solution, if he wanted out, was simply divorce. He opted to be halfway out, remaining married but sleeping around when he liked. As he summed up their new relationship in one of his memoirs, "Gradually we traded the fire of our first 10 years for a bond that was calmer but just as strong. . . . It was a time when we were happy to see one another, but without the thrill of desire. She was strong for both of us."[37]

On the evening of August 5, 1962, Montand called Signoret in Toulouse, where she was filming René Clement's *Le jour et l'heure / The Day and the Hour* (1963, US 1964), to tell her that Monroe had died the previous day. She was saddened, for she had felt real friendship for the woman who briefly had been her rival. "She never knew to what degree I never detested her," she wrote in her memoirs, "and how thoroughly I had understood the story that was no one's business but ours, the four of us."[38] This was a generous, classy attitude toward someone who had unintentionally caused her great, lasting pain. As her friend Catherine Deneuve, who acted opposite Montand in two films, saw clearly, "She bore Marilyn etched on her face like a permanent scar. It was too much—at once too big and too petty."[39]

Giovanni Livi and his broom shop workers in 1921. Standing behind his right shoulder is his wife, Giuseppina, who at the time was pregnant with Ivo. (Collection Yves Montand–Valentin Livi, droits réservés)

Impasse des Mûriers in Marseille, where Ivo spent much of his childhood. At right is the hairdressing salon that his sister, Lidia, started. (Collection Yves Montand–Valentin Livi, droits réservés)

Ivo with his big brother, Giuliano, and sister, Lidia, in the 1920s. (Collection Yves Montand–Valentin Livi, droits réservés)

Montand at eleven, when he quit school and took a job in a pasta factory. (Collection Yves Montand–Valentin Livi, droits réservés)

Montand began his show business career at seventeen in a vest-pocket local theater doing imitations of Popeye and popular figures. (Collection Yves Montand–Valentin Livi, droits réservés)

Montand impersonating the popular singer Charles Trenet. In these early years, he experienced the stage fright that would plague him all his career. (Collection cinémathèque française, droits réservés)

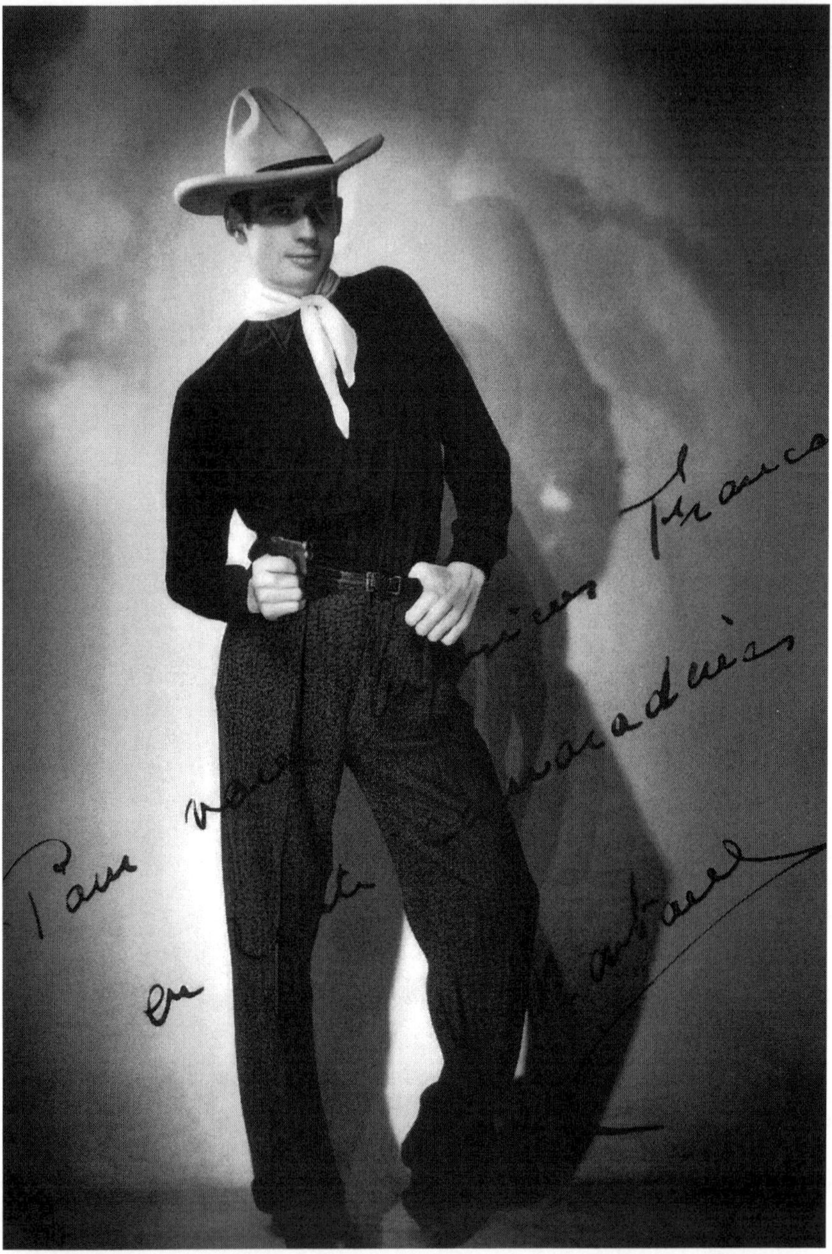

Montand's first big singing hit in 1939 was a number about cowboys around a campfire. It became a permanent part of his repertory. (Apic/Hulton Archive, Getty Images)

Montand literally swept Edith Piaf off her feet as he began his career in Paris. For two years, they were France's most famous lovers as she polished his act. (Collection Yves Montand–Valentin Livi, droits réservés)

Piaf wangled a small role for Montand in his first movie, *Étoile sans lumière / Star without Light* (1946). They broke up shortly thereafter. (United Archives GmbH, Alamy Stock Photo)

Montand and Nathalie Nattier in *Les portes de la nuit / Gates of the Night* (1946). The *glauque* film about postwar Paris flopped, and he was panned for poor acting. (Collection Yves Montand–Valentin Livi, droits réservés)

Montand was one of the first performers to place a scrim backcloth between himself and the orchestra. It focused the attention on him and served for dramatic projections of his silhouette. (Philippe Gras)

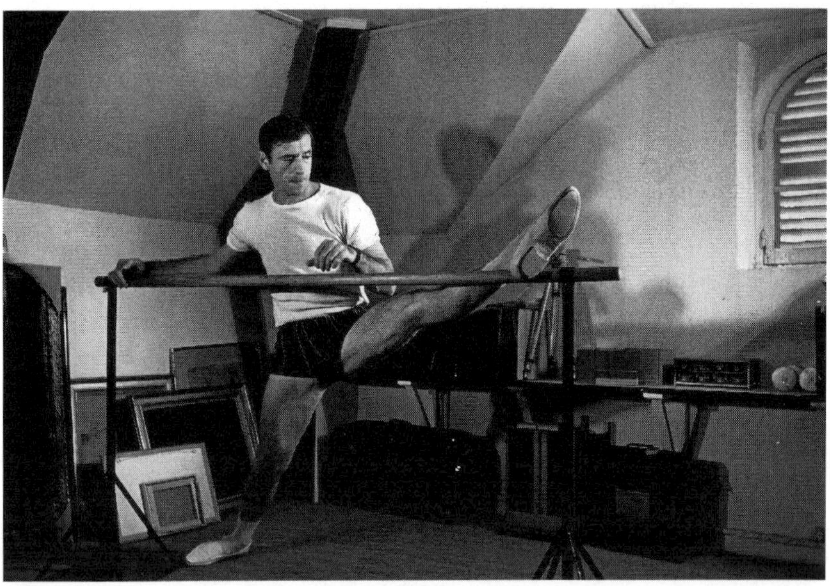

Montand worked hard at staying supple. It allowed him to surprise audiences with high kicks and other acrobatic moves. (Collection Yves Montand–Valentin Livi, droits réservés)

Montand showing off his athleticism with this jump/split on Paris's Quai des Orfèvres in the 1950s. (Collection Yves Montand–Valentin Livi, droits réservés)

Montand adopted plain brown slacks and an open-neck shirt for his performances, as in this show in 1962. It led to his being called "the singing prole" and "the working man's troubadour." (Daniele Darolle/Sygma, Getty Images)

Montand and Signoret in an outbuilding at their mansion in Normandy. The country residence served as a weekend retreat for themselves and their clan of show business friends. (© Fondation Folon/ADAGP, Paris, 2021)

Montand and Charles Vanel in the prize-winning film *Le salaire de la peur / The Wages of Fear*. The film made him a star. (*Le salaire de la peur*, Compagnie industrielle et commerciale cinématographique/Cinédis, 1953)

With Signoret in the film *Les sorcières de Salem*, the French movie version of Arthur Miller's play *The Crucible*. They saw the work as a vehicle for expressing their political convictions. (*Les sorcières de Salem,* Compagnie industrielle et commerciale cinématographique/DEFA/Variety Distribution, 1957)

Performing in Moscow in 1956. The trip opened Montand's eyes to the reality of life under Soviet communism. (Collection Yves Montand–Valentin Livi, droits réservés)

Arthur Miller and Marilyn Monroe get acquainted with the Montands after his performance in New York in 1959. They would meet again in Hollywood. (Collection Yves Montand–Valentin Livi, droits réservés)

Doing "Ain't We Got Fun" on *The Dinah Shore Chevy Show* in 1959. The program introduced Montand, "the idol of France," to Americans. (Everett Collection, Newark, NJ)

A dinner party tête-à-tête during the shoot of *Let's Make Love* (1960). The complicity is obvious. (Entertainment Pictures, Alamy Stock Photo)

A scene from *Let's Make Love*. Both Montand and Monroe disliked their roles, feeling they were underused. (*Let's Make Love,* Twentieth Century–Fox, 1960)

With Lee Remick in the controversial film *Sanctuary* (1961). William Faulkner said he had written "the most horrific tale" he could imagine. (Collection Yves Montand–Valentin Livi, droits réservés)

With Shirley MacLaine in *My Geisha* (1962). She fell under his European charm; he found her to be the All-American girl he had dreamed of. (Paramount Pictures, Collection cinémathèque française)

A Hollywood glamor shot promoting Montand in 1960. (Collection Yves Montand–Valentin Livi, droits réservés)

Getting used to driving a Ferrari racer for *Grand Prix*. Director John Frankenheimer refused to use doubles for the dangerous scenes. (*Grand Prix*, Joel Productions, John Frankenheimer Productions, Cherokee Productions/ Metro-Goldwyn-Mayer, 1966)

In 1968, Paramount was still promoting Montand as one of its big stars. (Collection Yves Montand–Valentin Livi, droits réservés)

Trying to help Daisy (Barbara Streisand) break her nicotine habit in *On a Clear Day You Can See Forever*. Montand felt he had been typecast once again as the French Lover. (*On a Clear Day You Can See Forever*, Howard W. Koch/Paramount Pictures, 1970)

With Charles Denner in *Z* (1968), the first of several politically themed films with the director Costa-Gavras. (Everett Collection, Newark, NJ)

For maximum realism, Montand lost nearly twenty-five pounds during the shoot of *The Confession* (1970). "He lived it," said Costa-Gavras. "He suffered night and day." (Paramount Pictures, Photofest)

Critics wondered whether Montand could hold the enormous stage of New York's Metropolitan Opera all by himself in 1982. He did. (Collection Yves Montand–Valentin Livi, droits réservés)

As a crafty Provençal peasant in *Jean de Florette,* Montand had one of the best roles of his career. (*Jean de Florette*, Pierre Grunstein, Alain Poiré/Orion Pictures, 1986)

Hugging a tree as a man with paranormal powers in *IP5: L'ile aux pachyderms* (1992). Montand died of a heart attack on the last day of the shoot. (United Archives GmbH, Alamy Stock Photo)

14

Three More for Fox

Having patched things up with Signoret as well as he could, Montand was back in Hollywood in July 1960. Twentieth Century–Fox was eager to capitalize on his growing reputation in the United States and wanted him to begin work right away. They proposed the male lead opposite Lee Remick in an adaptation of William Faulkner's novel *Sanctuary* (1931), a southern gothic tale of the degradation of a frivolous young woman in Mississippi.

Although *Sanctuary* would eventually become a succès de scandale and one of Faulkner's early breakthrough books after *As I Lay Dying* (1930), its author claimed to be not especially proud of it. In his introduction to it, he said he considered it "a cheap idea" that he wrote in three weeks purely to make much-needed money. To that end, he "invented the most horrific tale" he could imagine. When his publisher saw the manuscript, involving as it did sadism, rape, impotence, prostitution, murder, bootlegging, alcoholism, and nymphomania, he told Faulkner, "Good God, I can't publish this. We'd both be in jail." To make it more suitable for publication, Faulkner restructured and partly rewrote it, though retaining its violence.[1]

If this version was toned down, we can only imagine what the original was like. Over the years, critics and literati have seen it as an allegory of the South's decline, a reinterpretation of the Greek myth of the dread Persephone, queen of the underworld, an example of the literature of disgust, a hallucination full of expressionistic images, and a meditation on the discovery of evil.[2] Shortly after it came out, it inspired its first movie version, Paramount's *The Story of Temple Drake* (1933), directed by Stephen Roberts and starring Miriam Hopkins and Jack La Rue. Although the film left out some of the more shocking scenes, it was still thought indecent enough that it led to stricter enforcement of the newly adopted Motion Picture Production Code, better known as the Hays Code, dictating what was acceptable to show on the big screen. Controversial from the start, the film was banned in Ohio and

Pennsylvania; New York censors made cuts into scenes of violence and sex. Joseph Breen, head of the Production Code Administration, which would enforce the code, forbade that the film be rereleased once the code came into effect in 1934, thus keeping it out of circulation until the mid-1950s.

Producer Richard D. Zanuck paid $75,000 for the rights to *Drake* and acquired the movie rights to both Faulkner's *Sanctuary* and the sequel, *Requiem for a Nun* (1951, *nun* being an Elizabethan slang term for prostitute), believing that combining the two books would make a stronger screenplay. He sent people to Mississippi to consult with Faulkner, but they were unable to find him. Zanuck went ahead anyway, doing an outline and prologue. He turned the project over to James Poe, who recently had done the script for the film version of Tennessee Williams's *Cat on a Hot Tin Roof* (1958), also set in Mississippi and dealing with tormented characters. To direct the film, he chose the Oxford-educated Tony Richardson, a British New Wave director who had just done the film version of the realist *Look Back in Anger* (1959).

Combining the two novels involved merging three villainous characters into one named Candy, making Temple's father a governor instead of a judge, and altering other plot points, which resulted in a disjointed film. Richardson later rejected it, complaining that Zanuck interfered with his editing and had not let him work on the script. The convoluted structure included 70 percent flashback and only 30 percent the present, with 40 percent of the narrative coming from *Sanctuary*, 22 percent a transition between *Sanctuary* and *Requiem*, 8 percent from *Requiem*.[3]

Temple Drake (Lee Remick) is a giddy seventeen-year-old at the University of Mississippi in the 1920s. The daughter of the state's governor, she is a flirt and a tease who enjoys leading men on and then rebuffing them. One night after a dance, her beau, Gowan Stephens, takes her to a shack in the woods that serves as home base for bootleggers. While he drinks until he passes out, she encounters the dapper gang leader, Candy (Montand), a Cajun with a French accent who, the film suggests, rapes her in a corn crib. He then takes her to Miss Reba's brothel in New Orleans—Memphis in the novel, but the screenplay changed that to account for Montand's accent—where she discovers an unsuspected sensuality in herself. She becomes a willing white slave, Candy's kept woman at the brothel, an alcoholic-nymphomaniac reveling in lovemaking, gin, and the lacy underclothes he buys for her. "That dingy little room of Miss Reba's," she says at one point, "became for me a sanctuary of sin and pleasure."

Devastated when Candy's car has an accident during a rum run and he is believed killed, Temple returns to Gowan, marries him, and has two children. Five years later, Candy, who had survived the crash, returns and asks her to come away with him. She agrees and decides to take her second child, a baby, with her. Nancy, a Black servant, attempts to persuade her not to take the child. When Temple insists, Nancy suffocates the infant to save it from certain mistreatment, for which she is tried and hanged. Candy disappears after the murder, and Temple stays with Gowan—all is forgiven.

The film *Sanctuary* is a poor vehicle for Montand. He has no more than forty minutes on-screen out of an hour and a half, and seldom speaks lines of more than a dozen words—presumably the screenwriter was aware of his continuing difficulty with English. Candy is supposed to represent the character called Popeye in the novel, a vicious, sadistic, impotent racketeer who uses a corncob to rape Temple. Montand's Candy is none of these things. Although he slaps Temple around, he is far from impotent and gives every sign of being in love with her, covering her with kisses, and calling her tenderly "my woman, my only one." He commands her to act like a lady, not like the brothel "sluts." In other words, we once again have Montand the French Lover, as if Hollywood couldn't see him as anything else.

On its release, the film was coolly received by critics, the *New York Times* panning it as a "melodrama of the most mechanical and meretricious sort" in which it is difficult to see Temple as a credible human being.[4] Lee Remick does her best to speak Dixie, but she still resembles more a cool, New England–born, private-school-educated young lady of good family than a passion-driven creature who gives herself over to debauchery. Montand plays well the handsome, brusque bootlegger who runs his gang with an iron hand and lights his cigarettes with arrogant elegance, but his Candy is far removed from the original Popeye. The academic E. Pauline Degenfelder, who studied the movie closely, concludes that, on the whole, "the effect of combining these incompatible originals, as well as the extensive mutilation of the completed film, results in an artistic disaster."[5]

⊙ ⊙ ⊙

Montand moved right on to his next American film, the slick romantic drama *Goodbye Again*. It was produced and directed by the cosmopolitan, Russian-born Anatole Litvak, who had learned the trade in Saint Petersburg starting when he was thirteen. His early career reflected the political upheavals of

Europe: he moved to Germany in the 1920s to escape the Bolsheviks, then to France in the 1930s to avoid the Nazis. His success there with films such as the romantic tragedy *Mayerling* (1936) brought him to Hollywood's attention. He signed with Warner Bros. and became a leading director during the 1940s and 1950s.

For *Goodbye,* the screenwriter Samuel A. Taylor, who had just done the script for Alfred Hitchcock's *Vertigo* (1958), adapted the bestseller *Aimez-vous Brahms. . .* (1959) by the precocious, fast-living French novelist Françoise Sagan, who first burst on the French literary scene in 1954 at eighteen with the award-winning *Bonjour tristesse.* Although the film kept the book's original title when released in Europe, Litvak was concerned that American audiences might not understand the original—or even know, some advisers thought, who Brahms was—and sought a different title for its US release. He preferred *Time on My Hands* from the popular song of 1930 but refused to pay the $70,000 fee demanded by its publishers. *Goodbye Again* was finally chosen after Anthony Perkins recalled that it had been the title of a hit Broadway play in which his father had performed.[6]

Litvak picked Ingrid Bergman for the female lead. He had recently directed her in the highly successful *Anastasia* (1956), which had won her a Best Actress Oscar (and had also gained renewed acceptance for her in America for the first time in seven years after the scandal of her affair with Roberto Rossellini). For this love triangle, she played opposite two male actors, Yves Montand as Roger Demarest, her longtime but philandering lover, and Anthony Perkins as the idealistic young American lawyer Philip Van der Besh, who competes for her affections.

The casting was a good fit for all three. Bergman, at forty-five, incarnated the worldly-wise, long-suffering Paula Tessier, a still-attractive woman hitting the wall of middle age without the emotional security of a stable relationship. Montand slipped easily into his part, unlike his two previous American films, where he was a fish out of water. Now he was back in his element in France, playing a role—the elegant, insouciant French playboy who flees the commitment of marriage—that came naturally to him. Also, he would be directed by Litvak, who spoke French and whose favorite locale for filming was Paris, where thirteen of his thirty-seven films were set. For Perkins, it's possible that this was the ideal way to make his debut in European film after choosing to live in France to escape from what he felt was homophobic treatment in the United States. It was also a way to avoid being typecast as the horrific character he had just played in Hitchcock's *Psycho* (1960).

The plot of *Goodbye* is a cliché; the interest, rather, is in how the story is told. Litvak and his principal actors, with their intuitive feel for this very French kind of tale and its setting, manage to hold audience interest despite the plot's predictability. Paula has been in a relation with Roger for five years. He makes no effort to conceal his dalliances with the younger women he picks up in bars, and she goes along with that because they have an understanding that both will remain free. When she meets Philip, the twenty-five-year-old son of one of her clients, she is flattered by his callow infatuation. He insists that he is in love with her and that the fifteen years separating them doesn't matter. He follows her around like an amorous puppy, even showing up at Paula and Roger's table very drunk one evening at a chic nightclub—Perkins actually got inebriated to play the scene.[7]

When Roger goes off on yet another weekend tryst, Paula accepts Philip's invitation to a Brahms concert and begins sleeping with him. Roger gets wind of this and, referring to the fact that Paula is redoing Philip's mother's apartment, speaks one of the movie's better lines: "If you go in to do the young master's bedroom, why not do the young master? Makes the work so much more interesting." After some weeks, Paula and Roger are reconciled, and he proposes marriage. In the last scene, he calls Paula to say he has to go off on "a business trip," and she realizes that marriage won't change his behavior.

The chemistry among the three leads was good. "These two actors are wonderful for their parts," Bergman said during the shoot. "It's a long time since I worked with *two* actors I enjoyed so much. They are both charming, both great personalities and very different, and you understand why I—in my part as Paula—love them both."[8] Montand confided to Bergman during an interlude between takes that he preferred to be a singer, not an actor; when singing, he could hear and judge his performance, which he couldn't on a sound stage.[9] Perkins, however, seemed to fear that Bergman might go too far in pushing for a personal relationship with him. As he told *People* magazine, "She would have welcomed an affair. Every day she invited me to her dressing room to practice a love scene. I insisted on standing near the door, which I kept open."[10] In a biography written before that interview, however, Bergman explained the dressing-room rehearsals thus:

> I took Anthony Perkins into my dressing room—he was supposed to be my young lover—and I said, "For heaven's sake kiss me!" Anthony did a double-take, then he laughed and said, "Why, what

> for?" I said, "Because we've got to do it later in the film, and I don't know you. I'm hardly acquainted with you, and I'm shy and I blush. Much better we do our first rehearsal in my dressing room, so that I shan't start dreading the moment when we have to do it in front of a hundred technicians." He grinned, and understood, and said, "Okay," then kissed me, and said, "That hurt? No? Good." He was very sweet, and it was easier for me after that.[11]

In Sagan's novel, there is an encompassing sepia atmosphere of weltschmerz that constitutes much of the reading pleasure. Bergman was initially disappointed that the screenplay didn't have more action and wrote several pages of complaints to Litvak before the shoot. In the event, the problem of transferring the novel to the screen was largely overcome, and the film was well received in Europe. Perkins won the Best Actor Award at the Cannes Film Festival in 1961—upstaging Montand—and Litvak was nominated for the Best Director Award. American audiences and critics were more reserved, considering it too much of a "woman's film." Bosley Crowther found it "solemn and pedestrian."[12] In France, however, *Le Monde* thought it "old-fashioned and brilliant," with an ingenious adaptation and elegant direction. As for Montand, he was "aimable and nonchalant."[13]

⊙ ⊙ ⊙

As with *Let's Make Love,* Montand was not the first choice for male lead in his next film. When Paramount put out the word in August 1960 that it was preparing "a comic reworking of *Madame Butterfly,*" it said the film would feature Shirley MacLaine and James Stewart, with Maria Callas dubbing MacLaine for arias from Puccini. Stewart was to play MacLaine's husband, who was directing a film version of the opera. The screenplay for *My Geisha* by that master of wisecracking mistaken identity, Norman Krasna, had MacLaine disguising herself as a Japanese geisha. Negotiations with Stewart were supposed to be completed that autumn, but they didn't work out, and Montand was offered the part.[14]

Krasna's screenplay was based on an old comedy called *The Guardsman* by the Hungarian writer Ferenc Molnár first published in 1910. It previously had been the basis of a movie of the same name in 1931 with Alfred Lunt and Lynn Fontanne, who were nominated for Oscars. It tells of a jealous actor who disguises himself as a Russian guardsman with a thick accent to test his wife's fidelity. She goes along with the story and yields to him, afterward claiming she knew it was him all along. Krasna transposes the action to Japan, where a French director from Hollywood, Paul Robaix (Montand), plans to film *Butterfly*. For the first time in his career, he wants to do a film without his more famous actress wife, Lucy Dell (MacLaine), as leading lady, to prove that he can succeed without her star power. By doing this opera, he has a pretext for not choosing her for the female lead because as a blue-eyed redhead she is obviously not Japanese.

Lucy and the producer, Sam Lewis (Edward G. Robinson), think up a way to get her the part anyway by disguising her as a Japanese geisha named Yoko Mori. Paul comes across her in a Tokyo teahouse and, fooled by Lucy's convincing geisha manner and costume, plus the painstakingly applied makeup to transform her face and eyes, hires her as the lead. This works until he makes the painful discovery that his geisha is really Lucy. She salves his wounded ego during the presentation at the premiere, when she explains that Yoko Mori has retired to a convent and that all the film's success is due to Paul.

The film was produced by MacLaine's husband, Steve Parker, who spent most of his career in Japan—he was named Man of the Year in 1959 by the Japanese government for his Las Vegas stage show *Holiday in Japan*. *My Geisha* would be directed by the longtime British cinematographer and director Jack Cardiff, who had just done a highly praised film version of D. H. Lawrence's *Sons and Lovers* (1960), which won him a Best Director Academy Award nomination. Filming began on January 16, 1961. It constituted a virtual travelogue of Japan, being shot elaborately on locations in Tokyo, Yokohama, Kyoto, Nara, Hiroshima, and Nagasaki. The dubbing of Butterfly's arias was finally done not by Callas but by the Japanese soprano Michiko Sunahara; vocals for Lieutenant Pinkerton were by the American operatic tenor Barry Morell, who had recently performed the same role at the Metropolitan Opera.

Much of the credit also went to Hollywood's top makeup man, Frank Westmore, who found an ingenious way to make a non-Japanese American woman look Japanese. Brown contact lenses to change her eye color were no problem, nor was hiding her freckles with heavy rice makeup. Making her eye shape appear Japanese while allowing her to blink and close them was more complicated. His improvised solution: cutting almond-shaped prostheses from the soft, pliable rubber of condoms and gluing them to her eyelids.[15]

Montand was particularly happy to be playing opposite MacLaine, who had just done Billy Wilder's *The Apartment* (1960). It had been nominated for ten Academy Awards and won five, and she had won a Golden Globe for her performance. She had also received a star that year on Hollywood's Walk of Fame. He had liked her in Alfred Hitchcock's black-humor experiment *The Trouble with Harry* (1955) and had met her on the set of *The Apartment* while he was in Hollywood. To him, she was the funny, independent, all-American girl he had visualized when devouring movies in Marseilles as a youngster.

They enjoyed each other's company and laughed a lot together. His behavior was all the more impulsive because his state of mind was still in tumult, trying to put the Monroe affair behind him and dealing with the guilt over Signoret's hurt. As he described it, "When I left for Japan in mid-January 1961 to shoot *My Geisha,* my head was like a punching bag. Simone was in terrible shape. Marilyn, after trying to come to Paris, kept cabling that she would be landing in Tokyo. I was completely adrift, and I did a lot of stupid things all over again."[16]

MacLaine, aware of Montand's reputation for liking a certain degree of intimacy with his leading ladies, had told him before the shoot began, "No monkey business."[17] However, in her book *My Lucky Stars: A Hollywood Memoir* (1995), she devotes an entire chapter entitled "A Man I Loved. . . on Location" to relating in detail worthy of "a schoolgirl crush," as Montand might have put it, how she fell in love with him. In fact, she gives the impression of having half-expected it from the moment he showed up, if not actually laying for him. That's not too surprising for an actress who later told Oprah Winfrey that she frequently fell for her leading men, who had what she called an open marriage in which she saw Steve Parker only two or three times a year, and who enjoyed detailing her globe-trotting "sexcapades" with actors and prime ministers.

"I wondered whether he would arrive alone," she wrote. "He did. I wondered how long he would remain that way, and whether I'd be the next 'adventure.'" When he kissed her hand on arrival at the airport, she thought he might have held it a split second longer than necessary. She appreciated his charisma and "European charm." When she showed him how to use chopsticks, she noticed that "his hands were warm. I wondered about his heart."[18] When he told her of his stage fright before a one-man show, she found that attractive, and when he laughed at her jokes and showed understanding about her makeup problems, she found him irresistible. She loved it when he called her by his pet name for her, "Big Bird."

She wasn't seeing much of Steve Parker at the time, who, she noticed, wasn't around often, despite having an obvious interest in the film. Finally, one evening in Nara after the day's filming was over and actors and crew had gone to their respective hotel rooms, there was a knock on her door. "I opened it to find him [Montand] standing in the hallway, his arms dangling by his sides, looking lost and forlorn. I pulled him into my room and folded him gently into my arms. We melted together. Then, at long last, fell into bed. It was sweet—a relief more than anything. I wondered what it would mean in my life."[19]

As it happened, not much. The next evening, Parker, whose absences were due to his also having an affair, joined the group, and she told him about what had happened with Montand, saying that she really liked Montand and was unsure where that was going. He replied that Montand had flaunted his relationship with Monroe and, worse, that he had bet Parker that he could make MacLaine fall in love with him during the shoot. Whether that was true or the ploy of a jealous husband cuckolded one time too many, she was stunned and believed him. When she confronted Montand with the allegation, he chose to remain silent, not wanting to offend either her by admitting the truth of the story or his producer by denying it.[20]

In any case, the relationship, like the film, was over. Who had seduced whom must remain an open question. But callous behavior on the part of Montand, such as betting he could make MacLaine fall in love with him, would have been uncharacteristic. He liked and needed women, but usually it was the woman who took the initiative with him or at least gave him that impression, and he treated them with a certain gallantry; all his life he was seemingly often more seduced than seducing.

My Geisha / Ma geisha (US and France, 1962) had its world premiere at the Plaza Theater in London in January 1962. The critics were underwhelmed. *Variety* found that MacLaine was spirited but that playing a dainty, submissive geisha left little room for her vivacious personality, while "Montand has his moments."[21] The *New York Times* said the plot was rickety, MacLaine "more subdued than normal," Montand "still appear[ing] to find English and his surroundings somewhat uncomfortable."[22] Back in France, *Le Monde* called it "brilliant and amusing," one of the best American comedies in a long time, and in it Montand had found his best role of the four American films he had made.[23]

It was also his last American film for several years. He had fulfilled his contract with Fox, doing his best to break into American films. Non obstante the *New York Times* critic, he looks perfectly at ease in his part in *My Geisha,* his English fluent and clear, his timing for comic numbers perfect. But he had to admit that all four of his American movies were largely critical and box office flops. Like a number of French actors who dreamed of making it in Hollywood, Montand concluded that he would never be considered a star of the first magnitude but rather be typecast. After the shoot, he confided to MacLaine that he was through with Hollywood and its Tinseltown values. As she reported their conversation, "He'd rather have 'real' food, 'real' love, and 'real' conflicts. He said playing both sides of the Atlantic Ocean confused him and others."[24]

Unlike many of their European neighbors, the French generally do not transplant easily to other countries. Ivo Livi, becoming Yves Montand, was inextricably rooted in his adopted France and its dense culture. He would eventually do two more American films and perform his stage show in the United States and much of the rest of the world, becoming a global music hall superstar, but he knew that France was where he belonged.

15

Mixing Stage and Screen

Montand was still winding up the filming of *My Geisha* in February 1961 when he told the French press that he was already planning his return to singing. He would record ten new songs as soon as he was back in Paris, then begin preparing his next music hall tour for 1962. Asked his opinion of Japanese women, he replied wryly, "Don't you think I've had enough problems with women?"[1]

First, though, he had an engagement on Broadway to honor. *An Evening with Yves Montand* at the John Golden Theater on West Forty-Fifth Street opened on October 24, 1961, for three weeks. It gave him and Signoret the opportunity to enjoy together the New York they had known on his previous tour, from pastrami sandwiches at delis to the bridal suite at the Algonquin Hotel. His show with twenty-six songs, including two in English, was again standing room only, and the critics were just as crazy about him. "Yves Montand is one of the most potent love potions ever poured across the footlights," said *Time*. "He is a one-man theater of the performing arts."[2] *Newsweek* found that he "dizzied New York all over again with his masculine Gallic charm,"[3] while the *New York Times* raved, "Are you nostalgic for Paris? Join Yves Montand at the John Golden Theatre on a personally conducted tour that is almost as gay and sentimental as a visit. . . . But it is not the songs alone that charm you on this journey. It is M. Montand's gift for mime, his ease and plasticity of movement, his skills as an actor, and especially his personality."[4]

During the first months of 1962, Montand and Signoret were in England and Japan. His show in London, his first there in thirteen years, opened for four weeks at the Saville Theater on Shaftesbury Avenue. It was the predictable success, with audiences calling him back for as many as twelve curtain calls. It was over breakfast in his suite at the Savoy that he announced to the correspondent for *France-Soir* that his shows in Tokyo and then at the Étoile in Paris would be his last for a while. "Doing these shows is exhausting," he explained. "They take over your life: no more seeing friends or going out, or even time to read a book. A doctor told me that one performance is the equivalent of a three-mile run. So I'm going to concentrate on the theater and cinema." At that point, Signoret entered the room and asked what they were talking about. His reply showed that the healing process between them, never total, was at least having enough effect for them to joke about what had happened in Hollywood: "Nothing important, *chérie*, just that everything is fine and we're not going to divorce." They laughed together.[5]

Montand had not sung in Paris for four years, and the Parisians were glad to have him back after his time in America and Japan. "Yves Montand Is French Again," hailed the headlines when his show opened at the Étoile on November 14.[6] He celebrated the twenty-fifth anniversary of his music hall debut with twenty-five songs, including two new ones, and two sketches. In honor of the anniversary, he resuscitated the song that had been his first hit, "Dans les plaines du Far West." Congratulatory telegrams poured into his dressing room from friends and fellow show business pros such as Alain Delon, Maurice Chevalier, and Tino Rossi; backstage visitors ranged from Françoise Sagan to the filmmaker René Clair and Ingrid Bergman.

The show ran for six months into the spring of 1963. Its success was particularly important to Montand, proof that he and his repertoire were not passé. He could hold his own against the coming generation of singers, such as the great balladeers Georges Brassens and Jacques Brel as well as the rocker Johnny Hallyday. Despite his international status as the master of music hall and his repeated declarations—the latest being to Ingrid Bergman on the set of *Goodbye Again*—that he preferred singing to acting, he clearly itched to get back on the boards and before the cameras.

He also sang on special occasions, including the Second Inaugural Salute to the President, commemorating the second anniversary of John F. Kennedy's election. Montand immediately accepted the invitation to perform, being an admirer of Kennedy as an innovative leader who appeared to promise renewal and reform. He interrupted his show at the Étoile long enough to make a round-trip flight to Washington, DC.

Held at the vast, 10,000-seat National Guard Armory in Washington on January 18, 1963, the event attracted the city's political elite along with the usual power brokers and influencers in the capital. Besides Montand, performers included the New York City ballet, George Burns, Carol Channing, the folk group Peter, Paul and Mary, and the Welsh singer Shirley Bassey. At a dinner hosted by Vice President Lyndon Johnson, Montand was seated at the main table next to Jacqueline Kennedy. Before the evening ended, Kennedy sang an Irish ballad, Gene Kelly and Kirk Douglas danced, and Montand, inevitably, sang "Les feuilles mortes."[7] Shortly after Montand returned to France, a letter arrived at place Dauphine on White House stationery. "Dear Mr. Montand," it began, "Both Mrs. Kennedy and I are most grateful for your giving of your time and talent and for doing so much to make the evening a truly memorable one. John Kennedy."[8]

When Kennedy was assassinated on November 22 that year, Montand felt what he called "a bereavement, deep, real grief."[9] In the early 1960s, he had placed his hope in Kennedy, Khrushchev, and Pope John Paul XXIII, believing that with these new, more liberal leaders an era had begun that would produce a better, more just world. He was convinced that Kennedy was killed because he had a reform agenda that might jeopardize the profits of certain vested interests. "It was a question of money," he said. "They organized it in broad daylight as a way of saying, 'You see, we fear no one, not even a president. If anyone gets in our way, here's what we can do.'" For Montand, Lee Harvey Oswald was a patsy; the job was clearly the work of an organization.[10] Sixteen years later, he would do a film inspired by the assassination with the director Henri Verneuil, *I comme Icare* (1979).

Montand returned to acting in legitimate theater in a role unlike any he had played before. *A Thousand Clowns,* a five-act comedy by the young Herb Gardner, had been a hit when it opened at the Eugene O'Neill Theater in Manhattan on April 5, 1962, with the New York Drama Critics naming Gardner "most promising playwright of 1961–62." It was also made into a feature film in 1965 starring Jason Robards and directed by Fred Coe, which was nominated for four Oscars and won one. Robards was Murray Burns, an eccentric, nonconformist writer of a children's television show called *Chuckles the Chipmunk* with inane lines such as "Goshes and golly-goods, kidderoonies; now what are all us Chippermunkies gonna play first this fine mornin'?" He quits his job in favor of going to the movies, visiting the Empire State Building, watching ocean liners in the harbor, and playing his ukulele.

He is also raising his bright, twelve-year-old nephew, Nick, in a chaotic apartment cluttered with odds and ends such as broken radios, clocks, and hats. He instructs Nick that he must find his own special way in life, avoiding the suffocating middle-class conformity where he would learn only "how to be one of the nice dead people."[11] Investigators from the Bureau of Child Welfare have a different notion of how to raise a young boy, however, and give

Murray an ultimatum: get a regular job and give up his bohemian lifestyle or see Nick taken away and placed with a normal family. One of the social workers, a young woman, sympathizes with Murray, moves in with him, and tries to straighten him out. He reluctantly accepts the constraints of a job, a steady relationship, and even an orderly apartment so that he can keep Nick, though the audience is left wondering how long that will last.

Montand took on the role of Murray in *Des clowns par milliers,* the French adaptation by the playwright Jean Cosmos—who had also written songs for him—that opened on December 5, 1963, at Paris's venerable, mid-nineteenth-century Théâtre du Gymnase. With a supporting cast that included the excellent young character actors Michael Lonsdale and Marlène Jobert as the child-welfare inspectors, *Des clowns* was directed by Raymond Rouleau, who had directed Montand in in both the stage and film versions of *Les sorcières de Salem* eight years earlier. The role was an audacious choice for Montand, who had only *Les sorcières* as his total stage experience. Furthermore, he was playing a part that had been made famous by Jason Robards, a superb Broadway actor who had won a Tony Award in 1958 for his powerful role in Eugene O'Neill's *Long Day's Journey into Night.* Finally, the play's subject, nonconformism in the face of oppressive social norms, did not automatically resonate with French audiences; known for their individualism, they were accustomed to eccentricity and had not experienced the pressure to conform that was prevalent in the America of the 1950s.

Nevertheless, without drawing on the lithe physicality and romantic intensity that had marked his persona in most of his previous acting, Montand managed to bring off on a French stage the part of a whimsical eccentric defying social expectations in Manhattan, USA. The expressive, mobile face that made him such a successful mime served him well to compensate for the difficulty of translating American humor into French. His success was also due to the empathetic rapport he felt for Murray Burns as he struggled to retain his wistful, quixotic, idealistic identity while satisfying society's criteria for parenthood. Herb Gardner himself noticed this rapport one day while visiting Montand as he was rehearsing. "I looked at him, and he was in tears," Gardner recalled. "He said, 'This is very painful stuff. Do you know how sad all this is?'"[12]

The play and its male lead were well received by public and critics, responding to a character who thumbed his nose at humorless bureaucrats—something the French always admire. "How can we not enjoy the indolent, innocent charm of the 'big brother' when it is personified by the inimitable

Yves Montand?," asked *Le Monde*. "And how not to feel complicity when he and his nephew play tricks on the representatives of the powers that be?"[13]

⊙ ⊙ ⊙

True to his habit of keeping several irons in the fire, Montand was not only doing his show at the Étoile in the evening but also shooting a film in the afternoon. *Compartiment tueurs / The Sleeping Car Murder* (1965, US 1966) was the first film of an ambitious young graduate of Paris's film school, the Institut des hautes études cinématographiques (IDHEC), Konstantin Gavras, a name he had honed down to "Costa-Gavras." Born and raised in Greece, he was the son of a communist-leaning Resistance member during the war. That complicated his life because the country's postwar right-wing government refused him entry to a university, considering him tainted by communism. By the same token, he was denied a visa to the United States, so he immigrated to France in 1952 and enrolled at the Sorbonne to study literature with the goal of becoming a writer.

Costa-Gavras began frequenting the art cinemas around the Latin Quarter, decided that film would be his career, and transferred to IDHEC. He interned with directors such as René Clair and René Clément. While working as an assistant to Clément on *Le jour et l'heure / The Day and the Hour* (1963, US 1964), he met Simone Signoret, who had the female lead. That led to meeting Montand, after which a friendship developed, and he became a regular in their weekend outings at the country house in Autheuil.

One day Costa-Gavras picked up a crime thriller called *Compartiment tueurs* (1962) by the French author and screenwriter Sébastien Japrisot, who had dashed it off for a generous advance from his publisher to pay back taxes. It told of six people who take the night train from Marseilles to Paris. On their arrival in Paris, one of the young women in the six-berth sleeping compartment is found to have been strangled. The police investigation led by Inspector Grazziani, known as "Grazzi," has to find the murderer quickly because the latter has begun systematically killing the others who were in that compartment. Grazzi and his team question thirteen suspects in all, some of whom unintentionally give false leads, others just want to talk, and all have their own suspect secrets.

Costa-Gavras, looking to shoot his first professional film after graduation from IDHEC, decided to write an adaptation of the novel and film it as a police thriller. He added a lot of harried detectives working the phones to follow up clues day and night in a grimy police headquarters and ended the film with a nighttime car chase through the streets of Paris. Unsure of his own judgment, he took the train to Saint Paul and showed his screenplay to Signoret over lunch at La Colombe, where she and Montand were vacationing. She liked it and volunteered to play a cameo role as an aging actress. She also agreed to let her eighteen-year-old daughter, Catherine Allégret, play the female lead as one of the passengers being stalked by the murderer—as soon as she got her high school diploma.[14]

At that point, Montand dropped by their table and said, "I hear you've written a good screenplay. Anything in it for me?"[15] Costa-Gavras delightedly suggested he play Inspector Grazziani and do it with a Marseilles accent. Montand hesitated for two reasons: French leftists reflexively don't like the police, and he had spent years ridding himself of his accent. The young director overcame Montand's antiauthority reflex, though, and told him that if he didn't feel right with the accent, he could later dub himself without it. Costa-Gavras was giddy with excitement: "A few days earlier my screenplay was sleeping in a drawer," he recalled later, "and now it was associated with two prominent actors who were famous in France and throughout the world."[16]

With that kind of backing, Costa-Gavras was suddenly bankable. He convinced Julien Derode, who had produced *Othello* with Orson Welles (1951) and would later do the award-winning film *The Day of the Jackal* (1973), to put up a slim budget. The other main obstacle was the Paris Police Prefecture. It was necessary to have its permission to film in the city's streets, but when the chief of police learned that the story's villain was a police inspector, he refused. Montand called an assistant to the chief who liked show business—a part-time poet, the assistant had written songs for Edith Piaf and Gilbert Bécaud—and asked for help. The solution: make the murderer a police intern instead of a regular. Permission granted.

There was not enough money to sign top actors, but Montand and Signoret decided to put together a collaborative enterprise. They got out word of the project and suddenly their actor friends, members of the Autheuil weekend clan, were calling to say they wanted in on it. To help the debut director, they were willing to waive their usual fee and be paid in royalties, if any. Thus, Costa-Gavras fortuitously found himself with a stellar cast including Michel Piccoli, Jean-Louis Trintignant, Charles Denner, and Pascale Roberts, plus, of course, the Montands and Catherine. That cast, his well-wrought screenplay, and his taut direction produced a stylish, fast-paced thriller that keeps the audience involved and guessing the murderer's identity until the final scene.

The result was a surprise success from a first-time director that won an Edgar Allan Poe Award as Best Motion Picture in the US and was named Best Foreign Film by the National Board of Review. Comparing it to the best American gangster-detective films and the works of Henri-George Clouzot, *Film Quarterly* said a couple of years after it debuted that "Costa-Gavras's *The Sleeping Car Murder* is so polished a first film as to put off 'serious' critics who become easily chagrined by slickness."[17] One major critic, Bosley Crowther of the *New York Times,* called it one of the ten best films of the year, "one of those French mystery films that makes you marvel at the flashy versatility of the detectives and the cinematographers of France. . . . It races and pants like *Breathless,* it vibrates like *Alphaville.* And it ends in a chase that screams and screeches like something from the American 'underground.'"[18] Shortly afterward at a Paris dinner in honor of Crowther organized by the producer Ilya Lopert of United Artists, Crowther got up and went over to Costa-Gavras to shake his hand and congratulate him on the film. Impressed, Lopert then came over and told Costa-Gavras, "You can come to United Artists any time you like, with any project you want."[19]

Besides its critical and commercial success, *Compartiment* enabled Montand to reach a new plateau in his acting, feeling at home in his part as he had never before in any of his previous seventeen movies. He even felt free to add bits of business to his character, such as giving Inspector Grazziani a cold that has him continually wiping and blowing his nose with a large handkerchief. His new ease on the set might have been due in part to the film's being, as he put it, a family affair, in which most of the other actors were close friends—he could relax and concentrate on being Inspector Grazzi. It also might have been due to working with a young director with a light touch. Montand "was totally liberated," Costa-Gavras commented later. "I was not a superstar, so he felt safe. It was in this film that he really began to understand that an actor develops a character from the inside, not by imitating the way others had done it."[20]

This was a watershed in Montand's career. Friends who gathered at Autheuil on the weekends had heard him wondering aloud whether he wanted to do another film at all. He had had some good reviews for his earlier performances but still wasn't certain that acting was what he did best, compared with music hall. Costa-Gavras, giving him free rein and encouraging him to relax and be himself on the set, enabled him to put such doubts aside. Montand himself said that *The Sleeping Car Murder* marked the moment when he began taking acting in films seriously: "I only really dedicated myself to films in 1963, when I met Costa-Gavras and we did *Compartiment tueurs,*" he said during a television interview in 1978. "Before that, I was a dilletante."[21] From now on, he would in effect begin a second career. He was leaving music hall behind and concentrating on acting. During the next twenty-five years, he would do only two full recitals. It was an apt symbol of his departure from music hall that the Étoile, "his" theater for so long, would soon be demolished.

The film also was the beginning of a long and fruitful collaboration between the actor and the director. Over the years, it would produce some of their best work. As Costa-Gavras became the master of the political thriller, practically inventing a new film genre, Montand would be his protagonist and partner. His first political film, however, was done not with Costa-Gavras but with the Left Bank intellectual Alain Resnais, who was part of France's Nouvelle Vague of directors, along with Jean-Luc Godard and François Truffaut. Resnais was known especially for his skewed storylines, as in his first feature film, *Hiroshima mon amour* (1959, US 1960), and for surrealistic, jump-cut mixing of past and present, as in *Last Year at Marienbad* (1962).

La guerre est finie / The War Is Over (1966, US 1967) is the tale is of an aging, disabused, communist revolutionary fighting against Franco's dictatorial regime in Spain. The screenplay was by Jorge Semprún, who was a veteran of the communist underground resistance to Franco and many things besides. Montand had met him in the summer of 1963 in Saint Paul. Semprún was having lunch with Signoret, who had encountered him some years earlier in her circle of leftist intellectuals. It was one of the most important meetings of Montand's life, one that would lead to a mutually enriching, lifelong friendship between the French entertainer and the Spanish intellectual. As Montand described his feelings for Semprún,

> It was almost love at first sight between us. We met at the Colombe d'Or. He was sitting at our table, with Simone and his wife, Colette, and he was in my chair against the wall. I came in and thought, Who is this guy who's taken my seat? I gave him a dirty look. Simone introduced us. For half an hour I was curt with him, and then we found we had an amazing amount in common. It was a love story. He was a man I loved the way you love a woman. I truly loved him—without the slightest ambiguity—and he loved me back, even though in the background he was more reserved than me and showed his feelings less.[22]

The main thing they had in common was that they both were recovering communists going through a painful period of weaning from the ideology that had given meaning to their lives for decades. Montand admired the forty-year-old Semprún as a real militant and revolutionary representing the sort of engaged political action that he had respected so much in his father, Giovanni.

Born in Madrid, Semprún was the grandson of a former prime minister of Spain and the son of a liberal politician and diplomat. The family moved to The Hague during the Spanish Civil War of the 1930s, when his father represented the Spanish Republican government. After Franco's victory, they went into exile in Paris. Semprún enrolled at the Sorbonne to study philosophy and, already a political activist at eighteen, joined both the Spanish and French Communist Party. After the fall of France in 1940, he fought with the French Resistance until he was captured by the Gestapo and spent two years in Buchenwald, an experience he described in his first book, *The Long Voyage* (1963).

After the war he became a member of the Executive Committee of the clandestine Spanish Communist Party. For a decade, he worked in Paris as an interpreter for UNESCO, a useful cover while he slipped into Spain frequently under the nom de guerre "Federico Sánchez" to help organize the communist underground resistance to Franco. In 1962, the party hierarchy decided he had been in the field too long and replaced him over his objections. At about this time, he read Alexander Solzhenitsyn's novel *A Day in the Life of Ivan Denisovich* (1962) and learned the reality of Stalinist communism and the gulags. Like Montand, he could no longer believe that the party was infallible. According to his former comrades, he became a right-winger, an anti-Stalinist, and, worse, a social democrat. "I came to believe that communist rule was the most tragic event of the 20th century," he told the *Paris Review.*[23]

Semprún spent the next decades writing nine books, mainly fictionalized memoirs based on his experiences as a Resistance fighter, survivor of a Nazi death camp, and communist dissident. He did the screenplays for important films by directors such as Resnais, Costa-Gavras, and Joseph Losey, many of them starring Montand. "In the stories I tell," he said in an interview for the *New York Times,* "there are always two specific ideas, deportation and communism. Two things Americans do not understand."[24] He would also serve as the Spanish government's minister of culture from 1988 to 1991, much as the cultural figures André Malraux did in France and Melina Mercouri did in Greece.

On the face of it, Montand and Semprún were worlds apart. Montand was from the slums of Marseilles; Semprún was born into the bourgeois comfort of a distinguished, cultivated Spanish family, was raised by German governesses, and spoke several languages. But they were united by their passionate political commitment and their disillusionment with the Communist Party. There was also the fact that Semprún became estranged from both his father and his own son over his Resistance work. As his biographer Soledad Fox Maura sees it, "As Jorge's family relationships crumbled, Yves Montand became the most important male figure in Semprún's life. He played the protagonists Jorge created on the big screen. . . . Montand was Semprún's longest-lasting French friend . . . and the most important male influence on Jorge for nearly thirty years, between 1963 and Montand's death in 1991."[25]

Semprún described their friendship more simply in *Montand, la vie continue* (1983): "It worked not because there was an intellectual giving lessons on one side and a singer on the other. Not at all. I loved what he did on stage, and, what's more, I considered it important. He sensed that I felt no condescension toward a 'minor art.'" The book is a paean to Montand. In describing Montand's voice and his presence on stage, for instance, Semprún writes, "A voice of such musicality, such iridescence, that it becomes itself a language, even for foreigners and despite the difficulties of a foreign language. A dramatic physical presence so dense that it communicates what is left unsaid. A voice and a presence that become quite simply a universal language."[26]

Alain Resnais had read *The Long Voyage* and found it particularly interesting. He had done a documentary about the horrors of the Nazi concentration camps called *Nuit et brouillard / Night and Fog* (1956), using stock footage and contemporary shots of the camps. It had a commentary by the poet Jean Cayrol, who had fought in the Resistance before being captured and sent to the notorious Mauthausen-Gusen camp, where the life expectancy of prisoners was six months. Resnais contacted Semprún and asked him to do a screenplay based on his underground work in Spain. The result after three versions was the semiautobiographical *La guerre est finie / The War Is Over*.

In *La guerre*, a middle-aged clandestine Spanish revolutionary (Montand) with several names—Diego, Carlos, Domingo—and as many passports shuttles between Paris and Spain delivering propaganda pamphlets, money, and orders from the Paris-based Executive Committee in exile. He is losing faith in the idea that Franco can be overthrown by general strikes, popular uprisings, and other traditional communist tactics. He thinks the committee members and the young Marxist firebrands who still believe in such ideas are out of touch with a Spain that is visited by 14 million tourists every year. The only realistic hope for change is that the Franco regime will eventually pass, and Spain will become a social democratic state like France or Italy.

The committee members and Marxist firebrands, however, believe he is the one who is out of touch. He has been in the field too long and has lost the ability to see the big picture. They give him one more assignment to contact a clandestine operative in Barcelona and accompany him safely to Madrid. He is already on his way when his comrades learn that the Spanish police have laid a trap for him in Madrid. The film ends with his Swedish mistress (Ingrid Thulin)—it was a Franco-Swedish production—at Orly airport to catch a plane to Barcelona to try to warn him.

Guerre is an unusual film for Resnais in that it has a mostly linear progression—the action takes place during three days—even though he does use flashbacks and flash-forwards to fragment time and place and shoots it in his habitual severe black-and-white. It has his usual intellectualism, with voice-overs putting the audience in the head of Diego, so they are aware from his interior monologue what he is thinking and feeling. Montand convincingly embodies a haggard, world-weary spy, constantly looking over his shoulder and checking everything twice, getting fed up with the necessary stealth of a life underground. He identified with the character of Diego all the more because he personally was evolving that way in his relations with communism. Regarding his acting technique, it is clear that he has learned the importance of using his eyes to project reflection, doubt, anger. He has matured, and his lined face and heavier upper body add to his presence—he can now make the simple act of drawing on a cigarette an impressive gesture.

The critics cheered. As the French film historian Michel Ciment said later, "That was the film that really confirmed him as a serious actor."[27] *Le Monde* called *La guerre* "outstanding,"[28] and the film was well received in the United States, being nominated for an Oscar for Semprún's screenplay and named Best Foreign Language Movie by the New York Film Critics Circle, the Foreign Language Press Association, and the Independent Film Importers and Distributors of America. The New York Film Festival at Lincoln Center chose it for its closing presentation.

The subject was too sensitive for some. Czech authorities ordered the picture removed from competition at the Karlovy Vary Film Festival at the request of Dolores Ibárruri, "La Pasionaria" of the Spanish Communist Party; it was shown out of competition. Similarly, when the selection committee of the Cannes Film Festival picked it as one of France's official entries, the Ministry of Foreign Affairs intervened to have it removed for fear of offending Spain. It was projected in a local theater, and Spanish journalists, outraged by the French decision, invented a special prize for it on the spot, the Prix Luis Buñuel.

Montand himself was especially pleased with it, considering it a tough-minded, intellectual movie and one of the best he had made. "After *La guerre est finie*, I said to myself, even if I never make another movie, it won't matter," he commented later. "I'd had my revenge on the cinema, I've really made a film."[29]

16

The Sixties

The 1960s were a productive and pivotal decade for Montand. He quickly would do a run of six films, deal in his own way with the epochal political events in France, and give a new solo show at a new music hall.

The range of roles he played in the films was typically diverse, in keeping with his practice, whether on stage or on a set, of being unpredictable. Thus, he would be a tank commander in General Philippe Leclerc's famed Second Armored Division as it liberated Paris in 1944; a race car driver risking his life on Europe's Formula One tracks; a television reporter seeing action from Africa to Vietnam; a Flemish professor of linguistics whose world is turned upside down; an assassinated liberal politician in opposition to a dictatorial regime in a Mediterranean country; and a comic Italian gangster holed up in a French chateau. These roles would afford him the opportunity to work with directors such as René Clément, Claude Lelouch, and, especially, again with Costa-Gavras.

Paris brule-t-il? / Is Paris Burning? (France and US 1966) was a sprawling, ambitious, three-hour reenactment of the liberation of Paris in June 1944. Adapted by Gore Vidal and Francis Ford Coppola from the bestseller of the same name by Dominique Lapierre and Larry Collins published in 1965, it was produced by Paul Graetz for Paramount. A German-born French producer, Graetz had bought the film rights even before the book was published. With the innovative René Clément as director—who had done such memorable films about France during World War II as *La bataille du rail / The Battle of the Rails* (1946, US 1949), and *Le jour et l'heure / The Day and the Hour* (1963, US 1964)—and Paramount providing generous financial backing, the film had an all-star Franco-American cast. A virtual sampler of the big film names of the day, it included, besides Montand, Orson Welles, Kirk Douglas, Anthony Perkins, Glenn Ford, Jean-Paul Belmondo, Charles Boyer, Alain Delon, and many others in cameo roles too numerous to list.

(Clément asked France's biggest movie star at the time, Jean Gabin, who had actually fought in the war, to take a part. He refused, saying he had seen enough combat in real life and wasn't interested in playing soldier before a camera.) Simone Signoret played a Paris café owner.

Montand was Sergeant Marcel Bizien, an actual member of the Free French forces who had commanded a tank in the Second Armored Division during the Liberation and had died jousting with a German panzer on Place de la Concorde. The actor-singer had only a few minutes on-screen and even fewer lines as he rode atop his tank before being killed—he called his role a "symbolic participation" in the film.[1] Paramount planned a Franco-American military parade and big fireworks show for the film's Paris premiere in mid-October 1966, but they were rained out. Montand did his part in the promotion by singing "Chant des partisans," the hymn of the Resistance written in 1943 by Joseph Kessel and Maurice Druon—both future members of the Académie française—from the first platform of the Eiffel Tower at midnight, as hundreds gathered below on the Champ de Mars. That wasn't enough to save the film from being panned by the critics, however. *Le Monde* tried to be kind, admitting that it "doubtless will not be classed among the classics of world cinema."[2] The *New York Times* was less gentle, regretting that "there is such a confusion of characters and their connections in this vague, diffuse account of the liberation of Paris from the Nazis in 1944: such a mishmash of melodrama."[3]

⊙ ⊙ ⊙

Montand loved to drive his own flamboyant Ferraris in real life, but he got more driving action than he bargained for when he did John Frankenheimer's *Grand Prix* (1966, France 1967). His fifth American film and his only one for MGM, it follows four professional Formula One drivers through an entire racing season, from Monte Carlo to Monza, as they compete on the track and vie for the affections of several women off it. James Garner was the male lead as Pete Aron, the only American of the four, while Montand got second billing as the French driver Jean-Pierre Sarti. Eva Marie Saint, playing a writer with a fashion magazine, was the love interest opposite Montand.

Frankenheimer was at the time one of Hollywood's leading directors. He was known for idiosyncratic classics such as *The Manchurian Candidate* and *Birdman of Alcatraz* (both 1962). More recently he had done the high-kinetic, ultra-realist action movie *The Train* (1964), in which Burt Lancaster has to stop a trainload of French art from going to Nazi Germany. MGM gave him generous financing estimated at $9 million for *Grand Prix,* which would run for two and a half hours, be his first color film, and be shot in 70-millimeter Cinerama. Still, Frankenheimer had to overcome a great deal of doubt about the project.

> Everybody was skeptical about a movie being made about racing. In fact, Ferrari executives didn't want anything to do with it. They said, "Go make your movie but it has nothing to do with what we do, and you can't use the word Ferrari in this picture." And that was pretty much the attitude as well of all the professional drivers. Besides that, we had a big film unit and we got in their way. The mechanics didn't like film crews interfering with their work, either. There was a general air of disapproval. When I look back, I don't know how the hell we ever did that film.[4]

Later, Ferrari bosses changed their mind after seeing a thirty-minute clip of filming at Monte Carlo and gave Frankenheimer complete access to their Maranello factory and their cars. A former amateur race car driver, Frankenheimer was determined to make *Grand Prix* the most authentic, realistic racing film ever done. For starters, he wanted Steve McQueen, who had done his own motorbike and car-chase driving in *The Great Escape* (1963) and would do so again later as the lead in *Bullitt* (1968). That didn't work out, and McQueen went on to do his own racing film, *Le Mans* (1971). Frankenheimer engaged top drivers, from Bob Bondurant to Carroll Shelby, Stirling Moss, and Jackie Stewart, either as consultants or drivers during the filming at the tracks, which was done on Mondays and Tuesdays after the real weekend events. (Of the thirty-two professionals who participated, five died in racing accidents within two years after the film was completed.)

He refused, however, to use professional doubles for actors during the race scenes. His solution: train the actors to handle three-liter racers at 150 miles an hour. It was a dangerous idea even though all of them underwent intensive training at the Jim Russell Racing Drivers School in Britain for three weeks, eight hours a day. (Russell said of Montand, "He'll be okay. He's not a very good driver, but he's okay."[5]) Garner, Montand, and the Italian Antonio Sabàto liked being their own stuntmen, but the Brit Brian Bedford said wryly, "I do think this is carrying The Method a little far."[6] Montand nearly paid for the extra authenticity with his life. On the first day of the shoot in Monte Carlo, his car, off-balance due to a camera mounted on the front, hit a bump and went into a spin. It crashed into a trackside building, and the ruptured gas tank spewed him with gasoline. Luckily for Montand, the gas did not ignite, and he was pulled from the wreck uninjured.

Frankenheimer's use of car-mounted cameras put the audience in the race, giving the same view as the driver of the track speeding by, which occasionally gave members of the audience motion sickness—some theaters provided barf bags. The vicarious ride was especially intense through the narrow, twisting streets of Monte Carlo and in the Belgian race, when torrents of rain limited visibility and spun-out cars littered the countryside. No process shots or models were used for the spectacular accidents with cars crashing in flames; real cars with dummy drivers were projected at racing speed against obstacles or off the track by a "hydrogen cannon" devised by the special-effects man Milt Rice.

Montand, whose character dies in a crash during the final sequence at Monza, was convincing as an intense, forty-year-old driver pushing the limit and with his charisma stole the show from the more low-key James Garner. Both, however, are stock characters corresponding to the clichés about stoic, heroic race car drivers as magnets for pretty women—the romantic sequences look trite and dutiful compared with the edge-of-the-seat thrill of the races. The film earned three Oscars for sound, film editing, and special effects and is still the gold standard for racing movies. But Montand had had enough thrills for a while. "I felt very excited about the idea of doing a film at the wheel of a race car," he said afterward. "But I would never do it again for a million dollars a day. It was crazy to take risks like that. During the race at Spa we were driving full speed through the rain with practically no visibility. I said to myself, 'Stop Montand, you didn't sign up for this.'"[7]

⊙ ⊙ ⊙

Claude Lelouch was surfing on a sudden wave of popularity and fame when he proposed to Montand the role of the male lead opposite Candice Bergen in his new film. His film *Un homme et une femme / A Man and a Woman* (France and US 1966), a sappy, stylish love story about a widow (Anouk Aimée) and a widower (Jean-Louis Trintignant), had just won Oscars for Best Foreign Language Film and Original Screenplay and the Palme d'Or at the Cannes Film Festival. *A Man and a Woman* had all the elements that would become Lelouch's trademark: characters with glamor jobs—he's a race car driver, she's in films—who have a passionate love affair in difficult, tormenting circumstances; slick photography and long silences taking the place of dialogue; and soaring romantic music.

Montand accepted the role in *Vivre pour vivre / Live for Life* (France and US 1967) based on Lelouch's reputation and without thoroughly going over the script. He plays a dashing, philandering French television foreign correspondent named Robert Colomb, while Bergen is an American fashion model named, yes, Candice. He's married to a long-suffering wife, Catherine (Annie Girardot), who tearfully dumps him when she learns of his affair with Candice. His job takes him to some of the world's hot spots, such as Africa and Vietnam, which Lelouch films like some dramatic travelogue, giving the picture an air of social significance.

There are Lelouch's long, moody silences and tricky photography, including a sequence where he places the camera in the middle of a room and makes it go around. The whole is accompanied by the same sort of romantic music that the composer Francis Lai did for *Un homme et une femme.* The silences and sparse dialogue mean Montand spends much time looking thoughtful, world-weary, and guilty. He shuttles between Candice and Catherine, both of whom decide they are better off without him.

Although some critics admired Lelouch's lush photography and slick product, most were unconvinced. *Le Monde* tried to be even-handed toward the director, saying, "His vitality, gusto and glibness make us forgive the excesses and affectation of the film"; plus, "Yves Montand is consistently excellent and Candice Bergen has a nice smile."[8] *Variety,* however, compared it unfavorably to *Un homme,* finding that "*Live for Life* is very similar in subject matter and style but lacks the lyric sweep and charm of its predecessor, even falters technically despite a sizeable budget."[9] "The movie is more or less given over to mutual deceptions among these people," wrote Roger Ebert, the Pulitzer Prize–winning critic for the *Chicago Sun-Times.* "Yves lies to Annie, Candice lies to Yves, Annie lies to Candice and Lelouch lies to us. He achieves this by taking a tawdry little domestic tragicomedy (which could have been a good tawdry little domestic tragicomedy) and propping it up with film clips from Vietnam, shots of Nazi demonstrations, and other trademarks designed to make small events look significant. It doesn't work, and it's offensive."[10]

For Montand, doing the film was an unhappy experience: "Lelouch told me the story of one film, and he did a different one. I trusted him and signed for it without seeing the screenplay, something I will never do again for any director. He centered the whole film on 'my wife' Annie Girardot, making the young

American Candice Bergen a marriage breaker. The whole thing is thin, conventional, very caricatural, like the stuff in a gossip magazine. That said, Lelouch's talent as a director is undeniable. It could have been a different film. Too bad."[11]

⊙ ⊙ ⊙

Nothing could be farther from that than Montand's next film, *Un soir, un train / One Night . . . a Train* (France and US 1968). Instead of being in the saccharine, lachrymose glamorized world of Lelouch, he would be plunged into a bizarre, oneiric realm as a university professor of linguistics who suddenly experiences reality slipping away from him. Based on a novel from 1953 by the Belgian Flemish author Johan Daisne (the pen name of Herman Thiery), *Un soir* was directed by Daisne's compatriot André Delvaux. Montand's costar is Anouk Aimée, like him a Lelouch alumna.

Both writer and director had the traditional Flemish penchant for the grotesque going back to the sixteenth-century painter Hieronymus Bosch and his eldritch, nightmarish scenes mixing esoteric symbols and graphic horror, as in his famous work *The Garden of Earthly Delights*. In modern times, this style was carried on by Belgian painters such as René Magritte and Paul Delvaux (no kin to the director), whose surrealist works depicted ordinary objects and situations in ways that defied usual perceptions of time and reality. In literature, the Ghent-based writer Jean Ray (the pseudonym of Jean Raymond Marie de Kremer) also produced gothic fantasy works, such as the novel *Malpertuis / The Legend of Doom House* (Belgium 1971, US 1972), which was done as a film directed by the Belgian Harry Kümel and starred Orson Welles. André Delvaux had taken degrees in Germanic philology and law at the Free University of Brussels, had played piano accompaniment at silent movies, and had taught Dutch language and literature before doing his first feature films. Very much in the Belgian artistic tradition of exploring the mystical, irrational aspects of existence, he became identified with what he termed magical realism, which, as its name implies, mixes the fantastic and the real.

Montand's character encounters strangeness after a quarrel with his mistress, a French woman named Anne, played by Anouk Aimée in a cool, enigmatic manner. She feels uncomfortable in Flanders, where she has no friends and struggles with the language. Professor Mathias teaches in the fraught atmosphere of bilingual Belgium, with its constant tension and frequent hostility between Dutch-speaking Flemings and French-speaking Walloons.

Together, they take a train to attend a conference at another university. He dozes off, and when he awakes, she is absent from their compartment, and, for reasons unexplained, the train has stopped in the countryside.

Mathias gets off to see whether Anne might have left the train. She hasn't, but the train starts off, leaving him and two others stranded in a dismal, rain-soaked field. They stumble upon an odd, nameless village and enter a gruesome bistro where no one speaks their language. Mathias becomes increasingly uneasy as a young, expressionless hostess stares at them intensely. As they learn that her name is Moïra (Destiny, Fate), a lugubrious orchestra begins to play, and the bistro's patrons dance glumly. Suddenly they stop and leave, and Mathias tries to ask Moïra who she is. Looking at him blankly, all she tells him is that there has been a train wreck. When he goes to see, he discovers that Anne has been killed in the accident. Devastated by this trick of fate that had him leave the train while she went on to her death, he lies beside her corpse, weeping.

None of the plot makes literal sense, nor, being a perfect example of Delvaux's magical realism, is it supposed to. Montand's acting is deeply interior as his comfortable, middle-class life is turned topsy-turvy. Disoriented and bereft, Mathias grapples uncomprehendingly with an absurd, incomprehensible world, a no-man's-land between life and death. As Delvaux explained, "Basically, my film tells of the adventure of a man who, believing he knows everything, is obliged by circumstances to realize that he knows nothing, to be stripped naked."[12]

The part was an important new departure for Montand, unlike anything he played before or after. As Delvaux put it, "For three years Montand had been undergoing an important change. He was detaching himself from his usual persona to become a profoundly authentic actor, idiosyncratic, showing exceptional intuition. We understood each other right away. It's a role that takes him out of his traditional character to find something very profound in himself."[13] He had reached a new plateau of acting skill. Some French critics now put him in the same class as Henry Fonda.

⊙ ⊙ ⊙

Nineteen sixty-eight was a tumultuous year in a crucial time. Among other stunning events, it included the assassination of Bobby Kennedy and Martin Luther King Jr.; the Tet Offensive, which turned the tide against the United States in the Vietnam War; and the Soviet invasion of Czechoslovakia, which brutally ended the budding democratic reforms of the Prague Spring. In

Montand's France, it was the year that the equivalent of a university panty raid in suburban Paris spiraled out of control, bringing the country to the brink of chaos and nearly sparking the fundamental political change that he had long supported as a communist fellow traveler. There, as in many parts of the world, recent history would be divided between before and after 1968.

The students at the suburban Nanterre campus of the University of Paris were unhappy because the school's regulations forbade nighttime dormitory visits among male and female students. When the French minister of youth and sports suggested they cool their romantic ardor by jumping into the school's new swimming pool, the young campus firebrand Daniel Cohn-Bendit—dubbed "Danny the Red" by the press—denounced the government's "fascism" and mobilized a protest movement. French universities, where enrollment had nearly tripled to more than 500,000 in the preceding decade, were a tinderbox that spring. The Nanterre campus, where the main courses included sociology based on a critical Marxist analysis of capitalist society, was particularly restive and open to the new international youth culture whose heroes were Ho Chi Minh, Che Guevara, and Mao Zedong.

When the authoritarian government of President Charles de Gaulle defiantly closed the suburban campus and sent busloads of riot police to lock out some 2,000 protesting students at the Sorbonne in the Latin Quarter, they took to the streets. Few Parisians viewed their march down boulevard Saint Michel seriously, "Sorbonne in State of Siege" being a common newspaper headline.

What had been a relatively good-humored protest movement turned ugly on May 10. During what became known as the Night of the Barricades, students, now numbering nearly 30,000, built some fifty barriers with cobblestones, the trunks of felled trees, and the carcasses of nearly 200 overturned and burned-out automobiles in the Latin Quarter. The police charged, firing tear gas grenades and beating students with truncheons; students replied with cobblestones and Molotov cocktails thrown from rooftops. By the time the fighting was over the next morning, more than 500 students and 600 police were injured, and 468 people had been arrested. It had been, said the Paris police prefect Maurice Grimaud, "one of the most lamentable nights Paris has ever known."[14] To many who knew their French history, the situation recalled King Louis XVI's question after the fall of the Bastille: "Is it a riot?" To which the duke of Liancourt replied, "No, sire, it is a revolution."

Student leaders such as Cohn-Bendit certainly hoped so. Singing the "Marseillaise" and the socialist "Internationale," they strung up a banner saying, "Long live the commune of May 10." Haranguing the feverish, round-the-clock student debate in the courtyard of the Sorbonne, Cohn-Bendit called for nothing less than the total suppression of capitalist society. Sensing a rare opportunity for joint student–worker action, the communist and socialist labor unions called a wildcat general strike. Over the next several weeks, nearly 10 million workers walked out, leaving France paralyzed without public transport and gasoline or, periodically, gas and electricity, while factories closed from Brest to Belfort and Calais to Carcassonne.

De Gaulle, who had been in power for ten years—one of the popular anti-government slogans was "Dix ans, ça suffit" (Ten years are enough)—seemed disoriented and unable to grasp what was happening; he called the situation *insaisissable,* incomprehensible. Suddenly he disappeared on May 29 as rumors flew that he had resigned and fled the country. He had in fact left by helicopter, but only as far as Baden-Baden, near Strasberg, where he consulted with General Jacques Massu, commander of French occupation forces in West Germany. Assured of the army's support, he returned to Paris amid reports that tanks were converging on the capital to suppress the insurrection. Premier Georges Pompidou steadied the situation by buying off the labor unions with a 14 percent across-the-board increase of the minimum wage. Students were mollified by the relaxing of university regulations and the dumbing down of the curriculum. "After this," Pompidou concluded in a thoughtful speech to the National Assembly, "nothing in France can be quite the same as before."[15]

One might have expected Montand and Signoret, longtime ardent communist fellow travelers, to have been excited by this revolt in their own country against bourgeois capitalist society. But they were nowhere to be seen mounting the barricades, attending rallies, giving speeches, singing the "Internationale" with raised fists. Instead, they hunkered down at place Dauphine and followed events on television, refusing to be associated with the protestors. Asked during an interview whether he supported Georges Séguy, head of the communist-leaning CGT during the general strike, Montand snapped, "Never heard of him." When he, who had gladly sung at factories during his tour of the Soviet Union a dozen years earlier, was asked to sing for striking workers at a Renault automobile plant, he begged off, saying with questionable logic that "it would be arrogant and demagogic, and the fact that it would be so much elegant self-advertisement would make it even more shameful."[16]

After *les événements,* as the French still euphemistically call the protests, were over, Montand and Signoret issued a defensive-sounding press statement, saying, "Our age and situation did not incite us to play a part in the events of May 1968."[17] As he later explained his state of mind at the time, "To be sure, I still believe in a better tomorrow, but not in perfect happiness. I still criticize and say no when I disagree with someone's position, but they are not necessarily bastards. Among them there are also good people who are trying to be constructive and positive."[18]

Mature, prudent, reflective middle-age had set in.

17

"The Best Political Thriller Ever"

Montand now embarked on three very different projects, simultaneously, as was his wont. First, he would do a comedy for a change, his first foray into that genre, then make his second film with Costa-Gavras—the first of several with political themes—and then give a one-man show at a new venue, Paris's big Olympia music hall.

Le diable par la queue / The Devil by the Tail (France and US 1969) was a riotous romp in the light French manner directed by Philippe de Broca. Born Philippe Claude Alex de Broca de Ferrussac, he often did films with a strong escapist element about an eccentric, swashbuckling adventurer-hero. The actor Jean-Paul Belmondo fit this description perfectly and starred in several of de Broca's films, such as *L'homme de Rio / That Man from Rio* (France and US 1964) and *Le magnifique* (1973, US 1976), both over-the-top action films. Filmed in the vast seventeenth-century Château de Fléchères near Lyon, *Le diable* is a take-off on the story of a poor but noble aristocratic family making ends meet.

The marquise de Coustines, played by the sixty-eight-year-old, still vivacious theater star Madeleine Renaud, has turned the chateau into a hotel, but there are not enough guests to make real money. She persuades the owner of a local service station to sabotage the cars of passing travelers and then to suggest the chateau as a place to spend the night while he repairs them. One of them is the self-styled Baron César Maricorne (Montand), in reality a high-flying gangster traveling with the loot from his latest heist. The marquise and her family learn the truth and decide to kill him and get the money.

The stage is set for Montand to use his elegant presence and talent for mime as he plays the exuberant, hand-kissing baron with a strong Marseilles accent. With an excellent supporting cast including Maria Schell and Jean

Rochefort, the film is a series of sight gags, witty badinage, seductions, and merry chases around the grounds of the chateau. Montand had already signed for his upcoming show at the Olympia in the fall, but he squeezed in this film during the summer because he wanted to try his hand at comedy and develop his range. "Doing this film the same year as *Z* was exciting and risky," he said later. "But I don't want to be typecast, to become what I call a 'poster actor.' It was like an *exercise de style* that helped me develop for future films."[1]

His next film would be radically different in tone.

Costa-Gavras was returning to Paris after visiting his parents in Greece in April 1967, the same month that a military junta led by a group of army colonels launched a coup that put the country under military dictatorship for seven years. During the plane ride, he read a new political thriller by the prolific Greek writer Vassilis Vassilikos, a liberal political activist who would be forced into exile by the junta. The book, simply entitled *Z* (the first letter for the word *ζει* in ancient Greek, meaning "he lives"), is a novelistic treatment of the assassination of Grigoris Lambrakis in May 1963. A left-wing member of the Greek Parliament active in the pacifist and antinuclear movement, Lambrakis was murdered by right-wing thugs after he made a speech at a ban-the-bomb rally in Salonika. Costa-Gavras had been beaten by police as a child because he had put a hammer and sickle on his cap as a joke, and he had been denied admission to the University of Athens because his father had fought with a communist Resistance group against the Nazis in the Second World War. The story of Lambrakis's assassination thus resonated for him. He decided on the spot to make a film based on the book.

He asked Jorge Semprún, who had done the script for *La guerre est finie,* to write a screenplay with him. He would outline the scenes, underlining the psychology of the characters, the technical details of filming, and the direction; Semprún would add the dialogue and put it all in script form. The finished work ran two hundred pages. As Costa-Gavras described their method, "We holed up at a friend's house about 35 miles from Paris and worked every single day for five weeks. We stopped only to eat. . . . We argued a lot but Jorge came to see what he had already learned from working on *La Guerre est finie,* that you often do not need dialogue when an image will tell you all you need to know."[2]

Costa-Gavras was under contract to United Artists at the time. The studio initially responded favorably and agreed to finance the film but pulled out when its executives saw the finished screenplay, finding it too political and, above all, too leftist. Costa-Gavras then shopped the screenplay around to French producers for months, but for them a tale about a murdered Greek politician wasn't commercial enough. He received the same reaction in Italy and Yugoslavia. He was about to drop the project when Jacques Perrin, a twenty-seven-year-old French actor, took it in hand. He created a production company and suggested trying Algeria, where he had contacts. They visited Algiers to scout a location. Five years after the country had gained its independence from France following years of a brutal war, life in the city had returned to normal. Costa-Gavras liked what he saw: the architecture, the port, the sea—all made it ideal to represent a typical if unnamed Mediterranean country. Audiences would have no doubt that the country in question was Greece.

Like many former French colonies, however, the country had inherited a taste for complicated, nitpicking bureaucracy. Even though two Algerian producers, Ahmed Rachedi and Mohammed Lakhdar-Hamina, were found, and the cast and film crew would include Algerians, the project still had to go through the Ministry of the Economy and then the Ministry of Information and finally be approved by President Houari Boumédiène himself. Ironically, Boumédiène, a tough, take-no-prisoners colonel who had been one of the leaders in the fight for independence, had staged his own military coup to take power in Algeria in 1965. "So, you want us to produce a film about the colonels who came to power by a putsch?," he asked Costa-Gavras sternly as soon as the director entered the president's office. Then he burst out laughing. "Go ahead and do your film," he said. "I've got nothing in common with your Greek colonels. We're revolutionaries."[3]

For the film's musical score, Costa-Gavras wanted none other than Greece's most famous composer, who also happened to be a political activist of his own stripe. Mikis Theodorakis had composed works ranging from symphonies to chamber music, hymns to ballets, operas, and film scores, including one for the recent worldwide success *Zorba the Greek* (1964). He was also deeply involved in Greek politics, having founded the Lambrakis democratic youth organization after Lambrakis's assassination and becoming a left-wing member of Parliament.

Theodorakis's resistance to the Regime of the Colonels after their coup d'état earned him jail time and then internment in a concentration camp; playing and even listening to his music were banned. (With a touch of gallows humor, Greeks liked to recount the joke that an Athens cop on his beat is humming a banned song when a passerby says, "Officer, I'm surprised that you are humming Theodorakis." The officer arrests him for listening to illegal music.)[4] His imprisonment made Costa-Gavras's direct contact with him impossible, but the resourceful Jacques Perrin flew to Greece and was able to communicate the film's storyline to Theodorakis, who agreed to do the score from his prison cell. He hummed the film's themes on cassettes that he smuggled out to Perrin. They were then orchestrated by the French film composer Bernard Gérard, retaining the metallic Greek bouzouki coloration of *Zorba.*

The film, though thinly disguised as fiction, is virtually a documentary of the actual events that occurred during and after the assassination of Lambrakis. A charismatic member of Parliament whose only name is "Z" (Montand), a professional gynecologist who in his youth had won an Olympic gold medal (all of which describe Lambrakis), arrives in a provincial town (read Salonika) from the capital (read Athens) of a country under an extreme right-wing government (read Greece) to address an antinuclear rally. After his speech, as he is crossing the town square, he is fatally struck on the head by a man standing in the back of a passing pickup truck. The police class his death as a drunken accident.

An examining magistrate (Christos Sartzetakis, masterfully played by Jean-Louis Trintignant) thought to be friendly to the government is assigned to the case and begins digging into it. He smells something fishy, and his basic integrity prompts him to call in for questioning top members of the police hierarchy. Although key witnesses begin to disappear, he finally indicts four of the officers for complicity in the premeditated murder of Z. The trial is skewed by the fact that seven witnesses die violent deaths before they can testify. All of the officers and their civilian accomplices get off with light or only symbolic sentences. Faced with violent public reaction, the government falls, but a military junta takes power before new elections can be held. In case anyone still misses the point, the film ends with a split-screen image of Montand and Lambrakis.

Z (France and US 1969), a tough-minded political film with no love interest or other concessions to popular taste, had a lukewarm public reception when it was released in Paris in February 1969. Thanks to word of mouth, however, it caught fire and had a thirty-six-week run in theaters there, with audiences often rising and applauding at the end. It was immediately banned by the junta then ruling Greece (exiled opposition activists in London used it to raise money for their resistance to the colonels), by totalitarian regimes from Spain to Brazil, and by all communist countries. It would be 1975 before the Greek public could view it. When it opened there, it became one of the most popular and talked-about events since democracy had been restored six months earlier.[5]

French critics raved about what the weekly *L'Express* called "the first great French political film."[6] In the United States, not everyone knew quite what to make of it. For the *New York Times,* it was merely "an immensely entertaining movie—a topical melodrama that manipulates our emotional responses and appeals to our best prejudices in such satisfying ways that it is likely to be mistaken as a work of fine—rather than popular—movie art."[7] Roger Ebert had no such hesitation about its importance: "It is a film of our time. It is about how even moral victories are corrupted. It will make you weep and will make you angry. It will tear your guts out."[8] More recently, *The New Yorker* acclaimed it, saying, "*Z* may be the best political thriller ever made."[9] The critic David Thomson notes that "*Z* was a sensation in its day, a political thriller that seemed to combine authentic events, star players, and a restless mix of early Frankenheimer and cinéma verité . . . at that historical moment when filmmakers believed they were not just politicized but capable of affecting the outcome of events."[10]

Z won an impressive list of accolades, from two Oscars for Best Foreign Language Film and Best Film Editing to the Jury Prize at Cannes and Best Film for both the National Society of Film Critics and the New York Film Critics Circle. Its influence on American cinema was far-reaching. William Friedkin later said that he adopted his documentary-style realism in *The French Connection* (1971) as a result of seeing *Z*: "After I saw *Z,* I realized how I could shoot *The French Connection.* Because he [Costa-Gavras] shot *Z* like a documentary . . . it looks like he happened upon the scene and captured what was going on as you do in a documentary. My first films were documentaries too. So I understood what he was doing but I never thought you could do that in a feature at that time until I saw *Z.*"[11] Oliver Stone, too, felt the influence of *Z,* which he saw as a student in 1969. "It's the kind of film that hits you in the heart and head," he said in an interview with *Le Figaro* many years later. "When I filmed *JFK Revisited: Through the Looking Glass* (2021), I was thinking of *Z* and the way Costa-Gavras showed the assassination several times to analyze it better."[12]

Montand spent only a few days on the shoot in Algiers before returning to Paris to prepare his stage show. One of the unusual features of *Z* was that, although it was undoubtedly an important film, in it he made one of his shortest appearances—in a movie with two hours of running time, he is onscreen barely fifteen minutes and has minimal lines. To be sure, his presence and image pervade it, personifying as he does the film's hero. But the film really belongs to Costa-Gavras for his direction and tricky, film-school camerawork full of flashbacks and flash-forwards and to Jean-Louis Trintignant for his sober, understated playing of the determined magistrate. That acting earned Trintignant the Best Actor Award at Cannes in 1969, the only time he received a prize there.

This second film with Costa-Gavras helped cement Montand's relationship with him and underlined their common approach to filmmaking and political issues. Together they would be inventing the modern political thriller. The director particularly appreciated Montand's political commitment, which he sensed was genuine: "Montand is obsessed by politics because he's a passionate individual. Because he's sincere, just the opposite of those politicians who talk statistics, while he's speaking from the heart. For years he supported peace movements, criticized the wars in Indochina and Algeria, defended the Rosenbergs, condemned the totalitarian regimes in Chile and Spain. And the only public support he had in those days was [the communist newspaper] *L'humanité*."[13]

⊙ ⊙ ⊙

Montand was in Algiers for the shoot of *Z* when he learned that Soviet-led Warsaw Pact troops had invaded Czechoslovakia to end the liberal reforms known as "Socialism with a Human Face." The previous January the country's new first secretary of the Communist Party, Alexander Dubček, had eased censorship of the press and rehabilitated victims of the Stalin-era political purges. He followed those steps in April with sweeping reforms granting autonomy for Slovakia and a project for democratization of the government and a new constitution that would guarantee civil rights and liberties. Dubček tried to reassure Moscow and the Soviet Bloc that he could manage the move to more democracy, but once Czechs got a taste of freedom, they wanted more and sooner. The Kremlin viewed this movement as nothing less than a counterrevolution, so it ordered the invasion and occupation of Czechoslovakia on August 20, 1968, and appointed a puppet regime to oversee the curbing of the reforms. Dubček, lucky to escape with his life, ended up in the forestry service.

The news was a shock to Montand. He had already been struggling to keep some semblance of faith in the communist ideals he had absorbed from his father, but this occupation was too much. "I was knocked flat on my back.

Since 1956, [the invasion of] Hungary, and my visit to Eastern Europe, I had kept my distance [from the Communist Party], but I had stayed within the family circle. This was the last straw. I was disappointed, disgusted, nauseated. The Russian tanks in Prague were the coup de grâce, the end of the illusion that communism could be reformed. My reaction was instant, primal: I closed the communist chapter of my life."[14]

He said nothing publicly until he returned to Paris in September and was interviewed on a popular radio program. Then all his frustration and disappointment came pouring out. "Already there had been Budapest, which was difficult to swallow, but which I swallowed anyway when I went to Moscow. But the kick in the teeth last August without a word of explanation—never again! When things stink we have to say so. When people go on lying and killing and—what is even more disgusting—informing, then that damns a whole political system."[15]

The loss of faith is always wrenching. For Montand, this abandonment of political faith was made all the more painful by the fact that it meant a break with his physical family as well. He felt, first of all, that he was betraying his beloved father, Giovanni, whose political integrity and fidelity to the communist ideal he admired so much. But it was also to result in a rupture with his older brother, Julien, to whom he had always looked up and whom he esteemed for his staunch dedication to his work as a high official in the communist labor union, the CGT.

The break came to a head on the evening Montand gave his radio interview. Julien was informed while working at the union's headquarters that Montand had attacked communism in general and the head of the union in particular. He rushed to place Dauphine to confront Montand, furious. They had a shouting match and almost came to blows, Montand banging his fist on the dinner table so hard the dishes flew up and broke when they fell. He yelled so hard that he injured his vocal cords and couldn't speak, much less sing, for twenty-four hours. Julien stormed out and left for good the apartment they still shared. The brothers virtually never spoke again.[16]

This turbulent period in Montand's family life was made all the worse by the death of his father, Giovanni, a few weeks later at the age of seventy-six. Within a brief period, Montand lost or alienated the two men to whom he had been closest all his life. He did not attend Giovanni's funeral in Marseilles because of his contractual obligations to the Olympia during the show; that meant he would at least avoid the graveside altercations that surely would have occurred had he been there. His absence did, however, exacerbate the bad feeling within the family. "The break was terrible to live through," recalled his nephew, Jean-Louis Livi. "Everyone suffered. Everyone took it on the chin. Montand, Simone, my father, my mother, Catherine, and me."[17] Catherine Allégret said, "I saw terrible things done because of politics. They tore each other's guts out. Montand's hatred of Stalin was as violent as my uncle's primitive communism. There was no room for anything in between."[18]

The importance of the loss of his father can be measured by something his friend Jorge Semprún related to him. One day when they were discussing a project long after Giovanni's death, Montand mentioned to Semprún that he had consulted Giovanni about what to do. Incredulous, Semprún asked whether he meant that he actually had conversations with his dead father. "Yes, I sometimes talk with him," Montand replied. "I tell him about my doubts and describe my problems. Sometimes it's when I'm dreaming, but it can often happen when I'm awake. I talk to him often, and it helps me to sort things out." Conversations with the departed aside, Semprún speculated that Giovanni's death actually helped Montand in his break with communism, clearing the way for his apostasy by making unnecessary a confrontation with the redoubtable father figure.[19]

⊙ ⊙ ⊙

The family breakup and the aphonia that resulted from it came just as Montand was beginning his show at the Olympia music hall that September, his first recital since 1963—that evening all he could do was walk across the stage to the microphone and whisper his apologies to the 2,000 in the audience for being unable to sing.

Now that the Étoile was closed, the Olympia would be the venue of his increasingly rare Paris shows. Built in 1893, it had followed the familiar format of music halls, with the usual jugglers, acrobats, and mimes. La Goulue, Paris's star cancan dancer—and subject of Henri de Toulouse-Lautrec's famous Moulin Rouge poster—had performed there in the early twentieth century, as had the American Loie Fuller, who had made Paris her home. More recently, Louis Armstrong, Ella Fitzgerald, and Billie Holiday had starred at the Olympia, along with French singers such as Edith Piaf, Georges Brassens, and Juliette Greco.

For this show, Montand surprised his public by refusing to be topical, eschewing any numbers referring to either *les événements* that had rocked France only three months earlier or the Vietnam War. Not for him the

"Internationale" or the hymn to Che Guevara, "Hasta siempre, commandante," or any of the other political songs popular with Danny the Red and his cohorts of the day. It was a question of shunning everything facile, obvious, and opportunistic. Of being faithful to his own professional code of ethics. As he explained in an interview to the weekly magazine *L'Express* in mid-September 1968,

> My problem is to avoid falling into demagoguery or yielding to the temptation to be opportunistic. . . . I could have sung five songs about the revolution in May. No, it's too recent. That's opportunistic. I had prepared a song about Vietnam. I threw it out. Here, even De Gaulle is against that war. So what do I do? Take the easy way out and try to look like I'm courageously opposing it? Demagoguery. When Joan Baez takes a position, when she spends Christmas in jail, fine. It's her war, not ours. I think I showed courage enough when I sang "Quand un soldat" in the middle of our Indochina war. . . . My public has never been the masses as such. It's the educated masses. The professions, the bourgeois who live in Passy and Auteuil, the ones for whom I incarnate the metal worker with dirty hands and the pure heart. They either come to see me as I am or not. But attempting to be modern at all costs is to admit that you've grown old.[20]

Instead of trying to be topical, he seemed to enjoy mixing old favorites such as "Luna Park," "Les feuilles mortes," and even the thirty-year-old "Dans les plaines du Far West" with poetic new additions to his repertory. The latter included two difficult poems by the surrealist poet Paul Éluard. "L'amoureuse" (The Lover) describes a lover's surrealistic view of his lady love, who stands on his eyelids, whose hair mingles with his, and whose color is that of his eyes. In the other Éluard poem, "Je t'aime" (I Love You), the lover exclaims that he loves her for all the women he hasn't known and all the times he never lived, for the smell of the ocean and the odor of warm bread.

Montand's new political number was a poem by Nazim Hikmet, the Turkish novelist and playwright who spent years in prison for his support of revolutionary causes. Rather than singing it, Montand whispered into the microphone that if many are poor, oppressed, and tortured throughout the world, it's really because most people are apathetic and allow it to happen. As if to reward the audience for getting through such challenging material, he introduced "À bicyclette" (Cycling), a delightful new ditty about a group of childhood friends who go cycling with Paulette, whom they all are secretly in love with. As they roll through the fields, starting up clouds of grasshoppers and butterflies, the shy narrator vows that tomorrow he will try to take Paulette's hand. It became one of Montand's most popular songs and is still often heard and referred to in France.

Montand's style at the Olympia showed a new, more mature restraint, sculpting the air with his hands more rarely and only hinting at the occasional dance step. The critics noticed the different style. As *Le Monde* put it, "Yves Montand has changed. In the public mind, Montand was the proletarian, the political militant, the worker in a Renault factory, the truck driver behind the wheel. He had his union card, he read *L'huma-dimanche.* He had established a relationship between the elegant Étoile theater and the Maubert-Mutualité worker's hall, between [the working-class suburb] Saint Denis and Saint Germain des Prés. That character is finished. Instead of becoming bourgeois, the former worker has become more intellectual."[21]

After six standing-room-only weeks at the Olympia—a short run compared with his previous Paris recitals that usually lasted six months—he announced once again that he was going to stop doing his shows and concentrate on making movies. He was tired of going through the exhausting routine. Besides, he joked, "with the applause every evening I was starting to believe I was Yves Montand."[22] Except for a single benefit performance, he would not do another show for thirteen years.

18

The Other Political Films

Hardly had the curtain dropped on his last evening at the Olympia in October 1968 than Montand flew to Los Angeles to begin filming his fourth movie of the year—and the fifth and last American film of his career—*On a Clear Day You Can See Forever / Melinda* (US and France 1970) opposite Barbra Streisand. Directed by that master of the Hollywood musical comedy, Vincente Minnelli, it had a screenplay by the musical veteran Alan Jay Lerner, who adapted his own stage production of the same title from 1965.

This fantasy tale has Daisy Gamble (Streisand), a whimsical, twenty-two-year-old New Yorker who has extrasensory perception and can talk plants into growing more quickly, asking Marc Chabot, a practitioner of medical hypnotism, to help her break her nicotine addiction. When he hypnotizes her, she regresses to an incarnation of herself from early nineteenth-century England, Lady Melinda Winifred Waine Tentrees, a social-climbing adventuress at the court of the prince regent. Chabot begins to fall in love with the Melinda of the past and to believe in reincarnation. He finally breaks the spell when Daisy informs him that she has had fourteen previous lives and that she and he will be married in the year 2038.

Filmed in Minnelli's usual lush style, *On a Clear Day* was one of the last of the big-budget Hollywood musical comedies. It has some attractive musical numbers, such as Streisand's title song and "He Isn't You" and Montand's "Come Back to Me," sung incongruously atop New York's Pan Am Building. The picture is handicapped, however, by its complicated, convoluted plot and its reliance on weak one-liners ("Do you like painting?" "I don't know, I've gotten used to wallpaper."). It is also less than it could have been because it was cut by nearly an hour; Paramount had planned it as a three-hour roadshow theatrical release but decided belatedly that wouldn't work for the moviegoing public of 1970.

Furthermore, this was the first time Streisand was opposite a male lead who was himself a famous singer, which may have generated some tension between them, Streisand being accustomed to prima donna treatment. "Streisand's 'working relationship' with Montand was strained," her biographer Anne Edwards notes. "Seductive though he was, Streisand was not attracted to him."[1] (The feeling appears to have been mutual. When Paramount initially proposed the role to Montand, it offered $200,000. Not really attracted to the role and sensing that he would be typecast as a foil to Streisand, he countered by asking for $400,000, thinking he would be turned down. Paramount accepted, and he was in.)

Many of his numbers were deleted in the final cut, resulting in Streisand having twice as many as he did; Montand suspected that she had something to do with the cutting.[2] "When we commenced *On a Clear Day* I had the mistaken impression that I was the co-star," he said later. "I was Miss Streisand's first leading man who can sing, even though this was her third musical. I thought she was my leading lady, a partner."[3] The critics noticed this lopsided presentation. "It's apparently Montand's fate to be emasculated by big Hollywood actresses, and his role is largely that of a line-carrier for Streisand," said one.[4]

All in all, this film was another frustrating experience for the man who had dreamed of making it big in America. He now had done five films for Hollywood studios, and none had really amounted to the success hoped for. Even when the part had little romantic dimension, as in *Clear Day,* in the collective mind of the American moviegoing public and for the critics he was still the French Lover, the Gallic Charmer, not a first-rate actor in his own right. It was his own personal glass ceiling. He got the message and, not for the first time—he had said after *My Geisha* that he was fed up with Hollywood—declared his disappointment. "I doubt I shall ever choose to work again in Hollywood," he again said bitterly.[5]

This time he meant it. Montand would make twenty-three more films, but none of them was for a Hollywood studio. Altogether they form the usual actor's mix of potboilers, ego trips, and moneymakers, with the occasional genuine popular and critical success when the right man met the right script. It is beyond the scope of this book to examine them all; only the most significant are highlighted. A filmography is given at the end of the book.

⊙ ⊙ ⊙

During the 1970s, Montand would become not only the incarnation of the new political cinema but also, along with Jean-Paul Belmondo and Alain Delon, one of France's leading movie stars. He continued to take on a wide range of parts and to alternate seamlessly among genres, from tragedy to comedy, crime thriller to tales of star-crossed love, preferring to take risks than to become stereotyped. The only way he knew how to act was to *become* the character—a technique that would be especially evident in his political films. When he finished a movie, it took him several days to get out of character and back to being Yves Montand. "As I see it an actor doesn't act, he *is* the character," he once said. "To do that, he has to show his heart and soul, and be willing to let everyone criticize it. Every time I play a new part I have the same anxiety."[6]

That approach to acting explained in part his basic angst and why he often seemed unable to accept his own success. "What's fascinating about him is that he never really feels sure of himself on a movie set," observed the actor Bernard Blier, who did one film with Montand and was a member of the weekend clan at Autheuil. "I thought that a pro like him, with a career like his in theater, music hall and cinema, must arrive on the set full of self-assurance. But not at all. He still hesitates like a beginner, with the anxiety and insecurity of a beginner. Every morning of a shoot he concentrates on making it perfect."[7] Catherine Deneuve did two films with him and left this impression: "Montand is an uncomfortable man to work with because he is totally committed, into it to the hilt. And because he wants to direct or at least codirect. It isn't that he wants to control things, no. It's his one-man-show background: it gives him his own directorial vision. It's exhausting, and it's touching. . . . What astonished me was that Montand came to watch the rushes even on days he was not in them. . . . He's unique in his genre."[8]

Montand's commitment to authenticity was on view again in Jean-Pierre Melville's gangster film *Le circle rouge / The Red Circle* (1970, US 1993). The convoluted plot involves several mobsters played by Alain Delon, Bourvil, and Gian Maria Volonte, plus Montand as a former police sharpshooter who has quit the force and become a hopeless alcoholic. The gang draws up a detailed, foolproof plan to burglarize a famous Paris jeweler on place Vendome. They contact Montand's character, Jansen, to help neutralize the shop's security vault by shooting its lock out with pinpoint precision. He agrees only after going through a gruesome crisis of delirium tremens in which he imagines a grotesque tangle of nightmarish creatures come slithering and crawling out of his closet. It was unnecessary to show this hallucination in graphic detail, but Montand agreed for the sake of convincing realism to allow rats, serpents, lizards, and giant spiders—all live ones except for the mechanical spiders—to crawl all over him as he lay shivering and writhing in bed. This scene and the minutely detailed thirty-minute heist sequence in the night-time shop during which there is virtually no dialogue made the movie one of the top releases of the year in France and it became a cult movie for aficionados of the director's craft. It also cemented Montand's reputation as an actor willing to go the extra mile.

Of the many parts he played, the movies that most marked his career and meant the most to him were undoubtedly those that reflected the political convictions he had inherited from his father, intuited as a young man, and developed after he met Simone Signoret. The first of those films was *La guerre est finie* with Alain Resnais in 1965. Then there were *Z* and others, largely but not entirely thanks to his friendship and collaboration with Costa-Gavras and Jorge Semprún.

While Montand was still doing the *Clear Day* shoot, he received a telephone call in his bungalow at the Beverly Hills Hotel. Costa-Gavras and Semprún had just read a new book called *L'aveu* (*The Confession*) by the former Czech communist Artur London and decided immediately that they wanted to make a movie of it. They saw it as a way of showing graphically how Communist Party members could give up their own free will to the point of sacrificing themselves in the name of this new secular religion. The only actors they could imagine in the roles of London and his wife, Lise, were Montand and Signoret. After Montand heard Costa-Gavras's description of the real-life story of a faithful communist tragically caught in the web of a Stalinist purge, his reaction from Los Angeles was immediate: "If you and Jorge want to go ahead, count me in."[9] Of his politically themed films, this is the one in which he was most passionately involved, even at the risk of his own health.

Artur London had spent his life serving communism. As a young man from Czechoslovakia, he had joined the International Brigades organized by the Communist International, fighting with the Republicans in the Spanish Civil War of the 1930s. Then he joined the French communist Resistance against the Nazis until being captured and sent to the Mauthausen concentration camp. After the war, he returned to his native country, where he was rewarded for his loyal service to the party by being appointed undersecretary for foreign affairs in the communist government run by President Klement Gottwald.

Then in 1951 London was arrested on trumped-up charges of espionage as a Zionist agent. Thirteen other high officials, mostly Jewish, including the party general secretary, Rudolf Slánský, were also rounded up. The sweep was one of the last big Communist Party purges of the Stalinist era. In the case of Czechoslovakia, it appeared designed to blame scapegoats for the failure of Soviet-style communism, which clearly was not producing a standard of living comparable with that of the West. During what became known as the Slánský trial, all the officials arrested were tortured psychologically and physically until they confessed to crimes they had not committed; all but three, including London, were then hanged. He was given a life sentence, which he served until he was freed in 1956 following Nikita Khrushchev's de-Stalinization program. He and his wife, Lise, who had denounced her husband—so strong was her belief that the party was always right—went to live in exile in France, where together they wrote the book describing their ordeal, publishing it in 1968.

Both Montand and Signoret had doubts about taking the parts. During this period, they opposed America's war in Vietnam and its alleged support of dictatorships in Latin America. Might their participation in a film critical of a communist regime be interpreted as support for the "capitalist imperialists"? That was always the fallback argument of communist parties around the world: if you openly criticize us, you help the enemy. Montand no longer considered himself an ardent fellow traveler, but a residue of his old reflexes remained. Signoret's hesitation was more complicated. In addition to her reluctance to criticize communism directly, she couldn't imagine herself denouncing her husband under any circumstances. Finally, however, she overcame her misgivings and accepted the part, largely because Montand was so determined to assert the truth as he saw it. As he explained his state of mind at the time in an interview with the *New York Times*,

> The decision to make *The Confession* was a terrible one for Simone and me, because personally I would have preferred not to have done it. . . . But it was a film that had to be made. I can't go on voicing leftist, progressive—call them what you will—ideas and yet remain silent in the face of the flagrant, ignoble things that took place in Czechoslovakia as described by Artur London. . . . London's book is a very important document, but pictures are more powerful than words. The spectator gets to really feel all the humiliation, degradation, and destruction of a fellow human being. This picture forces the spectator to think—good or bad—but it makes him think.[10]

Costa-Gavras wanted to shoot on location in Prague, but in the summer of 1969 the totalitarian regime again began cracking down, so filming there was out of the question. After scouting other locations, he found that buildings in the old quarter of Lille in France resembled those in Prague. An abandoned hospice there could serve for the exterior and interior shots, in particular its gloomy underground cellars that resembled prison cells. The tribunal setting was created in a Paris studio. The quest for authenticity was aided by filmed records of the trial that Costa-Gavras obtained from a source in Prague, showing the décor of the courtroom and the exact places where judges and the accused sat, as well as by sound recordings of the proceedings.

Montand's own passionate search for authenticity during the eight-week shoot included fasting and going on approximately the same minimal prison diet that London had eaten, leading to a loss of nearly twenty-five pounds. He shunned staying in the hotel suite reserved for him and Simone, instead taking a small room where he slept on the floor and covered the windows with black cloth to block any light, as London had lived for months. He stopped washing and shaving, wore handcuffs that bruised his wrists, insisted that the actors playing his jailers throw him roughly against the cell's brick walls. In the scene where water is thrown on him to revive the unconscious prisoner, he asked that it be cold—that scene required twenty-one takes. At night, he woke up the cast and crew at the hotel with screaming nightmares. He had become Artur London so vividly that viewing the film was for many a painful experience. "He was completely sunk in his character," Costa-Gavras said later. "He lived it. He suffered night and day. I believe it's the furthest an actor has ever ventured into his part. I believe he must have dug deep within and come up with very personal issues to feed on."[11]

Montand agreed that doing the role that way was necessary for his own development, forming part of his long goodbye to the cause he had supported so sincerely:

> It was easy to get into that part. It came along at the right time, at a time when I wanted to tell subsequent generations how insane we had been. For me, *The Confession* was my farewell to the generous sentimentality of the left—a left that had been blind to its own crimes and had cultivated a Messianic pose, proposing to bring happiness to human beings even if it meant slaughtering them. Since I, too, had believed in it, there was naturally an element of penance in what I was doing. An internal cleansing. Through physical suffering.[12]

Jorge Semprún agreed that for Montand *L'aveu / The Confession* (France and US 1970) was much more than just another role. It was a very personal act of expiation. "He literally paid with his own person," Semprún believed. "He paid heavily, deliberately, for past ignorance, for blind faith, for his bad conscience, for repeating the standard stock phrases. . . . But he paid for all of us as well. He paid our debts and set us free. He purchased a new life for us with his passion as an actor. Rarely has an actor been so deeply engaged in this century's real stakes of human destiny."[13]

The Confession won the National Board of Review award as Best Foreign Film and was nominated for a BAFTA and a Golden Globe—even despite its long, repetitive sequences with flashbacks and flash-forwards in which London/Montand is thrown in his cell, taken from his cell for interrogation, and thrown back in his cell time and again. Such scenes made the film hard slogging for most American audiences, so it was seen mainly by those particularly interested in the era's ideological conflicts and in international affairs. Nonetheless, it was, the *New York Times* said, "a harrowing film of intellectual and emotional anguish, dramatized by the breathless devices of melodrama . . . much more complex, much more human. . . vastly more interesting than *Z*."[14] In France, it was in fact more popular and rated a respectable ninth in box office receipts in 1970. Montand's acting was unanimously saluted in the press, while the director Jean-Pierre Melville paid Montand a unique professional compliment: "Last year with *Z*, you brought glory to our profession; this year you bring honor."[15]

The movie became a political event in its own right when it opened on the Champs-Élysées in December 1970. The French Communist Party was painted into a corner, hating the film for its searing exposé of ruthless totalitarian methods but unable to refute London's detailed chronicle. It was all the more perturbed by the fact that the film's principal actors, Montand and Signoret, had long been party sympathizers and darlings of the French Left; they could hardly be accused of being capitalist stooges. The best the party newspaper, *L'humanité,* could do was claim that the film version of the book ignored the historical context and exaggerated its depiction of repression under a communist regime. Costa-Gavras, it said, had turned a "communist book into an anti-communist film."[16]

Prague's communist rulers immediately banned not only the film but also Montand's songs. Other Eastern Bloc countries followed suit, except the maverick Yugoslavia. It would be twenty years before *The Confession* was shown in Czechoslovakia, only after the Berlin Wall fell. Montand was invited to Prague in February 1990 to present the Jan Palach Prize, named for the twenty-year-old student who had immolated himself in the city's main square in January 1969 to protest the invasion by Warsaw Pact troops the previous August. The writer and anticommunist activist Václav Havel, elected the country's president in December 1989, gave Montand a hero's welcome and seized the opportunity of his visit to schedule a screening of the film. Besides Montand, also present were Costa-Gavras, Semprún, and Lise London.[17]

In June 1990, the scene was repeated in Moscow when the picture's makers were invited to attend a public showing of it. Following that, Mikhail Gorbachev decided that he wanted it to be seen by the newly elected members of the Congress of People's Deputies of the Russian Soviet Federative Socialist Republic. He had the assembly room in the Grand Kremlin Palace transformed into a movie theater for the occasion. Montand, who had said he would believe in democratization in Russia when the government allowed *The Confession* to be shown in Moscow, had every reason to be pleased.

In France, however, the blowback from the film was absorbed into the Livi family quarrel. Montand's alienated brother, Julien, who had a career devoted to the party and for whom it was still infallible, wrote an indignant letter to Costa-Gavras in which he roundly condemned both the director and Montand for the film's treatment of communism: "Basically this film could only be, one, an attack on the ideas of Communism in general and the Soviet Union in particular; and two, and most important, a good-conduct medal awarded to capital, to the old society, for the numberless crimes committed since time immemorial against those it crushes and exploits, foremost among them the Communists. It is plain as day that both the story and dialogue are designed to deal the heaviest possible blow against the Communists and their past and present struggles."[18]

Artur London had only praise for Montand's attitude at the time. "He remained constantly courageous and dignified," he said. "That was all the more difficult because the attacks came from the Left, which had always been his political home. He suffered a great deal during this period, especially due to his brother's criticism."[19]

⊙ ⊙ ⊙

Montand had distanced himself from the hotheads of France's *evenéments* of May–June 1968, but his next political film four years later was inspired by them. *Tout va bien* (1972, also known as *All's Well*) was Jean-Luc Godard's partly satirical, partly serious, but ultimately ambiguous look at French society following that brief spring psychodrama and at the subsequent swift deflation of hopes that suddenly everything would be better in a brave new Marxist world.

Montand played a burned-out filmmaker who had turned to making TV commercials he despised. He was opposite Jane Fonda—the same who had been turned on to political activism by Montand and Signoret in Paris in 1963—in the role of a conflicted American radio journalist based in Paris. Godard admitted frankly that he had offered the parts to the two of them because big-name actors helped him get the necessary financing to promulgate his political ideas. He also cast them in parts very close to the militant political roles they were identified with in real life.[20]

Montand had wanted to work with Godard for some time. When he saw the screenplay's political line attempting to sum up post-1968 France, he accepted the part immediately and agreed to do it simply for a share of the profits, without his usual fee upfront. Fonda, however, was reluctant and took considerable persuading. As she later recounted, it was "a movie I didn't want to make. I [i.e., her character] was homeless, structureless, loveless, and bulimic." Godard had offered her the role the previous summer. She agreed without reading the script because of his reputation as a political filmmaker. "But when I received the script, I found it incomprehensible," she said. "It read like one long polemic. Godard, I learned, was a Maoist." When she tried to back out, Godard asked his associate, Jean-Pierre Gorin, a radical leftist disciple of Marxist/structuralist philosophers such as Jacques Lacan, Michel Foucault, and Louis Althusser, to talk to her. Gorin, who served as Godard's political *maître à penser* at the time and coauthored the screenplay for *Tout va bien* with him, sought her out in the ski resort of Megève, where she was staying with her husband, Roger Vadim. She claimed that Gorin threatened her with bodily harm if she didn't do the film. She accepted but dissociated herself from the project as far as possible while honoring her contract.[21]

Godard had burst on the cinema world as a twenty-nine-year-old wunderkind of the New Wave with *À bout de souffle / Breathless* (1960, US 1961). He went into an antibourgeois funk after 1968 and refused to do anything that could be considered capitalist or commercial—or attract audiences. He was heavily influenced by Gorin's doctrinaire Marxism/Maoism. Together they wrote the screenplay for *Tout va bien* as an attempt, as Godard typically put it, to make political films politically.[22] It would be a different kind of *Love Story,* one that explained a couple's relational difficulties in terms of the class struggle, their feelings fluctuating as a function of each one's analysis of a factory strike. *Tout va bien* was billed as "the story of the crisis of a couple in a society in crisis, France in 1972."

The film is set, as a voice-over explains at the beginning, in a world where "farmers are farming, workers are working, and bourgeois are bourgeoising." Suzanne (Fonda), a.k.a. "Her," accompanied by her live-in partner, Jacques (Montand), a.k.a. "Him," go to a sausage factory on strike to interview the manager. As often happened during the events of May–June 1968, the workers sequester the manager in his office and the couple with him. The Maoists go on a rampage, destroying personnel files, defacing the offices, and comically arguing among themselves. Everyone—manager, workers, the couple—has the chance to explain their position in long, often caricatural, monologues addressed directly to the camera. Using jump cuts, Godard shows Montand and Fonda, outfitted in workers' coveralls, making sausages alongside the others before they go on strike. He then cuts to Jacques explaining at length why he left filmmaking to do commercials, and Suzanne similarly explaining why she is unhappy as a journalist who can't interest her editors in the stories she considers important. At the end, they wander off as the voice-over tells us they are rethinking themselves in terms of history as part of their self-discovery.

The shoot got off to a bad start. Shortly before it began, Godard was seriously injured while riding on the back of a motorcycle in Paris when a bus turned and caught him under a front wheel. With a broken pelvis and fractured skull, he was unconscious for six days and had to undergo treatment for the next two and a half years. Whether that accident affected his mood is an imponderable, but relations on the set between him and his two stars quickly degenerated into hostility. As Montand explained, "During the preparations for the film Jane and I had very cordial relations with Godard. But that good relationship ended as soon as we began the shoot. Suddenly there was a really dictatorial atmosphere, almost as if we were being punished, a contemptuous attitude toward us as actors. Jane and I worked for two weeks practically without a script, without knowing what we were supposed to be doing."[23]

It was as if Godard, having secured the participation of two big-name stars, despised them for having succeeded thanks to the capitalist system that he detested. Another problem were the briefings by Gorin, who tried to put them in context by explaining France's socioeconomic situation according to his doctrinaire Marxist ideology. That grandiose blather was incomprehensible to the two actors, but they just kept quiet and let him talk. Fonda kept her distance during the filming as well as she could. "I kept my head down," she said later, "staying under the radar, showing up on time, and keeping to myself on the set to avert outright hostility between Godard and me."[24]

Montand didn't like the finished picture, which he thought was simplistic and dismissive in its portrayal of France's very real social upheaval in 1968. It was a commercial disaster, the public finding it a pretentious bore. His former communist comrades and the CGT were furious, singling him out for blame for agreeing to participate in the film. A letter addressed to him and probably written by his brother, Julien, said in part, "You accepted to smear an organization and its militants who, unlike you, remain faithful to their class and their origins. Feel free to join the other side and try to do harm to those who have not changed, we know who is on our side."[25] He brushed off that condemnation as part of the price he was paying for his new independence. Despite his disappointment with the picture in general, however, he was glad to have been able to work with Godard and was ready to do so again if they could find the right working relationship.

⊙ ⊙ ⊙

Before doing his next political film, Montand took time out for a romantic drama that some consider one of his best roles. *César et Rosalie* (France and US 1972) is the sort of ménage à trois that the French do so well with a light, amoral touch. It has Montand playing César, a vulgar, voluble scrap-iron merchant who loves Rosalie (Romy Schneider), but she is torn between him and the artistic David (Sami Frey). It was directed by Claude Sautet, who trained as a painter and sculptor before enrolling at the French cinema school IDHEC and becoming one of France's premier directors.

Sautet had recently done the very successful romantic drama *Les choses de la vie / The Things of Life* (France and US 1970), with Michel Piccoli and Romy Schneider. He had done the screenplay for *César et Rosalie* eight years earlier with Jean-Loup Dabadie, a prolific writer and member of the Académie française. After the Italian actor Vittorio Gassman turned down the role of César, the script was ignored until Sautet fortuitously noticed Montand one evening at a film screening. Struck by something vulnerable and elemental in Montand's lined face, he proposed the part to him. Montand, sensing a complicity between the two of them, accepted immediately.

César et Rosalie, like *Les choses de la vie,* explores the tormented love lives of its three protagonists in their hesitation waltz toward and away from each other, depending on how they are feeling that day. Rosalie is living with César but gets back together with David, an old flame, when he returns from a long stay in America. The socially awkward, good-hearted César, broadly played by Montand with a Marseilles accent, is explosively jealous at first, alternately violent with both Rosalie and David, then penitent and cajoling as he tries to reconcile the sentimental equation. The film ends with a cliché of the typical French ménage à trois, the two men becoming friends as the independent-minded Rosalie leaves both.

Sautet was able to bring out Montand's temperament as no other director had before. In effect, he was simply letting Montand be Montand, full of volatile verve, by turns boastful, pitiful, cunning, inept, touching, and exasperating. Montand himself said that César was the character that most resembled him, and those who knew him best agreed. "It was what he was like in real life," his late-life partner and mother of his only child, Carole Amiel, said. "He could be at once tender and funny, marked by a certain naivete and even childlike, irritating and at the same time prone to terrible temper tantrums."[26] His nephew Jean-Louis Livi, who was also his agent for many years, concluded, "Montand is all there, with his bad faith, his bad temper, his tenderness and generosity. It's a classic."[27] The Academy of Italian Cinema—the film was a Franco-Italian production—awarded Montand its coveted David di Donatello Prize as Best Foreign Actor, putting him in the company of other recipients such as Laurence Olivier, Burt Lancaster, and Spencer Tracy.

⊙ ⊙ ⊙

Costa-Gavras was reading a newspaper in August 1970 when a brief item caught his eye. It was about an official at the US embassy in Montevideo, Uruguay, Daniel Anthony Mitrione, who had been executed by members of the Tupamaro urban guerilla group. The story said he was an American policeman, but a later edition referred to him as a diplomat. Costa-Gavras's curiosity was piqued. Which was he? Could Mitrione have been both? And why was he killed by the guerrillas when they had freed fifteen others they had kidnapped?

Costa-Gavras and the Italian journalist and screenwriter Franco Solinas, who had done the scripts for Gillo Pontecorvo's two films about anticolonial rebellions, *La battaglia di Algeri / The Battle of Algiers* (1966, US 1967) and *Queimada / Burn!* (1969), made a two-month trip to Latin America to get answers. They gathered documentation and interviewed police officials, politicians, journalists, eyewitnesses, and members of the Tupamaros National Liberation Movement. They followed up with further research in South America; Washington, DC; and even remote Richmond, Indiana, where Mitrione had been chief of police before joining the US government.[28]

The more they learned, the more they were convinced that they wanted to make a film about the incident. It would form part of a political trilogy: in *Z*, Costa-Gavras had taken on the military dictatorship in his native Greece; in *The Confession*, he showed up Soviet communism's vicious violation of human rights to retain power; and now he intended to expose US support of Latin American dictatorships. Moreover, Costa-Gavras had a personal interest in the subject: his wife, Michèle, had been kidnapped by revolutionaries and held for three days while covering the Uruguayan elections in 1971. Though set in an unnamed Latin American country and with individuals' names changed, Solinas's script used Costa-Gavras's usual investigative documentary style and closely followed what they had learned in their search for answers to what had happened to Mitrione. (Jorge Semprún, busy writing a book, was not available to work on the screenplay.)

Mitrione, an official in the Office of Public Safety of the United States Agency for International Development, had been assigned to the embassy in Montevideo after serving in Brazil and the Dominican Republic. As in his previous assignments, his official job was to work with the local police as an adviser on traffic and communications. The Tupamaros, however, had learned that his real mandate, under the cover of US development aid, was to train the police in counterinsurgency techniques using systematic repression and torture, as he had done in his two previous Latin American posts. President Jorge Pacheco Areco of Uruguay had imposed emergency measures—a virtual state of siege—beginning in 1968 to try to deal with Tupamaro kidnappings and raids like the one in which they attacked a quarry explosives depot and took a load of dynamite and detonators. The situation came to a head when the rebels kidnapped Mitrione in August 1970, along with an American agronomist and the Brazilian consul. As ransom, they demanded that a five-page Tupamaro manifesto be published in six specified newspapers and on radio and television and that 150 political prisoners be released. When the Uruguayan government, backed by Washington, refused to yield to their demands, the rebels put two bullets in Mitrione's head.[29]

To be authentic, the film had to be shot in South America, but Uruguay was out of the question. Chile, under the socialist government of President Salvador Allende, seemed the best candidate. Costa-Gavras had not reckoned, however, with the reaction of the Chilean Communist Party. It had already protested against the showing of *The Confession* in 1971. Perversely, it now saw the proposed film as favorable to the CIA and Mitrione, a propaganda vehicle for the anticommunist stance of the Nixon administration. When Costa-Gavras, Montand, and the film crew arrived in Santiago in April 1972, the party ordered those Chilean actors who were card-carrying members to go on strike.

Costa-Gavras threatened to take the shoot to Mexico. Before that, however, he worked his local contacts to get him and Montand invited to dinner at La Moneda, the presidential palace. Allende welcomed them cordially. He had read the script, was proud the shoot would be in Chile, and told Montand how much he loved his songs.[30] With the president's support, filming could proceed normally, including participation by the army for certain scenes and access to the National Congress Building for a day of filming.

État de siège / State of Siege (France and US 1973) is not a suspense thriller. The first time we see Philip Michael Santore/Mitrione (Montand), he is lying dead in the back of a car, so we already know that he's not going to get out alive. Using flashbacks and newsreel footage, Costa-Gavras produces an almost documentary look at US advisers' covert activities, their hand-in-glove work with authoritarian governments to prevent leftist/communist takeovers that would produce a regime less friendly to Washington. In an unusual twist, Montand plays not the film's hero, but its villain, and the character he creates is the opposite of what might be expected.

His Santore is not a ruthlessly wicked henchman but a normal family man with nine children, a patriot who sincerely believes he is serving his country. "As he often did, Montand surprised me by the way he completely metamorphosed into the character of Santore," Costa-Gavras noted. "He had the haircut, the suit, the way of moving of an American official. It was an impressive change."[31] He got into the part so thoroughly that he warned the crew he would be unpleasant to deal with, and, indeed, during the shoot he was brusque, cutting, and generally hard to get along with. As he explained his approach to the part, "I'm a poker player, so I found it exciting to play a character on the other side. . . . He was a good father, a perfectly honest guy convinced he was doing the right thing. I think that by approaching the character from that angle, and not by making him obviously a villain, that the film helps the audience draw their own conclusions, to seek to understand why and how such a thing could happen."[32]

Although the film treats Santore/Mitrione fairly as an individual, Costa-Gavras makes little effort to be objective about the Tupamaros. They get much of the screen time and are portrayed as generally idealistic, attractive young activists sincerely motivated by their political ideology. If they resort to violence, the film seems to imply, it is the fault of the government and its callous, careerist American puppets and the sadists who assiduously carry out their orders to torture. But he avoids appearing to support violence and assassination as the key to regime change. At film's end, Santore's coffin is being shipped back to the United States, and on another plane his replacement is seen arriving. Nothing has really changed. Killing him has served no operational purpose.

State of Siege generated the predictable controversy when released, particularly in Washington. The State Department denounced it as anti-American propaganda and denied its claim that US advisers trained Latin American police in repression and torture tactics.[33] The American Film Institute boldly scheduled it for the opening of its new theater at the Kennedy Center for the Performing Arts in April 1973 as part of a retrospective of several prominent directors' films. The showing was canceled at the last minute, however, by officials fearful that the subject was too incendiary. As a result, twelve filmmakers, including François Truffaut, Franco Zeffirelli, and Michael Anderson, withdrew their works from the festival in protest. The cancellation was condemned for its "foolishness . . . which suggests incompetence on the part of the institute, if not censorship."[34] Theodore Sorensen, a former adviser and speechwriter for President Kennedy, had the last word: "Costa-Gavras's *State of Siege* is a provocative, disturbing film that will shake most viewers out of their slumbering indifference to Latin America and make them think. For that reason alone, it is worth seeing."[35]

19

From Music Hall to the Met

Barely eighteen months after welcoming Costa-Gavras and Montand to the presidential palace in Santiago and agreeing to support the *State of Siege* shoot, Salvador Allende was dead by his own hand. Elected president in November 1970, he had quickly implemented a radical socialist restructuring of Chile's economy. He expropriated without compensation copper mines owned by US companies, froze prices of consumer goods, raised workers' wages, nationalized basic industries, and printed money lavishly to pay for it all. Soon the Chilean economy was a shambles, with production, exports, and private-sector investment all down. Workers protesting food shortages and rising inflation hit the country with nationwide strikes.

On September 11, 1973, General Augusto Pinochet, whom Allende had appointed commander in chief of the army only days earlier, led a military coup d'état. The air force bombed La Moneda palace, the army rounded up hundreds of civilians and imprisoned them in the national stadium, and Allende chose to commit suicide rather than be taken prisoner by the military junta now headed by Pinochet. In the first three years of Pinochet's sixteen-year dictatorship, some 130,000 people were arrested, and many were tortured.[1]

The coup was a painful disillusionment for many in France. Chile had appeared to the French Left as proof that a country could, after all, implement radical socialist policies while remaining democratic and shunning Stalinist totalitarianism. So closely was the French socialist-communist union of 1972 aligned with that experiment that its program copied word for word certain points of the Chilean Popular Party's election platform of 1969. As news of the military takeover sank in, anti-Pinochet demonstrations began to rage through the streets of Paris, while the major French newspapers inveighed against the coup. As sympathy for Chilean political refugees welled up, France welcomed nearly 10,000 of them.

In January 1974, Montand made a snap decision to do a benefit performance at the Olympia music hall with proceeds going to the Chilean refugee relief fund. He hadn't done a show for six years and didn't expect to do one anytime soon. With the concert date set for February 12, he had only a short time to prepare. He went to the country house in Autheuil with Bob Castella and members of the orchestra to begin a regimen of jogging, exercise, and stretching at the barre in the mornings, rehearsing his program in the afternoon.

In a surprising move, he gave the French documentary maker Chris Marker carte blanche to film in detail both his preparations at Autheuil and then his recital on the Olympia stage. The resulting hour-long documentary, *La solitude du chanteur de fond* (The Loneliness of the Long-Distance Singer, 1974), gives a unique look at Montand's meticulous, disciplined preparation for a show. We see him relentlessly questioning the best way to deliver a number even though he has sung it for years, occasionally exploding at the orchestra when he thinks they get a detail wrong.

There wasn't time to create new songs. He sang the old favorites: "Le temps des cerises," "Quand un soldat," "À Paris," "Mon frère," "Les grands boulevards," among others, and the benefit audience loved it. He concluded with the wartime Resistance anthem "Le chant des partisans," the first time he had ever sung it onstage. As he did it softly with minimal musical accompaniment, the following spot picking out only his face, a tight closeup by Chris Marker caught a tear running down his cheek—involuntarily revealing the feeling he had for Chile and its dead leader he had so admired only months earlier. The end of Marker's film has a voice-over of Montand explaining why he did the exceptional performance: "I'm not a philosopher or a politician, but I live in the real world with my feet on ground. The injustice and pain of this world resonate in me as it does in you. Maybe I'm just an entertainer, but I'm aware of what's happening in the world around us. There are thousands of Chilean refugees near you who seek a little bread and human warmth. I'm singing today so we won't forget the blood shed yesterday, so we can remain united and aware of the danger, so that blood won't be ours tomorrow."[2]

The statement typified Montand's turn to greater human rights activism in the 1970s and 1980s, going beyond the mainly French political controversies that had occupied him heretofore. Now he began condemning all forms of repression throughout the world, whether by the Right or by the Left. To be sure, he still had accounts to settle with French communists over what he considered their culpable hypocrisy in denying the brutal repression under Soviet-style communism. Reading Aleksandr Solzhenitsyn's *The Gulag Archipelago* in 1974 only confirmed his conviction that communism as it was being practiced was rotten at the core. When he spoke out, he struck hard. There was, for example, his interview on a French radio station in December 1976:

> It's especially hard for me to hear men of my generation, particularly those who headed the Party, say that they didn't know. I don't understand the attitude which consists of perpetuating an inadmissible lie. When they try to make me believe that the kind of things we saw yesterday are simply past history that we now condemn, and today everything will be different, I'm sorry but I'm not at all satisfied with that. Today in Czechoslovakia there is still institutionalized informing on neighbors, and psychiatric hospitals where hundreds of people are incarcerated and perfectly healthy human beings are reduced to eating their own excrement.[3]

Declarations like that outraged his brother, Julien, and some of his former fellow travelers, but he was in no mood to be conciliatory. "Someone had to take a stand, so I did," he wrote in an angry letter to Julien—the brothers now communicated only in writing—days later. "And I took a stand against you, my family and friends, and I've taken it for the last 20 years! And for the last 20 years I, along with many others, have committed the crime of being right before it was time."[4] This stand was another nail in the coffin of Livi family relations, but it seemed to liberate Montand once and for all.

He now went so far as to suggest that maybe the United States wasn't guilty of all the world's ills, which sounded radically new in the France of the 1970s, where much of the population was still in thrall to Marxism and communist propaganda. He dared call for more common sense and less ideology. In interviews, he said the French should stop dreaming that they were a great independent nation and admit that there were many things they couldn't do without help from the United States. If the United States seemed to bear responsibility for the well-being of western Europe, it hadn't asked for the role. It was the Europeans who had exhausted themselves with their wars.[5] From there, it was only a step to declaring that he was revolted by those who said capitalism was moribund. All you had to do, he said, was look around at the dynamism of countries he visited on tour, such as the United States,

Japan, and West Germany. *L'humanité* suggested in its editorials that France forbid American-made Boeing airliners to land at French airports? He retorted that the communist paper was treating its readers like imbeciles, given that Air France itself flew mainly Boeings.[6]

When one of the Cold War's worst crises erupted in the late 1970s, he knew which side he was on, unlike many others in western Europe who were confused by partisan claims and counterclaims. The Soviet Union ignited the crisis in 1976 by deploying a new medium-range missile, the SS-20. With a range of 5,000 kilometers, or about 3,000 miles, it could hit any target in western Europe from launch sites in the Soviet Union. Highly accurate and capable of being moved around on mobile launchers to escape detection, the SS-20 suddenly gave Moscow the upper hand in offensive firepower. The West had nothing comparable.

European leaders called on Washington to do something. In response, President Ronald Reagan ordered deployment in West Germany, Britain, Holland, Belgium, and Italy of a new intermediate-range missile, the Pershing II, and ground-launched cruise missiles, both capable of striking the Soviet Union within minutes. This decision caused a furor among antinuclear protest groups, who adopted the slogan "Better red than dead."[7] Montand, exercising the common sense he had called for earlier, asked, "Why didn't the pacifists demonstrate when the Soviets deployed their SS-20s? Better red than dead? No! Neither red nor dead! Free!"[8]

Whenever and wherever Montand saw human rights in danger during this period, he mounted the bully pulpit that his fame and popularity accorded him. Often accompanied by Simone Signoret, he spoke out, demonstrated, signed petitions endlessly. The Franco regime in Spain was a particular bête noire. He had vowed never to set foot in that country as long as Franco was in power. But in 1975 several young men accused of plotting against the regime were sentenced to death. As soon as Montand heard of the case, he headed to Madrid. He took along Costa-Gavras, the philosophers Régis Debray and Michel Foucault, and a few other human rights activists. They were armed with a petition supporting the condemned men and signed by such prominent figures as André Malraux, Jean-Paul Sartre, Louis Aragon, and the former French prime minister Pierre Mendès-France. When they arrived, Montand began a public reading of the text before a crowd in a main square in the capital, but the police forcibly broke up the demonstration and expulsed the group from the country; the young Spanish men were executed.

Other causes espoused by Montand and Signoret during these years included the plight of political dissidents being hunted down, kidnapped, or killed during the so-called Dirty War waged by Argentina's military junta from 1976 to 1983; the protests against Moscow's aggression in Afghanistan and its harassment of the human rights activist and Nobel Peace Prize winner Andrey Sakharov; the campaign to welcome the Vietnamese boat people fleeing the communist takeover of the country; and the founding, along with Graham Greene and Arthur Miller, of the International Support Committee for the signers of Charter 77, which called on the communist regime in Czechoslovakia to respect the 1975 Helsinki Accords on human rights. His engagement was active, not just sound bites in front of television cameras and signing petitions. Sometimes it meant on-the-spot support for causes Montand strongly believed in.

When Pinochet sought an additional eight-year term as president of Chile in a plebiscite in 1988, Montand flew to Santiago to join the democratic opposition in calling for a "no" vote. During a three-day visit, he consulted with human rights groups, met Salvador Allende's widow, and walked in the March of Hope with 500,000 Chilean opposition activists. Later that year he went to Israel at the invitation of Prime Minister Shimon Peres to promote the peace project of opening a road to Jordan through Aqaba and was invited to participate in the celebration of the country's fortieth anniversary. Months later he was in Warsaw to support the Solidarnosc (Solidarity) campaign against the Communist Party in the country's first elections since the 1940s; there, he met Lech Wałęsa, whose Solidarnosc independent trade union he had long championed, visited the grave of the murdered opposition leader Father Jerzy Popieluszko, and delivered a speech to university students. "You must force the authorities not to step back from this," he told them. "What is happening in Poland is a springtime that could turn into summer."[9]

⊙ ⊙ ⊙

After concentrating on films for years, Montand decided in 1980 to return to singing. As he recounted to his friend Jorge Semprún, he made the decision almost accidentally while spending a weekend at Autheuil. Semprún wrote later, "He said he was alone, walking through the house, when he opened a closet, saw a top hat and took it out. Just playing around, he put it on and suddenly caught a glimpse of himself like that in a mirror. Instinctively he tried out a few dance steps, some hand gestures, and finished with a sweeping bow with the hat. When he straightened up his heart was beating with excitement. At that moment he decided to go back on stage, with all the work that implied."[10]

To start with, he did his first album in fifteen years as a trial balloon to get the public's reaction. *Montand d'hier et d'aujourd'hui* (Montand Yesterday and Today) had fourteen songs. They included his version of the old First World War popular number "Roses of Picardy," which he revised as "Dansons la rose" and dedicated to Signoret, and the powerfully anti-Soviet "Le mégot" (The Cigarette Butt), about a political prisoner in the infamous Kolyma Siberian gulag camp, "a white hell." The prisoner comes across a windblown butt from a nearby town with a trace of lipstick, and, before he is beaten again, he dreams of the women he has known. The album sold more than a million copies.

In March 1981, Montand made his announcement during a television interview. His hour-and-a-half show would be in Paris at the Olympia beginning in October and comprise a mix of old and new numbers. He wanted to avoid nostalgia and show a younger audience a new Montand. The risk he was taking, gratuitously, was enormous. Instead of resting on his laurels as France's uncontested star of music hall entertainment, he was putting his title on the line at the age of sixty. In terms of reputation, he had nothing to gain. As one Paris paper put it, "In undertaking this adventure, Montand has everything to lose. If he gets it wrong or even just disappoints, he risks tarnishing forever the marvelous Montand myth that, without this act of pure panache, could have gone on forever."[11]

He was aware of the risk and also of the work and nervous stress that going back on the Olympia stage meant. He revealed his own doubts about the wisdom of trying to do such a thing in an interview with a Belgian journalist. "What an idea, going back to the Olympia!" he said, as if to himself. "Why am I going to take on all those worries, all those problems, all that work, when I don't even have ten years to live? But, merde, I want it!"[12] Montand had developed mild heart trouble but otherwise had no serious health problems. Was he going purely by the insurance companies' actuarial tables? Or did he have a premonition? In any case, the Olympia show and the marathon national and international tour that followed—including a surprise invitation to New York's most prestigious musical institution—would unintentionally constitute Montand's spectacular farewell to the stage.

Immediately after his announcement, lines began forming at the Olympia's box office, some fans arriving as early as 5:00 a.m., armed with folding chairs as the waiting line snaked down boulevard des Capucines for a hundred yards. On the first day, the theater's switchboard shorted out under the tsunami of calls. Women dropped everything and queued up in house slippers and curlers—despite French women's notorious abhorrence of appearing like that in public.

Travel agencies organized charters from the United States and Japan. Sacksful of letters requesting tickets were returned unopened; hundreds of blank checks were addressed directly to Montand's place Dauphine address by those willing to pay anything. Scalpers made a fortune. The whole bizarre phenomenon was, as one magazine put it, "abnormal, passionate, irrational . . . Montand madness."[13] It was also, perhaps, simply due to the feeling among many, especially the young, that this was their last chance to see the man who had personified French show business, both music and cinema, for three decades.

Besides going through his routine of hours of physical exercise and stretching in the morning followed by rehearsals, he supervised every detail at the theater. He specified exactly how he wanted the spotlights and sound, how fast the curtain should open and close. He walked the stage as a technician in the balcony checked whether he was visible from all the seats; if not, he forbade the Olympia to sell tickets for those seats. By May, he had tape-recorded a first version of the recital, and each of his eight musicians had a copy to work with and memorize. Montand himself had always had trouble with tempo, so Bob Castella made him a special cassette with each song so he could work at keeping time mentally; he played it when he shaved in the morning, he played it on his car radio when he was driving.

The old preshow anxiety was always there, as was the childlike wonder at what he was doing. "For the first three weeks," he told an interviewer later, "I swear that I hoped I would break a leg to have an excuse for not going on stage, I was so afraid, physically afraid. I never was really cut out for this. Why the son and grandson of peasants like me should have become an entertainer, I'll never know."[14]

Sold out six months before the first curtain went up, the show would be standing room only from October 7, 1981, to January 3, 1982, followed by a return summer engagement from July 20 to August 14. The show was taped for television and recorded for an album. Despite his declared intention of showing the younger members in the audience a new Montand, the program was basically his new album plus a virtual sampler of all his well-known hits for nearly four decades, from "Je vais à pied" to "Battling Joe," "Luna Park," and "À Paris." He performed the first part of the show in black trousers and velvet vest over an ample white shirt, before donning his habitual brown slacks and open-neck shirt.

He made no effort to conceal that he had aged, that the hair was thinner, the cheeks hollow, the eyes puffy, the forehead deeply lined, the skin slack, his expression fatigued. Cameras filming the show from the wings caught him returning to the wings between numbers gasping for breath, perspiring profusely as he grabbed a towel to wipe his face. But the voice was still the smokey baritone, burnished with ripe maturity, and there was a dense pathos and gravitas to his gestures when he traced the air with his hands. This was evident when he did a new number entitled "L'addition" (The Bill or Summing Up) about the sum of a life, its joys, disappointments, injustice, the aimless violence of war, with a deceptively jaunty musical accompaniment by Michel Legrand. And when he sang "Les feuilles mortes," it was with a profound poignancy that resonated with memories of loves lost.

Geopolitics intruded in December, when Poland's new premier and commander in chief, General Wojciech Jaruzelski, imposed martial law and arrested members of Solidarnosc. Montand had supported the movement's effort to bring a modicum of freedom and democracy to communist-ruled Poland and had welcomed its leader, Lech Wałęsa, to his Olympia dressing room only weeks earlier. Within days, Montand went on a radio broadcast to thunder against the French government's position that events in Poland concerned only Poles, declaring, "They have asked for free elections. Free elections! The most elementary of things."[15] Thereafter, a giant banner emblazed with the movement's name was unfurled onstage at the end of each performance. Wherever he went, he wore a Solidarnosc button in his lapel.

After Paris, he was off on a whirlwind tour of the French provinces, where the local theaters weren't large enough to accommodate the demand; in cities such as Bordeaux, Tours, Rouen, and Marseilles, he performed in hastily erected tents that could hold up to 5,000 spectators. Following his return to Paris for his summer engagement at the Olympia, Montand began his international tour, starting with Brazil on August 25, 1982. True to his support for the working class and conscious of those in Rio de Janeiro's teeming favelas, Montand insisted that his concerts be held in the biggest locales possible. In the case of Rio, that meant the vast, 12,000-seat Maracanãzinho sports arena. Dissatisfied with the stadium's acoustics, he had the organizers spread thousands of empty potato sacks on the stadium's concrete bleachers to dampen an annoying echo. From there, it was on to New York, where Yves Montand was awaited for one of the most prestigious events of his career.

The previous spring, just after the Olympia show, his agent, Charley Marouani, received a call from Jane Hermann, the presentation director of the Metropolitan Opera. She was in Paris, had seen the show, and wanted to talk about it. He invited her to lunch at Maxim's, where she extolled the importance of the Met, complete with photos from her handbag, as if he had never heard of it. The point was, she wanted Montand.

Both Marouani and Montand were astonished at the idea. In the Met's ninety-nine-year history, no popular singer, much less a French one, had ever performed at New York's opera house. Montand agreed on one condition: he had to see the theater and be sure that it fit his criteria for his kind of show. They took the supersonic Concord to New York, where Hermann welcomed them with a bouquet, a limousine, and a tour of the premises. Accompanied by a stage manager he knew who could give him technical advice, Montand walked the stage, tested the lighting and sound equipment. He would do it.[16]

As soon as word got out about the show, entitled *Paris in the Fall: Yves Montand,* tickets began selling so fast that within days a red ribbon announcing "Sold Out" was hastily plastered over the poster. Scalpers were soon asking upward of $120 for seats; charter flights were booked from Paris for opening night. Some in the press were skeptical. "Can Yves Montand fill the Metropolitan Opera House all by himself?" questioned the critic Moira Hodgson in the *New York Times.* "And can he—alone in front of an enormous auditorium—hold that stage which is large enough to accommodate the elephants in *Aida*?"[17] Hermann had no doubts. "Montand has a classicism that supersedes the normal pop artist," she said. "He belongs here, where the greatest artists in the world perform, and he's played bigger houses before."[18] The artist himself had his own ruminations, as he confided to a reporter: "I don't know why I am doing this. Sometimes I look in the mirror in the morning and I think, you're crazy. What do I want? Money? I've got it. Success? It's O.K. I want to win, to give the best I can. And it's exciting to give these young audiences something that's almost disappeared: the tradition of the music hall."[19]

In the opening-night audience of nearly 4,000 were many of New York's great and good, along with luminaries such as Robert De Niro, Paul Newman, Mikhail Baryshnikov, Joanne Woodward, and Ben Gazzara. There was also Simone Signoret. Hoping to avoid stealing the show to the detriment of Montand, she attempted to slip in unnoticed after the lights had dimmed and take her eighth-row seat next to Catherine Allégret. It didn't work. Someone noticed and began to applaud. It grew to a five-minute standing ovation while Montand waited nervously in the wings. When the curtain finally went up, another ovation began, this time for him. As he stood there waiting to begin, the old *trac* hit him, and his knees were shaking so hard he was afraid the audience could see the movement in his pant legs.

After that, the professional reflexes took over, and he took New Yorkers to Paris with twenty-nine songs, from "À Paris" to "Les feuilles mortes." "It's an excursion to the vanished world of Chevalier and Trenet and Piaf," decided Frank Rich, the chief theater critic of the *New York Times*, "a world that Montand perhaps knows better than any performer still at work." As for the man himself, he "looks terrific—vigorously sexy—and his voice doesn't sound discernably different from the one we hear on records made a generation ago. . . . A graceful dancer, as well as an adept mime, he can create dramatic poetry out of the most economic of gestures."[20] *The New Yorker* found him "trim and explosively energetic at sixty . . . still an improbable mixture of theatrical shrewdness and political idealism."[21]

No one knew that Montand's portable microphone had a temporary glitch that inhibited his movement on the stage for a while. Or that when he headed toward his dressing room afterward, shouting the name of his twenty-two-year-old technical assistant, Carole Amiel, with whom he wanted to discuss the issue, he came up against Signoret, waiting to congratulate him. She suspected, correctly, that the young woman, whom Montand had known for years in Saint Paul, was more than an assistant, and she was shocked to hear him calling for Amiel instead of for her.[22]

After the Met, it was on to Washington for performances at the Kennedy Center, followed by a reception for Montand at the residence of the French ambassador, who toasted his political engagement as exemplified in the films *Z* and *L'aveu*. The tour went on for the next two months: Ottawa and Montreal, San Francisco and Los Angeles, then across the Pacific to Japan for shows in Osaka, Tokyo, and Yokohama. Everywhere it was the same sheer showmanship that overcame the language barrier with foreign audiences, the majority of whom couldn't understand the nuances of the French poetry they were applauding. As much as the music, it was the man they came for: after his performance in San Francisco on October 13, they stood and sang "Happy Birthday" to Montand.

⊙ ⊙ ⊙

An unwittingly prescient line in *Z* took on increasing meaning for Montand throughout the 1970s: "How is your wife?," a character asks, to which Z

(Montand) replies, "She's fine. We have our problems." It sums up the last fifteen years of France's celebrity couple. Montand, whether on stage or on film sets, went from strength to strength, while Signoret deliberately let herself get old, sick, and unattractive, a period that her daughter Catherine called her "slow descent into hell." Never a heavy drinker before, she now consumed a bottle of alcohol a day, mostly scotch—plus an aperitif, wine with meals, a digestif afterward.[23] Still only in her forties, she became puffy faced, bloated, and irascible as her systematic self-destruction continued.

The inescapable conclusion is that this was her passive-aggressive expression of years of pent-up anger, her revenge for her husband's unending, flagrant, continuing infidelities, for the public humiliation of his affair with Monroe. He must have sensed this, but his attitude was one of bewilderment and hurt. "It wasn't seeing her get old that I couldn't stand," he told his biographers after her death. "It was her tendency to self-destruct, the methodical nature of that self-destruction. I told her so. I asked what had happened to our so-called great love now that she was letting herself go. She smiled and said: 'Yes, I'm letting myself go, yes, I find myself ugly, so what? Might as well accelerate as step on the brakes, no?'"[24]

And yet she kept on acting until two years before her death and had some of her finest performances during this period. Particularly notable was *Le chat / The Cat* (France and US 1971), opposite Jean Gabin, in which she played a former circus performer who is physically disabled and trying to retain the love of her alienated husband. She won a Silver Bear as Best Actress for the part at the Twenty-First Berlin International Film Festival. Just as impressive was *La vie devant soi / Madame Rosa* (1977, US 1978), for which she deliberately put on weight and used makeup to accentuate her bloated, devastated face in her role as a former Jewish prostitute who raises an Algerian orphan in Paris. Based on the prize-winning novel of the same title by Romain Gary, the picture won an Oscar as Best Foreign Language Film, while in France Signoret was awarded a César for Best Actress.

Montand and Signoret now had separate bedrooms—as his affairs became more overt, he rarely spent the night at home, anyway—and communicated mainly by written messages. In one of hers, she spelled out with clear, clinical precision what she thought of him:

> You like to make me feel guilty because you are not happy. You are not happy because you're built that way. I have seen you enthusiastic, funny, anxious, passionate, jealous, angry. I have

> never seen you "happy." Happy to while away the time, happy to loaf, happy to listen, happy to share. You are the most selfish person I have ever known. You are the most arrogant, the least grateful toward those who love you, the cruelest toward those who love you. You are the sweetest toward people you do not give a damn for, the most wounding toward people who love you. You loathe yourself for being yoked to this too-old, too-fat "contemporary." Shake off the yoke. I won't love you any the less.[25]

They fought ferociously, she with scathing, tongue-lashing sarcasm, he with physically violent temper tantrums, both going for the jugular. Signoret's grandson Benjamin Castaldi recalled one memorable fight at Autheuil when Montand, red-faced with anger, grabbed Signoret by the hair and dragged her down a hallway while she howled in pain. Everyone in their circle of habitual weekend visitors dreaded such scenes, which were frequent. And yet between these two who couldn't live with or without each other, there were still moments of tenderness. He often held her hand while they watched television.[26] And there was the night in March 1985 when Signoret, as president of France's César awards ceremony, couldn't read the names of winning films due to increasing blindness, and Montand whispered them to her discreetly.

Signoret and Catherine decided not to tell him that she was dying, perhaps to avoid disturbing him that September while he was doing a shoot in the South of France. He visited her bedside at Autheuil frequently, thinking she was recovering from her recent surgery for pancreatic cancer. He had just returned from there to filming in Provence when Catherine called him on September 30, 1985, to say that she had died that morning at 7:30.

As he rushed back to Paris, France's media devoted most of their coverage to her life and her importance as an actress, political activist, and writer. On the evening news, her death was the lead story, ahead of a coming Reagan–Gorbachev meeting and threats of a nationwide strike. In the United States, the *New York Times* said that "her sensuous face, with its full lips and heavy-lidded eyes, was a recurrent image through four decades of French movies, becoming a sort of symbol of her country's postwar film renaissance."[27] President François Mitterrand sent a telegram to Montand, saying, "During more than 40 years she has spoken to the hearts of the French people," while his minister of culture, Jack Lang, said she "embodied to perfection all those who fight, to the end, for all the most desperate causes."[28]

The next day at Paris's Père Lachaise Cemetery, the resting place of many other French cultural figures from Molière to Sarah Bernhardt and Edith Piaf, Montand, accompanied by Catherine, quietly made his way through the media circus and the crowd of Parisians come to pay their respects. He kissed a rose, dropped it on her casket, and left discreetly. Back at the place Dauphine apartment, he discovered in a closet the shoes Signoret had worn during their first visit to New York twenty-five years earlier, their stiletto heels blackened from sinking into the soft, Indian summer asphalt of the city's streets. He kept them along with some of her clothing and other mementoes.

During his period of mourning, he would occasionally go to the apartment to lie on their bed and remember. At the house in Autheuil, he wandered through the rooms as if attempting to sense her presence. He left undisturbed her office, where she wrote her books—her memoir, *La nostalgie n'est plus ce qu'elle était* (1976) / *Nostalgia Isn't What It Used to Be* (1978), and a novel, *Adieu Volodia* (1985)—in her last years, her typewriter sitting on the desk, a cardigan hanging on a chair.

He would get on with his life, do more pictures, take more lovers. He continued his relationship with Amiel, eventually asking her to move into the house at Autheuil, to the displeasure of Catherine and other members of the family. But the pain was deep and permanent. His father, Giovanni, had been his idol, Edith Piaf had taught him showmanship, even his affair with Marilyn Monroe had left its imprint, but for thirty-five years it was Signoret who had been his guiding compass, the single most important person in making him what he was. She had seen his tremendous potential and opened the sophisticated Parisian world of culture, ideas, and politics to the uncouth, unlettered yokel from the slums of Marseilles.

Castaldi recalls instances when, walking through the grounds at Autheuil together, a grieving Montand would suddenly stop and cry aloud, "Why did you leave me?"[29] After the funeral, he never revisited Signoret's grave.

20

Montand President?

The film Montand was working on in the South of France when Signoret died was a double-header, a cinematic diptych entitled *Jean de Florette* (France and US 1986) and *Manon des sources / Manon of the Spring* (France and US 1986). Running two hours each, they took nine months to film back-to-back and cost $15 million to produce, making them together the most expensive movie project ever done in France until then. They would also provide Montand one of the best roles of his life.

Claude Berri, the director, was perhaps best known in the United States for *Le vieil homme et l'enfant / The Two of Us* (1967, US 1968), *Le sex shop / Sex Shop* (1972, US 1973), and *Mazel tov ou le mariage / Marry Me! Marry Me!* (1968, US 1969), all giving a caustic, quirky look at social mores. He got the idea for the new project by accident when in a hotel room he picked up a book by Marcel Pagnol called *L'eau des collines,* which contained both halves of the diptych. In a twist on the usual book–movie sequence, Pagnol had done *Manon des sources* as a film in 1952 but, unhappy with how it turned out after the distributor cut it down from four hours, decided in 1963 to do the story as a novel about avarice, property, and deceit in the Provence that he knew so well.

Berri loved the novel and decided it had to be done as two films. *Jean de Florette* would be the prequel and *Manon des sources* the climax of a tale of implacable, ironic fate worthy of Greek tragedy. "I was bowled over by Pagnol's book, by the characters, by their complexity, and by this notion of fate, its universal and contemporary aspect," he explained. "Pagnol, starting from a story about the search for water, managed to unleash a devastating tragedy. In the end, the story is about the destiny of a man, a life, that becomes visible only in the long term, over a large number of years. That's what destiny is."[1]

Although it appears obvious in hindsight that Montand was made for the role of a scheming, crafty Provençal peasant with a strong southern accent, he initially rejected it when Berri made the offer. He didn't like the idea of looking old beyond his years, fearing that the younger members of the audience who hadn't seen him in his prime would think of him only as an old codger. A false mustache did the trick. When he put it on, he was flattered to see that it made him look a little like his father. That, plus Simone's urging him to take the part—she and Pagnol's wife, Jacqueline, had gone to school together—and Pagnol's standing in as witness at Montand and Signoret's wedding in Saint Paul, convinced him to accept the role of César, known as "le Papet" (Grandpa) in the local patois.

For the part of César's nephew Ugolin, the Pagnol family wanted someone originally from Provence. Daniel Auteuil, who was from Avignon, was chosen, but Berri waited until Montand, who had the last word, approved. The part of Jean Cadoret, known as Jean de Florette, went to Gérard Depardieu; Emmanuelle Béart was to be the adolescent Manon. Berri picked the picturesque Provençal village of Mirabeau in the rocky, arid hills behind Aix-en-Provence as the location.

Jean opens with Ugolin returning from his military service—the setting is the early 1920s—with the idea of raising carnations on his property near César's. The flowers are profitable, and together Ugolin and César want to buy an adjacent property where there is a spring, but it's not for sale. Eventually it is inherited by Jean de Florette, a naive, idealistic clerk from the city with a hump on his back who wants to start a new life in the country with his opera singer wife and small daughter, Manon. César and Ugolin, determined to make this outsider fail, plug the spring so he won't have water for his crops. Jean tries digging a well, but when he uses dynamite to blast through rock, he is killed by falling debris. César and Ugolin buy the farm cheaply from the widow and celebrate by unplugging the spring, while Manon secretly observes them.

The sequel, set ten years later, has Manon living in the area and tending goats when Ugolin falls in love with her. She loathes him for obvious reasons, and as the tragedy unfolds, the rejected Ugolin hangs himself in disappointment. Shortly thereafter, César learns that a village girl named Fleurette he unknowingly had gotten pregnant decades earlier had given birth to a child with a humped back after he had left the village for military service in Africa. Stunned by the realization that Jean, whom he had indirectly killed, was the son he had always wanted in order to continue the family line, César loses the will to live and dies. In his testament, he leaves everything he has to Manon. As the film ends with him on his deathbed holding a comb Fleurette had given him, the haunting musical theme from Verdi's *La forza del destino* swells.

Perhaps inevitably, the two parts are uneven. *Jean de Florette* benefits from the energetic, passionate presence of Gérard Depardieu, who nearly takes over the film. In *Manon des sources,* he is replaced in third billing by Béart—surely the prettiest goatherd in France—who spends most of her on-screen time in closeups looking pensive, wary, or vengeful and speaks relatively few lines. The sequel is also weakened by occasional dips into melodrama, as when the handsome young local schoolteacher falls in love with Manon, and they have an implausibly lavish village marriage, and when César decides to die and does so by will alone. That said, the villagers are authentic while avoiding caricature, the rocky, scrub-brush Provençal terrain beautifully evoked.

Montand's César is pitch-perfect, from the first shifty-eyed advice he gives Ugolin on how to ruin the newcomer to his muted, entirely interior reaction to the revelation of his paternity—he is practically alone on the screen for the last twenty minutes as the full extent of the tragedy takes hold. The part was arguably the finest achievement of Montand's sixty-film career as it drew to a close. "Ah, the old rascal, he's had us again," concluded *Le Monde.* "Overcome by a delicious emotion, we let the tears flow. Pagnol, Berri, and Montand have won."[2] Montand himself seemed to rate it higher than his much-praised performance in *The Confession:*

> I had to get as close as possible to the truth of the character. You put on a costume, like the corduroy jacket of le Papet, but it's inside that you have to wear the character, and you're never certain to succeed. The critics praised my losing weight for my part in *The Confession,* but that's beside the point. Any idiot can lose weight. But bringing a character like that to life, doing it all the way to the end of the film, being up to what the director demands and the image the public has of you, that's something else.[3]

Jean won four BAFTAs, including Best Film and Best Scenario. Best Actor in a Supporting Role went to Daniel Auteuil, who also won a César for Best Actor. *Manon* won Best Foreign Language Film by the National Board of Review of New York, and a César went to Emmanuelle Béart for Best Supporting Actress. Montand received no official recognition, just as he never received a major award in France or the United states for his acting, although he was often nominated. He had to content himself with a special nostalgic treat when he went to New York in June 1987 for the film's American premiere: a lunch of hot pastrami on rye and pickles with cheesecake for dessert at a delicatessen on the Lower East Side. It was a taste he had acquired with Signoret during their happy first visit to the city in 1959.

⊙ ⊙ ⊙

In the 1980s, Montand's passionate voice was raised in the public discourse to the point that he became, to his own surprise, one of France's foremost opinion leaders.

The decade opened with the election of François Mitterrand to the presidency in May 1981. As the Fifth Republic's first socialist president, he began, with the support of his communist political partners, to implement economic and social policies based more on ideology than on the country's actual needs. He nationalized certain key sectors of the economy, such as banks; increased the minimum wage by 10 percent; boosted pensions and other social benefits; shortened the workweek from forty to thirty-nine hours; gave everyone five weeks of vacation per year; and imposed a wealth tax that created a new class of "economic emigrants" as many of France's top earners fled the country.

It was a virtual replay of Salvador Allende's radical socialist policies a decade earlier in Chile—and with similar results. Within two years, the franc had been devalued by 15 percent, inflation and unemployment were skyrocketing, and there was an abrupt U-turn toward economic "rigor" (the term *austerity* was avoided). The government suddenly had to raise income taxes, levy sales taxes on gasoline, alcohol, and tobacco, and impose exchange controls to limit the amount of money French citizens could take abroad.

The country was in crisis, the French were increasingly restive, and the government needed some way of getting its message across about the situation's causes and solutions. But that message necessarily consisted of eye-glazing data on work productivity, public debt, technological change, deregulation, and other subjects guaranteed to bore the public. A state-owned television channel hit on the idea of a ninety-minute program in February 1984 mixing fiction with documentary footage and interviews to explain why France was in economic trouble and what should be done about it. To make the program palatable, the channel chose Montand as the narrator of *Vive la crise!* (Long Live the Crisis).

Playing the role of an ordinary Frenchman who understood little of economics and less of finance, he explained in simple layman's terms that the good times of cheap oil, plenty of jobs, and easy prosperity—the thirty-year period from roughly 1950 to 1980 known as "les Trente Glorieuses"—were over. He interviewed economists and politicians and posed the questions that everyone was asking. A certain period of rapid postwar development was indeed finished, he concluded, but now was the time to transition to a new, more innovative, and mobile economy. At the end of the program, he faced the camera squarely and said no super state or superman was going to save the country. The French had to do it themselves.

Today that conclusion sounds simplistic and evident. But in a socialist country whose citizens were accustomed to cradle-to-grave protection by the government nanny, it was an unheard-of call for a more capitalistic approach relying on individual initiative. Surprisingly, the program was an unprecedented success, with a 31 percent audience rating, compared with 23 percent for the latest television appearance of President Mitterrand. It sparked a national debate, beginning within the family. Signoret, unhappy with what she considered the program's conservative line, let Montand know she didn't like it at all. The French Communist Party demanded equal airtime to rebut the call for a more free-market economy. But the program also had its defenders. "Yves Montand tells us the solution is you," said an editorial in the leftist *Le Monde.* "That's the essential point to remember from this fine program. Thank you, Monsieur Montand!"[4]

Montand had spoken his mind on French politics and foreign affairs for decades, which was often brushed off as simply his private opinion. Now he was increasingly a voice the public listened to, a viewpoint to be reckoned with because what he said cut through the official claptrap and made sense. His next subject caused an even greater uproar.

Europe was in the depths of the Cold War. Even when the Soviet Union provoked a crisis with its deployment of new medium-range missiles that upset the balance of terror, there was little real public debate in France about how and whether it could defend itself. Since the presidency of Charles de Gaulle and acquisition of the atomic bomb, the French were lulled with expressions such as *force de frappe* (strike force), *dissuasion,* and *national sanctuary.* But was that enough? Would either France or the United States start a nuclear war to protect Europe if the Red Army attacked with classical weapons? The subject was taboo.

Again, a state-owned television channel chose Montand to explore and explain the issue. In an hour-long program entitled *La guerre en face* (Facing

War) in April 1985, he dared question the official line that nuclear dissuasion was sufficient. What, for example, if the Soviet Union massed 15,000 tanks on the border of West Germany and decided to roll? There was no alternative to massive—and self-destructive—retaliation, Montand argued, because Europe had lost the will to defend itself with classical weapons, claiming it was too expensive to finance a modern army compared with a single atom bomb. "The Europeans spend less for defense per capita than the US, the USSR, Sweden, or even the Swiss " he said. "And nobody gives a damn. A country or a continent that is no longer able to ensure its own defense automatically loses its independence. Personally, I don't want to live on my knees or groveling on my belly." And he repeated his slogan, "Better red than dead? No! Neither red nor dead! Free!"[5]

The show was more than a provocative television program, more even than a French political event. It took on an international dimension when the Soviet embassy in Paris sent an official note of protest the same day to France's Foreign Ministry on the Quai d'Orsay. The embassy had gotten wind of the program while it was being prepared and, feigning ignorance of such a thing as freedom of the press, had warned the ministry against it. Now, the embassy fulminated in an official statement, "This sordid calumny against the Soviet people had nevertheless been broadcast by a French public-service channel." According to the embassy, the lack of action against the television station by the French authorities bordered on culpable complacence in the face of such animosity and distrust toward a friendly country.[6] The Soviet news agency TASS took up the cudgels against Montand, claiming that his commentary aimed to arouse hysterical fear among the French. Using epithets usually reserved for German revanchists and other neofascists, TASS called him a renegade who had abandoned his former support for Soviet communism and now engaged in "filthy antisovietism."[7]

No matter. Montand, who had been on the public stage for forty years and was now in his sixties, had never been more popular. As his friend Françoise Sagan put it, he had aged like fine wine, acquiring "vulnerability, understanding, modesty and indulgence, while keeping his force, his decisiveness, his virility."[8] After his down-to-earth explanations of France's economic and geostrategic problems and options, he was praised for speaking on the big issues in language everyone could understand. Wherever he went, the press asked him not only the usual questions of a top entertainer but also for his opinions on world affairs. "Suddenly we had the impression that someone was asking the right questions," *Paris-Match* enthused. What it called the "Montand effect" was a welcome change from the usual dreary repetition of *idées reçues*. He was emerging as an important political player, it said, one proof of which was that he was attacked by Soviet government press organs such as TASS and *Izvestia*.[9]

Opinion polls even before the two television programs bore out this assessment. In one, 55 percent of French citizens believed that what Montand thought about politics was more important than the opinion of professional politicians.[10] Another found that he was the fourth most famous man in France after François Mitterrand, Valéry Giscard d'Estaing, and Jacques Chirac. One poll presented a list of thirty-four French men and women to a thousand people and asked them to name their favorites in different categories. Montand was the number one pick for intelligence, masculinity, the most moving, the most charm, the strongest personality, and, for women, the most desirable father of their child. "Montand has become a myth," *Paris-Match* wrote. "What a president we would have with him (after all, Reagan was an actor too)."[11]

From there, it was only an easy step in this hyperpoliticized country to start seriously considering Montand as a possible candidate for the presidency. He was urged on by behind-the-scenes political counselors such as Marie-France Garaud, who had been an éminence grise to Presidents George Pompidou and Jacques Chirac. Also pushing him to declare candidacy were Bernard Kouchner, who later served as foreign minister, and Jacques Seguela, one of the country's leading public-relations specialists. The political moment appeared propitious, with parties of both the left and the right divided, exhausted, and largely discredited, leaving the public hungry for someone new and different with pragmatic ideas. He was on magazine covers with titles such as "Montand homme politique?" (Montand the Politician?), "Montand de plus en plus politique" (Montand More and More Political), and simply "Montand parle" (Montand Speaks).[12]

Polls of the early 1980s had shown that people thought he was right to speak out on public issues and that he dared say things publicly that everyone thought secretly. Would he mind awfully being called the "French John Wayne," an inquiring American reporter asked. "Go ahead, whatever, I don't care," he replied. "I want to wake people up."[13] Another caught him vacationing on the Côte d'Azur and popped the question: President Montand? "Politics is a lot of work," he said. "I have no party or organization, I'm all alone. But maybe. Why not?"[14]

John Wayne wasn't the only American he was being compared to. Many in his circle cited the case of Ronald Reagan, an actor who became president, or even Clint Eastwood, who recently had been elected mayor of a town in California. He said he admired Reagan for restoring America's confidence in itself and the world's respect for America, which he called the last rampart of democracy. When asked to define himself as either on the left or the right, he would reply that he was intellectually on the left but viscerally on the right, a position he called "Reagan leftist."[15]

He was, in sum, a political maverick, refusing to act like a conventional politician. "If I enter the race for the presidency, it won't be by creating a party," he told a magazine. "Those who followed me would have their party membership card in their heads and hearts. That might be amateurish, but it wouldn't correspond to any of the usual rules. But maybe I'm dreaming."[16] Costa-Gavras encouraged the dream. He suggested they do a film with the working title *Montand President.* It would be about an actor who became president thanks to his unconventional new ideas but soon finds to his disgust that it means he has to engage in the usual base politicking to get his programs through. Semprún was called in to work up a script, but the project fizzled.

Reality began to raise its ugly head. He was an outsider in a rigidly structured society where political leaders are bred from a young age for the role—and they are not the sons of working-class Italian immigrants. That usually means attending the exclusive Institut d'études politiques for an initial cull, followed by the even more competitive École nationale d'administration, the alma mater of most of the country's politicians and technocrats. Montand was considering politics as a way of getting a hearing for his ideas, but was it really necessary to go through all that travail?

As the presidential election scheduled for May 1988 approached with Mitterrand the heavy favorite, he began to distance himself from the idea. He wasn't, after all, a politician and had no stomach for jumping into the political arena at the age of sixty-five. Not only did he have no party organization or campaign financing, but he also never directly criticized Mitterrand, his government, or its policies—surely the first thing expected of a political opponent. Invited to participate in a television interview in December 1987, with 29 percent of voters saying they would favor him and an overall approval rating of 78 percent, he decided to quash the idea once and for all. "Let's be serious," he said. "I have never had such an ambition. I know my limits. I have neither the education nor the experience to be president of France."[17] Or as he might say in his native tongue, "*Basta!*"

Bursting the bubble after such a heady buildup must have been painful. His nephew, Jean-Louis Livi, talked with him often and was convinced that

Montand was seriously tempted by the idea: "He believed in it, and I understand why he would have. France was following him. That must have been intoxicating."[18] Costa-Gavras recalled discussing the movie project with him one day when Montand began outlining a scene for it. It was clear, he thought, that Montand was in fact rehearsing not for a film but for a campaign he was preparing in his mind.[19]

In retrospect, it seems apparent that he had been irresponsibly manipulated by certain people in his circle to the point where he thought he really could make it as a presidential candidate. But that illusion was also due in part to Signoret's death in 1985. She would have helped him keep things in a more realistic perspective. With her disappearance, he had lost the compass that, despite their deteriorated relations, had maintained him on course for so long.

⊙ ⊙ ⊙

For a presidency, Montand had to settle for being president of the jury for the Fortieth Cannes International Film Festival in May 1987. The situation was ironic: *Jean de Florette* and *Manon des sources* had just been released to high praise on two continents, and his own interpretation of César was universally applauded, but neither was selected as one of the twenty films in competition for the Palme d'Or. As usual, the festival jury preferred to honor little-known directors and obscure pictures. The award went to *Sous le soleil de Satan / Under the Sun of Satan* (1987, US 1989), the tale of a tormented young provincial priest directed by the idiosyncratic Maurice Pialat and starring Gérard Depardieu as the priest. The festival had its usual cohort of movie glitterati who climbed the twenty-six red-carpeted steps to the auditorium, including Elizabeth Taylor, Jeanne Moreau, Paul Newman, Robert De Niro, Bo Derek, and Isabella Rossellini. One important attendee who did not get the red-carpet treatment and, indeed, tried to remain as discreet as possible was a comely young brunette named Carole Amiel.

She was the same "technical assistant" who had accompanied Montand to New York for his performance at the Met in the fall of 1982; only this time he wanted to make her status unambiguous—this was to be her coming out. Elegant in an understated black dress by Jean-Louis Scherrer, she was on his arm at the festival's receptions, cocktail parties, dinners, and other events attended by the jury's president, with Montand making a point of introducing her all around. This formalized an intimate relationship that had begun in 1980, when she was still a twenty-year-old student at the University of Paris and he had invited her to an austere, sparsely furnished bachelor's pad he had set up at place Dauphine, near the apartment where Signoret still lived when not at Autheuil. As they began meeting there regularly, she assumed the housewifely tasks of cleaning and shopping.[20] She would be, in effect, his official romantic partner for the last ten years of his life. Whether she was the only one seems doubtful.

They had met in 1980 at Saint Paul, where her parents, originally from Épernay in the Champagne region, had bought a house several years before. Their paths crossed from time to time when she was riding her bicycle to school, and he was strolling on the same country road. Their friendship developed slowly during casual meetings in the village, encounters that she increasingly planned, timed, and looked forward to as, by her own account, she became totally infatuated with him. Tongues began to wag. That was brought home to her one day when the owner of La Colombe d'Or winked and asked what she was waiting for to present Montand with a beautiful baby.[21]

When Amiel went to Paris to continue her studies in economics, there was the invitation to place Dauphine. Shortly thereafter, she was being introduced as his new press attaché for his Olympia show in 1981, then as technical assistant for his world tour starting in New York. As Montand explained to *People* magazine, "Simone could not go. I needed someone to trim my hair. To bring food at 4:30 p.m., not at 6 p.m. So I took Carole along. . . . Simone knew about us, but she didn't want to know, vous comprenez? She didn't like it, but she understood. You cannot leave a man like me for eight years without certain things."[22]

After the presidential fever dropped, Montand spent more time in Saint Paul taking care of "certain things" with Amiel, playing the Provençal form of *boules* with the locals, and making notes for his memoir, which he never got around to writing. What he liked about Amiel was her discretion, her common sense, and even her ordinariness—he called her "Mademoiselle Tout le Monde," Miss Everybody. It was restful being with someone not caught up in the tinsel of show business. Still, he had never been able just to loaf for a while, as Signoret had observed bitterly. Around the time that he declared he would not be a presidential candidate, he took Amiel to Mauritius for a short vacation, but he was bored. "We wanted to be alone together, away from all the tumult," she remembered. "But Montand on vacation was like an animal in a cage. He didn't know the meaning of the words 'doing nothing.'"[23]

She had her own agenda for their life together, however. That included having his child. When she told him in the spring of 1988 that she was pregnant, he exploded in anger, refusing to accept the idea. He had often said he wanted children with Signoret but abandoned the idea after her two miscarriages. Now he found it ridiculous to be facing fatherhood at an age when men usually are becoming grandfathers. He also feared that people would think he had fallen into a pregnancy trap set by her. For three weeks, it was unclear whether they would stay together. As she explained later, "He did not want a child, but more because of his age than from any deep-seated reluctance. Admittedly, I made the decision, not Montand. . . . It was the only thing I could give him that he had never had before, and also the only way of being with him my whole life long."[24]

His sister, Lydia, took Amiel's side, as did others, including his agent, Charley Marouani, who, when asked for his advice, reminded Montand that he bore his part of responsibility in the matter. He finally relented, although, contrary to a common belief, he never married Amiel—his way, perhaps, of being faithful to Signoret. He spent the next six months adding a room to the house in Saint Paul and fretting over things such as whether his son or daughter might inherit a nose as big as his. On December 30, 1988, a television channel broadcast *Manon des sources*. As they watched it together, she was overcome with emotion during the sequence in which le Papet is on his deathbed.[25] The contractions began, and Valentin Giovanni Jacques Livi, weighing a hefty nine pounds four ounces, was born at a hospital in Nice the next day. That at least reassured Montand about his virility: "With that size, they can't say he's the son of tired old loins."[26] He discovered the joys of fatherhood, calling it fabulous, an inexplicable happiness, the real point of living. And if his fans thought he was going gaga over Valentin, that was fine with him.[27]

Becoming a father was consistent with Montand's philosophical attitude about the turn his life had taken after Signoret's death. He was convinced that a life can't be remade or started over after such a loss. The choice was either to give up and end it or cope and continue. He would continue with his new family. He also began tying up loose ends. He legally adopted Catherine, who had never known any other father; she then took the surname "Allégret-Livi." He visited his brother, Julien, at the hospital where he was being treated for heart trouble. They spent three hours together recalling the good times they had had and became reconciled. Montand also cast a cold eye on the persona that had served him so well in his life. In a conversation with a reporter who had covered him for years, he summed up his feeling about the "singing proletarian" label that the press had stuck on him:

> I never liked my physique or my "nice working-class guy" image, but even if it bothered me, I couldn't do otherwise on stage because that's what people expected of me. When I did "Luna Park," I wasn't trying to be the singing prole, but that's how people perceived me. Coming from the social class I did and with the political ideas I had, I just continued in that style. . . .To some extent, I had the same problem as Marilyn, who was obliged to play scatterbrained idiots because of her voice, that high-pitched little girl's voice in a superb body.[28]

He was at an age when in France a man of his accomplishments often receives the Legion of Honor, but he had previously turned it down. It should be reserved for exceptional servants of the nation, he replied to the invitation, and he did not consider himself one such. He was willing, however, to accept the tribute paid to him by New York's Film Society of Lincoln Center in April 1988. Held annually since 1972 at the Avery Fisher Hall (now the David Geffen Hall), home of the New York Philharmonic Orchestra, the Chaplin Award Gala has honored many of the movie industry's top talents, beginning with Charlie Chaplin, who returned to the United States from his self-exile in Switzerland to receive it. The award put Montand in the company of such recipients as Fred Astaire, Federico Fellini, Alec Guinness, Alfred Hitchcock, John Huston, and Laurence Olivier.

His friends Louis Malle, Costa-Gavras, and Claude Berri accompanied him to the gala, which included showings of excerpts from several of his films, including *Jean de Florette* and *Manon des sources.* American reporters covering the event found that he had lost none of his charisma. "Yves Montand is one of those rare individuals who looks more important than the limousine he arrives in," wrote one. And a lady journalist who watched him arrive gasped to a companion, "My God! If I told you what just happened inside my body!"[29]

⊙ ⊙ ⊙

Maybe fatherhood really did rejuvenate him. In any case, as he approached seventy in 1991, he got the itch to do another big show, if only so his son could see what his father could do. He began serious preparations for one, which he envisaged as the biggest he would ever have done in Paris. It would be staged at the Bercy sports arena and concert hall with a capacity of 20,300—the equivalent of New York's Madison Square Garden. An opening date was set for May 1992, with a dozen performances scheduled. Posters were printed and plastered all over Paris. It was sold out as soon as he made the announcement during a television interview. When the interviewer asked whether this was his goodbye to the stage, he replied, "Look, at seventy years old I'm not going to pretend I'm a young matinee idol. But when it's time to say goodbye, I'll do it feet first. Like everybody else."[30]

His voice was still warm and strong despite warning signs about his health. When he went to visit Julien and climbed the steps to the hospital, he suddenly felt unwell and had difficulty breathing. There had been pulmonary congestion in April 1989, followed by a serious cardiac incident in October that required ten days of hospitalization. He seldom saw doctors or took medication, believing that the human body has its own defenses and should be left alone. But in early 1991 he called Lydia and admitted in the Italian they often spoke together that he didn't feel very well: "Non me sente troppo bene."[31]

While he was getting ready for his show, the film director Jean-Jacques Beineix asked him to read a script he had written. Beineix had done the successful psychological drama *37.2 C in the Morning / Betty Blue* (France and US 1986), which received BAFTA and Oscar nominations for Best Foreign Language Film. Montand had long been interested in working with him. He impressed Beineix with his serious approach to reading the script: "At our first meeting, Montand read the whole thing through for three hours, word for word. He acted out all the parts, sometimes stopping at points where he was uncomfortable with it. As he read the script, I saw my film and its characters come alive in my mind. No other actor had ever done that for me."[32] Montand accepted the male lead, although it meant a strenuous routine of doing the shoot during the day and rehearsing for the show in the evening. By now, he was visibly waning, his face cruelly tired and wrinkled, so it also meant accepting being filmed looking far older, grayer, and decrepit than he had in *Jean de Florette*.

IP5: L'Ile aux pachyderms / IP5: The Island of Pachyderms (1992, US 1993) is a wistful, whimsical road movie about three characters searching for an impossible dream. (The obscure "IP5" is an abbreviated reference to L'Ile aux Pachyderms, a place mentioned in the film, and Beineix's fifth film.) The delinquent Tony (Olivier Martinez) falls in love at first sight in Paris with a nurse who rejects him. Together with his sidekick, a young Black rapper and tagger named Jockey (Sekkou Sall), they set out to find her in Toulouse, where she has gone to work in a hospital. They come across Léon (Montand), a strange old man tramping through the forest hugging trees, listening to the stars, and bringing dead rabbits back to life. Escaped from an asylum where his family had him committed, he, too, is looking for a lost love, a girl he had known briefly forty years earlier.

The unlikely trio becomes a mutual support group in their quest, with Léon imparting bits of wisdom to the two skeptical youngsters, who are more interested in stealing cars. Tony finds his nurse, but Léon discovers that his beloved drowned herself after he left her. He has a heart attack and dies. A doctor called in to give pointers to Montand on how to mime the attack was impressed by how realistic he made it: "Montand was extraordinary. He had the same spasms as an actual victim would have had. I was flabbergasted by his performance."[33]

It would be hard to make up an uncannier case of life imitating art. After Montand finished the film's last shots on November 8 on location in a forest near the town of Senlis, which involved several takes in which he plunges into the chill waters of a lake, he headed back to his improvised dressing room to change. He promised Beineix he would return to say goodbye before returning to Autheuil. When he didn't, film crew members grew concerned and discovered him around midnight lying in the dressing room suffering from a myocardial infarction. An emergency medical team arrived and found him still conscious and even talkative. He told them not to inform Amiel and Valentin and added, "If something happens to me at my age, I've lived long enough and well enough to have nothing to regret."[34]

Georges Dognon, Montand's chauffeur, picked up Amiel at Autheuil in the middle of the night and drove her the eighty-five miles to Senlis. Doctors in the intensive-care unit reassured her that he was doing well after receiving a thrombolysis to dissolve a clot in a cardiac artery. He asked that a television set be installed in his room so he could watch *César et Rosalie,* which was being broadcast later that day. During the morning, Catherine and a few close friends from the Autheuil clan, including Bernard Kouchner and his wife, the television journalist Christine Ockrent, and the actor François Périer, visited him and then waited at the hospital for better news. Instead, the ICU doctors came to tell them Montand had had a second, fatal infarction at 1:10 p.m. on November 9.

French radio stations interrupted their programming to announce the news, followed by endless repetitions of songs such as "Les feuilles mortes." Television channels broadcast his greatest films, including *Le salaire de la peur* and *Jean de Florette.* President François Mitterrand declared in an interview, "For many French citizens, Yves Montand was part of their family. They had an affectionate relation with him. His songs, his movie roles, his always passionate stands on issues were part of their lives."[35] Minister of Culture Jack Lang said, "He formed part of our history. Every time a people or an individual suffered, he took up their cause. His hopes, his doubts, his utopias all made up one entity. He will be with us for a long time to come."[36] His friend Jorge Semprún, in Madrid, said, "He was honest and, what's more important, he knew how to recognize his own mistakes."[37]

His passing was headlined in much of the world's press, which saluted not only his career as a singer and actor but also his passionate activism for the causes he believed in during the turbulent twentieth century. For the leftist *Liberation,* "If Yves Montand is so celebrated today, it's also because with him disappears a great witness to our century . . . of a time that began with Auschwitz and ended with the collapse of the communist bloc."[38] *Paris-Match,* devoting most of an issue to him, called him "the most perfectionist of entertainers, the most passionate of the thinking class."[39] In Italy, his death was covered like that of a native son, with Milan's *Il corriere della sera,* the country's biggest daily, calling him "a voice become a myth."[40] The *New York Times* termed him "the quintessential French romantic, half-adventurer, half-intellectual."[41]

Montand's body was transferred the next day, a Sunday, to the second-floor apartment at 114 boulevard Saint Germain that he had bought for his new family, which caught by surprise a small crowd that had gathered at 15 place Dauphine, thinking he would be brought there. They then crossed the Seine on the centuries-old Pont Neuf and stood on the sidewalk opposite his new apartment. He was not a rock star; there were few young people. Most of those who came were old enough to have hummed his songs in the 1950s and 1960s and to have followed his career and political evolution since the 1950s. Many laid bouquets at the building's door and signed the book of condolences put at their disposal—"Thank you for having helped me recognize my mistake," wrote one, alluding to Montand's own courageous reappraisal of his belief in Soviet communism.[42]

Amiel and Catherine prepared the twenty-four-hour wake attended by all the Autheuil clan, supplying an abundance of food and pastries, making available bedrooms where the mourners could nap. Many kissed his forehead or touched his hands crossed on his chest. A woman sang a lament. Everyone recalled anecdotes about him, some provoking laughter amid the tears. Before they closed the casket, Catherine placed inside it a mohair blanket that Signoret had crocheted for their bedroom at place Dauphine. Montand had prized it and had asked to be buried with it.

The funeral cortège with its flower-laden hearse left the apartment at 10:00 a.m. on November 13 for the forty-five-minute trip to the Père Lachaise Cemetery in eastern Paris, where a crowd estimated at 7,000 waited. It was a good crowd, but only one-third as large as the one for Signoret, and nothing compared with the 100,000 who had turned out for Edith Piaf. The casket was taken to avenue Aguado in the forty-fourth division of the garden cemetery, which placed him not far from Oscar Wilde and, more appropriately, Gioachino Rossini. Signoret's gray granite tomb was made ready, Montand's casket was lowered into it beside hers. Among the bouquets piled around it was a life-size composition of red and white roses forming his stage silhouette, top hat in hand at a jaunty angle. On the tombstone below Signoret's name was engraved only "Yves Montand." No dates of birth and death were given, nor his real name.

Ivo Livi had been subsumed in Yves Montand—the man who, against all odds, had not only entertained much of the Western world and incarnated Gallic charm for four decades but also become the passionate voice of individual freedom at a crucial time when it was in the balance. All his life he remembered the circumstances that led to his being French rather than Italian. Several times the town of Monsummano Alto, hoping to capitalize on his fame, offered him the title of honorary citizen. He flatly refused. True to himself and to the memory of his beloved father, he never forgave the craven neighbors who did nothing to help when the Blackshirts came.

Epilogue

The years following Montand's death have not always been kind to him. As a harbinger of things to come, on the very night of his wake in Paris burglars broke into the house at Autheuil. While Valentin lay sleeping and unharmed in his bedroom, they took all the valuables they could stash, plus souvenirs of his career and family mementos. Days after that, family squabbling broke out over his will concerning an estate estimated at about $3.5 million. Montand had left the house at Autheuil to Catherine's children, Clémentine Vaudaux and Benjamin Castaldi, while the apartments in Paris and Saint Paul went to Valentin, which left no one satisfied.

Then began a years-long series of posthumous slurs and unprovable allegations. By their very nature, no one could be sure where the truth lay, and they inevitably tarnished Montand's image.

In 1989, two years before his death, he was named in a paternity suit. Brought by a B-movie starlet with a talent for fabulation, Gilberte Drossart, who also went by the names "Anne Drossart" and "Anne Fleurange," the suit claimed that she had had a two-year affair with him beginning in 1974. As a result, she said, a girl, Aurore, was born. She had waited fifteen years to bring the matter up, she explained, because she didn't want to disturb Montand's relations with his wife. Now she demanded one million francs (about $161,000) in damages, plus 10,000 francs (about $1,600) a month in child support.

The court rejected the suit as violating the two-year statute of limitations but, in a quirk of Gallic juridical logic, simultaneously ordered Montand to submit to a blood test for DNA examination. Montand filed a countersuit for libel and declined to show up for the test. There was no tangible trace in Drossart's suit to support her allegation of a two-year affair—no photo, no letter, no gift, no evidence whatever of a relationship. Montand died three days before he was due to testify in the trial.

Still, in 1994 a judge ruled that his refusal to submit to the test amounted to a confession. The judge also saw what seemed to be a convincing physical resemblance of Aurore to Montand. Aurore was declared to be his daughter, with his name to appear on her birth certificate, and eligible for one-sixth of his estate. The family appealed and asked for more testing. Samples taken from Montand's sister, Valentin, and Amiel were compared with those from Gilberte and Aurore Drossart showed that there was only one chance in a hundred that Aurore could be his daughter, whereas Valentin had a 99.9 percent chance to be his son.

Even with this evidence, carrying the matter as far as possible, the court ordered in 1997 that Montand's body be exhumed and samples taken for DNA examination. This unprecedented ruling in a paternity case was termed outrageous by the then minister of health and Montand's friend, Bernard Kouchner, who said it was more a question of inheritance money than of using science to get at the truth.[1] The exhumation became a national controversy, with scientists arguing over whether the DNA would still be valid. Polls showed nearly two-thirds of the French were shocked by the indignity being perpetrated on a national icon, and three-quarters holding that he should not be obliged to submit to an exam that he refused while he was alive.[2]

Under the cover of darkness on the night of March 11, 1998, behind a gray plastic shroud that left gawkers and television crews frustrated, grave diggers opened the granite tomb, raised Montand's casket, and turned it over to a laboratory for testing. Bones, teeth, and decomposed body parts were cut, sawed, and torn out and put in sealed containers as lawyers for both parties observed. There was no legal reason for them to be present, but Drossart *mère et fille* insisted on watching, the better to have stories for the gutter press. On July 12, 1998, the whole danse macabre ended: test results proved Montand could not be Aurore's father.

The French weren't scandalized that a woman claimed to have had a love child by Montand but by the lack of respect and grisly horror with which his remains were treated. In fact, many, knowing his reputation as *un grand séducteur, un homme à femmes,* would have been surprised that he had *not* sired one or more children. But now that he was safely underground and fair game, writing scabrous allegations about him became a virtual cottage industry.

First to do so was Catherine Allégret's son, his grandson by adoption, Benjamin Castaldi. His book *Maintenant, il faudra tout se dire* (Now We Must Tell Each Other Everything) in 2004 was mainly about his life as a spoiled kid in the Montand–Signoret celebrity milieu. But in the final pages he dropped a little bomb of insinuation: relating a conversation with Allégret, he said, "Then she revealed bluntly and without beating around the bush that Montand had not always had with her the attitude that one expects of a stepfather. That that situation had lasted for some time with the knowledge of many in their circle. . . . Since then it had poisoned her existence."[3]

Well, what exactly were Castaldi and Allégret—she had approved the text in a postface, referring vaguely to "that terrible revelation that I made to you"—alleging? The press was quick to fill in the blanks. "Yves Montand had raised Catherine as his daughter, then loved her as a woman," screamed *Paris-Match,* "as Simone watched."[4] In an interview with the magazine, Castaldi conceded that he would never know exactly what happened between Allégret and Montand, but few readers got that far.

Allégret denied publicly that she had ever had sexual relations with Montand and successfully sued the magazine. After the success of Castaldi's book, though, she decided five months later—fourteen years after Montand's death—to write her own story. In *Un monde à l'envers* (A World Upside Down, 2004), she describes what she calls her troubled relations with him, beginning when she was four or five years old. He was giving her a bath, she writes: "He is washing me all over. He is leaning toward me, his face very close to mine, he looks at me, and his finger probes me."[5] She never mentioned it to anyone, she admits; the memory was vague; she couldn't remember whether it happened again. She also implicates Signoret, claiming that when she was an adolescent, she told Signoret that Montand was bothering her sexually but that her mother encouraged it. Then there was the time at place Dauphine when, she alleges, he threw her on the bed and reached under her skirt. She resisted, he stopped.[6]

Her account might be true. But during his lifetime, Catherine had always given the impression of enjoying a normal, loving relationship with Montand, considering him as her father, even aiding to organize his last big international tour and helping Amiel during the difficult moment of his death. Moreover, in 1998 she had written in a book inveighing against Anne Drossart and Montand's exhumation, "Montand can rest in peace, like the decent man he always was, . . . and my children will continue to be proud of their grandfather."[7]

So, inevitably, the question is: Why the public change in attitude over the six years between 1998 and 2004? She reportedly demanded a share of royalties for her postface to her son's book. Then she did her own quickie, consisting of only 152 large-type, well-spaced pages and having a print run of 60,000 copies, for which she was said to receive an advance of some 100,000 euros (about $124,000).[8]

Montand's reputation continued to be battered that year when the openly homosexual actor Jean-Claude Brialy declared that not only had Montand slept with everyone who wore a skirt—"He jumped the housemaid, assistants on the set, the hairdresser"—but he was also bisexual. Brialy offered as "proof" that a male friend told him he had had an affair with Montand.[9]

That juicy new angle was picked up by the writer Emmanuel Bonini, a specialist in digging up the dirt on showbiz celebrities from Josephine Baker to Edith Piaf and Romy Schneider. For the book *Le veritable Yves Montand* (The Real Yves Montand), published in 2021, he found two women in Marseilles who were sure that Montand had lived for three months with Reda Caire, a popular singer of operettas and known homosexual. Or at least they were certain that they lost track of Montand for a while and assumed he was with Caire. Besides, wrote Bonini, a muckraking American journalist named Doug Ireland said so in a blog. Case closed.[10]

Perhaps the best way to treat the more obviously sensationalist efforts to demolish Montand's reputation is the way taken by his son, Valentin. A sensible young man who started his own business in Montpellier, far from Paris, and lives there with his wife and son while avoiding the media, he jokes, "What's more, Montand was a zoophile. From 1948 to 1953 he raped the pet cat, the tortoise, and the guinea pig. And don't get me started on how he did it."[11]

Today few in France younger than fifty seem aware of Yves Montand's extraordinary career as singer, actor, and political activist. His films are rarely rerun on television or in the art cinemas, his songs seldom heard amid the modern cacophony on the radio. His political image is blurred, with the Left considering him a traitor because of his turn to conservatism and the Right recalling mainly his support for Stalinist communism and his concerts in Moscow—the price he paid for hewing to the line of truth as he saw it.

In any case, the collective memory of Yves Montand in France has not always received the nurture it deserves. Following his death, a few streets and schools in the provinces were named for him, but none in Paris. There was an attempt to rename place Dauphine in his honor, but the Paris city hall wasn't having it. Ditto in Saint Paul, where they refused to name a square of street for him to avoid jealous reactions by the other famous names associated with the town. In Marseilles, Square Yves Montand was renamed in 2020, and the bust of him that graced the garden went into storage.

In 2017, Catherine Allégret and her two children sold the house at Autheuil, synonymous with Montand, Signoret, and their show business clan. They then sold more than three hundred lots of objects from the interior, including the piano Montand used for rehearsing, the original screenplays of some of his movies, a pair of platinum, diamond, and sapphire earrings belonging to Signoret, letters and telegrams from Piaf to him, and other invaluable memorabilia. With so much of his patrimony dispersed to the four winds, there is no longer any possibility of a museum devoted to his life and career, unlike the ones for artists such as Jean Gabin and Georges Brassens or, in the United States, James Stewart.

What will always remain, something that nothing can extinguish, is the passionate voice of a man above all true to himself, who lived and loved intensely and incarnated many of the most important issues of his era. That, plus his legacy of songs and movies that are essential to anyone who wants to understand the popular culture of France during the twentieth century.

Acknowledgments

I thank the following for their kind responses to my requests for interviews and other assistance with this book.

Carole Amiel, Yves Montand's companion in his last years and mother of his son, Valentin Livi, welcomed me into her Paris home for a discussion of his life, career, and character. She also made available her exclusive collection of photos of Montand and helpfully provided contacts for further research. Valentin spoke with me from his home in Montpellier and described his feelings about the famous father who died before he could get to know him.

Further inside information on Montand's career and the relations within the Livi family were provided by Jean-Louis Livi, the artist's nephew and agent, who shared with me some of the material he has been saving for his own memoir. His position as both family member and professional associate gave special relevance to his unique insights into both sides of Montand's life. Similarly, Catherine Allégret-Livi, Montand's stepdaughter, provided perspective on the Montand clan from her home in Brittany.

Claude Gauteur, one of France's most prominent film historians, generously shared his encyclopedic knowledge of the history of French cinema to help me understand Montand's place in it. He also provided invaluable sources for further research. Another French movie historian, Michel Ciment, discussed with me his analysis of the films he considered Montand's best.

I am especially grateful to Ana Guigui, an associate professor of voice at the Berklee College of Music in Boston and a professional performer. She took the time to listen to several of Montand's performances and then give me in several discussions her informed analysis of his baritone.

The prominent Paris lawyer Dominique Piwnica, a specialist in France's complicated family law who represented Montand's family and was an official witness at the exhumation of his body, assisted me in understanding the convoluted suits and countersuits involved in the paternity case brought against him.

Stéphane Korb, the son of Francis Lemarque, kindly filled me in on his father's evolution from young communist sympathizer fighting with the Resistance to nightclub singer and then prolific writer of some of Montand's most successful songs.

Thanks also to Véronique Chauvet, director of the Iconothèque department at the Cinémathèque française, the world's largest depository of film documents. She and her colleague, Bertrand Kerael, made available their photo archives for my research. Further aid in my research for illustrations was provided by Luc Larriba, coauthor with Carole Amiel of the recent biography *Yves Montand: La force du destin* (2021).

This book benefited greatly from the support, encouragement, and guidance of Patrick McGilligan, an expert, prolific writer on film and the editor of the Screen Classics series at the University Press of Kentucky. Likewise, the press's director, Ashley Runyon, and her thoroughly professional team were a pleasure to work with.

A final word of appreciation goes to the American Library in Paris. Thanks to its uncommon depth for a small library as well as to its staff's friendly, helpful attitude, it was possible to do much of my research with its extensive resources.

Filmography

Yves Montand's films are listed here in chronological order according to initial release date, with the director's name following the title. If a film was released in both France and the United States, both titles are given, separated by a forward slash. If it was not but had a generally accepted English worldwide title, I have added an "also known as" title.

1946

Étoile sans lumière / Star without Light. Director Marcel Blistène.
Les portes de la nuit / Gates of the Night. Director Marcel Carné.

1948

L'idole (also known as *The Idol*). Director Alexandre Esway.

1950

Souvenirs perdus (also known as *Lost Souvenirs*). Director Christian-Jaque.

1951

Paris chante Paris (also known as *Paris Still Sings!*). Director Pierre Montazel.

1952

Paris est toujours Paris (also known as *Paris Is Always Paris*). Director Luciano Emmer.

1953

Le salaire de la peur / The Wages of Fear. Director Henri-Georges Clouzot.

1955

Quelques pas dans la vie (also known as *The Anatomy of Love*). Director Alessandro Blasetti.
Napoleon. Director Sacha Guitry.
Les héros sont fatigués / Heros and Sinners. Director Yves Ciampi.

1956

Marguerite de la nuit (also known as *Marguerite of the Night*). Director Claude Autant-Lara.

1957–1958

Hommes et loups (also known as *Men and Wolves*). Director Giuseppe De Santis.
Les sorcières de Salem / The Crucible. Director Raymond Rouleau.
Un dénommé squarcio (also known as *The Wide Blue Road*). Director Gillo Pontecorvo.
Premier mai (also known as *The First Day of May*). Director Luis Saslavsky.

1959

La loi / Where the Hot Wind Blows! Director Jules Dassin.

1960

Let's Make Love / Le milliardaire. Director George Cukor.

1961

Sanctuary / Sanctuaire. Director Tony Richardson.
Goodbye Again / Aimez-vous Brahms? Director Anatole Litvak.

1962

My Geisha / Ma geisha. Director Jack Cardiff.

1965

Compartiment tueurs / The Sleeping Car Murder. Director Costa-Gavras.

1966

Paris brule-t-il? / Is Paris Burning? Director René Clément.
La guerre est finie / The War Is Over. Director Alain Resnais.
Grand Prix. Director John Frankenheimer.

1967

Vivre pour vivre / Live for Life. Director Claude Lelouch.

1968

Un soir, un train / One Night . . . a Train. Director André Delvaux.
Mr. Freedom. Director William Klein.

1969

Le diable par la queue / The Devil by the Tail. Director Philippe de Broca.
Z. Director Costa-Gavras.

1970

On a Clear Day You Can See Forever / Melinda. Director Vincente Minelli.
L'aveu / The Confession. Director Costa-Gavras.
Le cercle rouge. Director Jean-Pierre Melville.

1971

La folie des grandeurs / Delusions of Grandeur. Director Gérard Oury.

1972

Tout va bien (also known as *All's Well*). Director Jean-Luc Godard.
César et Rosalie. Director Claude Sautet.

1973

État de siege / State of Siege. Director Costa-Gavras.
Le fils (also known as *The Son*). Director Pierre Granier-Deferre.

1974

Le hazard et la violence (also known as *Chance and Violence*). Director Philippe Labro.
Vincent, François, Paul et les autres / Vincent, François, Paul and the Others. Director Claude Sautet.

1975

Le sauvage / Lovers Like Us. Director Jean-Paul Rappeneau.

1976

Police Python 357. Director Alain Corneau.

Le grand escogriffe (also known as *The Big Operator*). Director Claude Pinoteau.

1977

La menace (also known as *The Threat*). Director Alain Corneau.

1978

Les routes du sud / Roads to the South. Director Joseph Losey.

1979

Clair de femme / Womanlight. Director Costa-Gavras.
I comme Icare (also known as *I . . . for Icarus*). Director Henri Verneuil.

1981

Le choix des armes / Choice of Arms. Director Alain Corneau.

1982

Tout feu, tout flame (also known as *All Fired Up*). Director Jean-Paul Rappeneau.

1983

Garçon! (also known as *Waiter!*). Director Claude Sautet.

1986

Jean de Florette. Director Claude Berri.
Manon des sources / Manon of the Spring. Director Claude Berri.

1988

Trois places pour le 26 / Three Seats for the 26th. Director Jacques Demy.

1992

IP5, L'ile aux pachyderms / IP5: The Island of Pachyderms. Director Jean-Jacques Beineix.

Notes

Introduction

1. Moira Hodgson, "Yves Montand: From the Music Hall to the Met," *New York Times,* September 5, 1982.

2. John Phillips, "France Mourns Montand," *The Times* (London), November 11, 1991.

1. The Blackshirts Come

1. Yves Montand, with Hervé Hamon and Patrick Rotman, *You See, I Haven't Forgotten,* translated by Jeremy Leggatt (New York: Knopf, 1992), 3–7.

2. Paola E. Signoretta, James M. Powell, and Martin Clark, "Economic and Political Crisis: The Two Red Years," section in "Italy," *Encyclopedia Britannica* online, updated April 20, 2023, at https://www.britannica.com/place/Italy/Economic-and-political-crisis-the-two-red-years.

3. Harold Henry Fischer, *The Communist Revolution: An Outline of Strategy and Tactics* (Stanford, CA: Stanford University Press, 1955), 13.

4. Jasper Ridley, *Mussolini* (London: Constable, 1997), 112–20.

5. Ridley, *Mussolini,* 106.

6. Quoted in Montand, with Hamon and Rotman, *You See,* 9.

7. Office of the Historian, US Department of State, "The Immigration Act of 1924 (the Johnson-Reed Act)," at https://history.state.gov/milestones/1921-1936/immigration-act.

8. Yves Montand, with Jean Denys, *Du soleil plein la tête* (Paris: Editeurs francais réunis, 1955), 7.

9. Montand, with Hamon and Rotman, *You See,* 14.

10. David Crackanthorpe, *Marseille* (Oxford: Signal Books, 2012), 150.

11. Crackanthorpe, *Marseille,* xii–xvi.

2. Amateur Night

1. Yves Montand, with Carole Amiel, *Montand par Montand: Confidences et entretiens présentés par Carole Amiel* (Paris: Nouveau monde, 2016), 19; all translations of non-English material are mine unless otherwise indicated in note source citations.

2. Montand, with Hamon and Rotman, *You See,* 45.

3. Montand, with Hamon and Rotman, *You See,* 52.

4. Montand, with Hamon and Rotman, *You See,* 53.

5. Montand, with Hamon and Rotman, *You See,* 55–57, quote from Elvire on 55.

6. Montand, with Hamon and Rotman, *You See,* 56–57.

7. Quoted in Russell Miller, *World War II: The Resistance* (Alexandria, VA: Time-Life Books, 1979), 81.

8. Quoted in Miller, *World War II,* 29

9. Quoted in Alan Riding, *And the Show Went On: Cultural Life in Nazi-Occupied Paris* (New York: Knopf, 2010), 38.

3. "I Discover My Career"

1. Justus Rosenberg, *The Art of Resistance: My Four Years in the French Underground* (New York: William Morrow, 2020), 110.

2. Quoted in Riding, *And the Show Went On,* 77.

3. Michèle Morgan, *Avec ces yeux-là* (Paris: Robert Laffont, 1977), 146.

4. Quoted in Riding, *And the Show Went On,* 58.

5. Quoted in "La peine et l'argent," *Candide,* May 22, 1967.

6. Quoted in Montand, with Hamon and Rotman, *You See,* 62.

7. Quoted in Montand, with Hamon and Rotman, *You See,* 67.

8. Reproduction of Montand's scrapbook in Michel Giniès, *Yves Montand* (Paris: Vade retro, 1995), 22.

9. Quoted in Montand, with Hamon and Rotman, *You See,* 72.

10. Giniès, *Yves Montand,* 6–8.

11. Maurice Rajsfus, *La police de Vichy: Les Forces de l'ordre françaises au service de la Gestapo, 1940/44* (Paris: Cherche midi, 1995), 209–17.

12. Quoted in Crackanthorpe, *Marseille,* 153.

13. Benjamin Castaldi and Frederic Massot, *Je vous ai tant aimés: Montand et Signoret, un couple dans l'histoire* (Paris: Éditions du Rocher, 2021), 40.

14. Montand, with Hamon and Rotman, *You See,* 81.

15. Montand, with Hamon and Rotman, *You See,* 89.

4. Edith

1. Larry Collins and Dominique Lapierre, *Is Paris Burning?* (New York: Simon & Schuster, 1965), 236.

2. Jacques Pessis and Jacques Crépineau, *Le Moulin Rouge* (Paris: Hermé, 1989), 12, quoting the local paper.

3. Simone Berteaut, *Piaf: A Biography* (New York: Harper & Row, 1972), 216–18.

4. Edith Piaf, *Au bal de la chance* (Paris: L'Archipel, 2003), Kindle ed., loc. 1267–68.

5. Edith Piaf, *My Life* (London: Penguin, 1992), 89.

6. Montand, with Denys, *Du soleil plein la tête,* 198.

7. Montand, with Hamon and Rotman, *You See,* 107.

8. Montand, with Hamon and Rotman, *You See,* 109.

9. Montand, with Hamon and Rotman, *You See,* 110

10. Montand, with Hamon and Rotman, *You See,* 119.

11. Quoted in Berteaut, *Piaf,* 241.

12. Carole Amiel and Valentin Livi, *Yves Montand—Il y a ceux qui rêvent les yeux ouverts et ceux qui vivent les yeux fermés* (Paris: Michel Lafon, 2011), 63.

13. *La dépêche de Paris* and *Opéra* quoted in Montand, with Hamon and Rotman, *You See,* 133.

14. Quoted in Berteaut, *Piaf,* 248.

5. First Films

1. Telegram and Piaf quoted in Carolyn Burke, *No Regrets: The Life of Edith Piaf* (New York: Knopf, 2011), Kindle ed., loc. 1901.

2. Hodgson, "Yves Montand."

3. Quoted in Richard Cannavo and Henri Quiquéré, *Montand: Le chant d'un homme* (Paris: Robert Laffont, 1983), 92.

4. Eon Wood, *Dietrich: A Biography* (London: Sanctuary, 2002), 247.

5. Quoted in Norma Bosquet and Michel Rachline, *Marlene Dietrich: Les derniers secrets* (Paris: Nouveau monde, 2007), 58.

6. Wood, *Dietrich,* 247.

7. Marcel Carné, *La vie à belles dents* (Paris: Jean-Pierre Ollivier, 1975), 267.

8. Carné, *La vie à belles dents,* 268.

9. Quoted in Montand, with Hamon and Rotman, *You See,* 149.

10. Henry Magnan, "*Les portes de la nuit,*" *Le Monde,* December 6, 1946.

11. Quoted in Alain Rémond, *Montand* (Paris: Henri Veyrier, 1982), 44.

12. Reproduced in Montand, with Amiel, *Montand par Montand,* 16.

13. Henry Magnan, "Yves Montand à l'Étoile," *Le Monde,* September 25, 1946.

14. Quoted in Amiel and Livi, *Yves Montand,* 73.

15. Montand, with Hamon and Rotman, *You See,* 154.

16. Photo caption, *Motion Picture Herald,* February 1, 1947.

17. Details about the lawsuit and the quote from Reissar are given in Patricia A. DeMaio, *Garden of Dreams: The Life of Simone Signoret* (Jackson: University Press of Mississippi, 2013), 85.

6. Simone

1. Quoted in Montand, with Hamon and Rotman, *You See,* 161.

2. Montand, with Denys, *Du soleil plein la tête,* 226.

3. Quoted in DeMaio, *Garden of Dreams,* 84.

4. Montand, with Hamon and Rotman, *You See,* 188.

5. Simone Signoret, *Nostalgia Isn't What It Used to Be,* trans. Harper & Row (London: Weidenfeld and Nicolson, 1978), 83.

6. Montand, with Hamon and Rotman, *You See,* 187.

7. Montand, with Hamon and Rotman, *You See,* 192.

8. Quoted in DeMaio, *Garden of Dreams,* 83.

9. Signoret, *Nostalgia,* 83.

10. Signoret, *Nostalgia,* 87–88.

11. Quoted in Laura Bergquist, "The Lives and Loves of Simone Signoret," *Look,* August 1960.

12. Quoted in DeMaio, *Garden of Dreams,* 45.

13. Signoret, *Nostalgia,* 40.

14. Signoret, *Nostalgia,* 88.

15. Quoted in Castaldi and Massot, *Je vous ai tant aimés,* 100–101.

16. Claude Gauteur, conversation with the author, July 10, 2021.

17. Quoted in Castaldi and Massot, *Je vous ai tant aimés,* 90.

18. Quoted in "La femme de sa vie," *Paris-Match,* November 21, 1991.

19. Quoted in Montand, with Hamon and Rotman, *You See,* 214.

20. Quoted in Hélène Delye, "Mémoires pour Simone," *Le Monde,* October 14, 2013.

21. Quoted in "Signoret–Montand, le couple mythique du cinéma français aurait cent ans," *Le Figaro,* March 25, 2021.

22. Quoted in Eric Pace, "Simone Signoret Dies in France at 64," *New York Times,* October 1, 1985.

23. Quoted in DeMaio, *Garden of Dreams,* 92.

24. DeMaio, *Garden of Dreams,* 115.

7. Political Activist

1. Jane Fonda, *My Life so Far* (London: Ebury, 2006), 138–39.

2. Montand, with Hamon and Rotman, *You See,* 238.

3. Quoted in Montand, with Hamon and Rotman, *You See,* 241.

4. Montand, with Hamon and Rotman, *You See,* 240.

5. DeMaio, *Garden of Dreams,* 98; Walter A. McDougall, "The Stockholm Appeal of 1950," section in "20th-Century International Relations," *Encyclopedia Britannica* online, updated April 2, 2023, at https://www.britannica.com/topic/Stockholm-Appeal-of-1950.

6. Montand, with Hamon and Rotman, *You See,* 232–35.

7. Montand, with Hamon and Rotman, *You See,* 246.

8. Laurent Delahousse, announcer, "Alliance(s), couples de pouvoir, Signoret et Montand," *13h15 le Dimanche,* France 2 (television), September 6, 2020, at https://www.francetvinfo.fr/replay-magazine/france-2/13h15/13h15-du-dimanche-6-septembre-2020_4078813.html.

9. Signoret, *Nostalgia,* 98.

10. Quoted in Signoret, *Nostalgia,* 98.

11. Quoted in Cannavo and Quiquéré, *Montand,* 186.

12. Quoted in Cannavo and Quiquéré, *Montand,* 188.

13. Quoted in Patrick Rotman, "Il était d'abord un solitaire," *Paris-Match,* November 21, 1991.

14. Signoret, *Nostalgia,* 88.

15. Henry Magnan, "Yves Montand montreur d'images," *Le Monde,* March 10, 1951.

8. Star

1. Quoted in José-Louis Bocquet and Marc Godin, *Clouzot cinéaste* (Paris: Éditions de la table ronde, 2012), Kindle ed., loc. 226.

2. Quoted in Samuel Blumenfeld, "Cannes 2017: 'Le salaire de la peur,'" *Le Monde,* May 19, 2017.

3. Blumenfeld, "Cannes 2017."

4. Bocquet and Godin, *Clouzot cinéaste,* loc. 1370; Signoret, *Nostalgia,* 102.

5. DeMaio, *Garden of Dreams,* 106.

6. Bocquet and Godin, *Clouzot cinéaste,* loc. 1384.

7. Bocquet and Godin, *Clouzot cinéaste,* loc. 1384.

8. Blumenfeld, "Cannes 2017."

9. Signoret, *Nostalgia,* 102.

10. Jean de Baroncelli, "*Le salaire de la peur,* un coup de foudre," *Le Monde,* April 17, 1953.

11. Quoted in Bocquet and Godin, *Clouzot cinéaste,* loc. 1522–25.

12. Ted Loos, "The Most Suspenseful Movie Ever Made," *Esquire,* November 2005.

13. Vincent Canby, "Review/Film: Clouzot's 'Wages of Fear' Version Complete," *New York Times,* October 18, 1991.

14. Rémond, *Montand,* 52.

15. "Billboard Year-End Hot 30 Chart for 1953," Music Outfitters, n.d., at https://www.musicoutfitters.com/topsongs/1953.htm.

16. Anthony Bonner, introduction to *Songs of the Troubadours,* ed. Anthony Bonner (London: Allen & Unwin, 1972), 3, 15.

17. Ezra Pound, *A Walking Tour of Southern France* (New York: New Directions, 1992), 84, 93.

18. Ana Guigui, conversation with the author, August 21, 2021.

19. Signoret, *Nostalgia,* 118.

20. Montand, with Denys, *Du soleil plein la tête,* 238.

21. Signoret, *Nostalgia,* 117.

22. Périer quoted in Emmanuel Bonini, *Le veritable Yves Montand* (Paris: Pygmalion, 2021), 254; Reggiani quoted in Amiel and Livi, *Yves Montand,* 44.

9. Salem

1. Signoret, *Nostalgia,* 123.

2. Arthur Miller, "Why I Wrote 'The Crucible,'" *The New Yorker,* October 21 and 28, 1996.

3. Montand, with Hamon and Rotman, *You See,* 254.

4. Cannavo and Quiquéré, *Montand,* 78.

5. Signoret, *Nostalgia,* 126.

6. Quoted in Miller, "Why I Wrote 'The Crucible.'"

7. Quoted in Miller, "Why I Wrote 'The Crucible.'"

8. Miller, "Why I Wrote 'The Crucible.'"

9. Quoted in Montand, with Hamon and Rotman, *You See,* 256.

10. Robert Kemp, "*Les sorcières de Salem,*" *Le Monde,* December 18, 1954.

11. Signoret, *Nostalgia,* 127.

12. Signoret, *Nostalgia,* 128.

13. Arthur Miller, *Timebends: A Life* (New York: Grove Press, 1987), 349.

14. Bosley Crowther, "Screen: French 'Crucible,'" *New York Times,* December 9, 1958.

15. Jean de Baroncelli, "*Les sorcières de Salem,*" *Le Monde,* May 2, 1957.

10. Moscow

1. Signoret, *Nostalgia,* 145–46.

2. Montand, with Hamon and Rotman, *You See,* 265.

3. Quoted in DeMaio, *Garden of Dreams,* 135.

4. Montand, with Amiel, *Montand par Montand,* 36–37.

5. *Yves Montand Is Singing,* 1956, at https://www.net-film.ru/en/film-4886/?search=qyves%20montand%20is%20singing.

6. Signoret, *Nostalgia,* 160.

7. Montand, with Hamon and Rotman, *You See,* 275.

8. Montand, with Hamon and Rotman, *You See,* 275.

9. Signoret, *Nostalgia,* 167–72.

10. Montand, with Hamon and Rotman, *You See,* 272.

11. Signoret, *Nostalgia,* 169.

12. Montand, with Hamon and Rotman, *You See,* 273.

13. Quoted in Cannavo and Quiquéré, *Montand,* 207.

11. New York

1. Montand, with Hamon and Rotman, *You See,* 282.

2. Quoted in Montand, with Hamon and Rotman, *You See,* 278.

3. Signoret, *Nostalgia,* 200.

4. Signoret, *Nostalgia,* 208.

5. Montand, with Hamon and Rotman, *You See,* 281, ellipses in original.

6. Quoted in Cannavo and Quiquéré, *Montand,* 204.

7. Montand, with Hamon and Rotman, *You See,* 403.

8. Quoted in Giniès, *Yves Montand,* 43.

9. Quoted in Rémond, *Montand,* 77.

10. Montand, with Amiel, *Montand par Montand,* 39.

11. Claude Sarraute, "À l'Étoile," *Le Monde,* October 8, 1958.

12. Pace, "Simone Signoret Dies in France at 64," quoting the earlier *New York Times* article.

13. Quoted in DeMaio, *Garden of Dreams,* 166.

14. Signoret, *Nostalgia,* 227.

15. Montand, with Hamon and Rotman, *You See,* 291.

16. Giniès, *Yves Montand,* 76.

17. Signoret, *Nostalgia,* 250.

18. Montand, with Hamon and Rotman, *You See,* 295.

19. Excerpt from the *New York Post* review on an advertising poster for the show reproduced in Giniès, *Yves Montand,* 71.

20. Quoted in Giniès, *Yves Montand,* 71.

21. Quoted in Giniès, *Yves Montand,* 71.

22. Kenneth Campbell, "Theater: Yves Montand; Gallic Actor-Singer Opens One-Man Show," *New York Times*, September 23, 1959.

23. Kenneth Tynan, "Direct from Paris," *The New Yorker,* October 3, 1959.

24. Signoret, *Nostalgia,* 257.

25. Quoted in Montand, Hamon and Rotman, *You See,* 300.

12. Hollywood

1. Yves Montand, guest appearance on *The Dinah Shore Chevy Show,* November 15, 1959, at https://m.ina.fr/video/CAF88034264/yves-montand-aux-usa-ok-mister-montand-video.html.

2. Montand, with Hamon and Rotman, *You See,* 306; also quoted in Barbara Leaming, *Marilyn Monroe* (New York: Crown, 1998), 337.

3. Quoted in Donald Spoto, *Marilyn Monroe: The Biography* (New York: HarperCollins, 1993), 411.

4. Signoret, *Nostalgia,* 286.

5. "*Let's Make Love,*" *Variety,* December 31, 1959.

6. Bosley Crowther, "The Screen: Milton Berle Steals Show in 'Let's Make Love,'" *New York Times,* September 9, 1960.

7. Jean de Baroncelli, "*Le milliardaire,*" *Le Monde,* October 12, 1960.

8. Montand, with Hamon and Rotman, *You See,* 333.

9. Quoted in Spoto, *Marilyn Monroe,* 358.

10. Quoted in Leaming, *Marilyn Monroe,* 330.

11. Miller, *Timebends,* 483.

12. Leaming, *Marilyn Monroe,* 329.

13. Quoted in Spoto, *Marilyn Monroe,* 411.

14. Quoted in Leaming, *Marilyn Monroe,* 329.

15. Quoted in Spoto, *Marilyn Monroe,* 414, emphasis in original.

16. "Powerful Stars Meet to Play-Act Romance," *Life,* August 15, 1960, cover.

17. Montand, with Hamon and Rotman, *You See,* 306.

18. The card is reproduced in Amiel and Livi, *Yves Montand*, 127.

19. Montand, with Hamon and Rotman, *You See,* 307.

20. Signoret, *Nostalgia,* 269.

21. Quoted in Spoto, *Marilyn Monroe,* 413, emphasis in original.

22. Spyros P. Skouros, "Design for Perpetuity," *Fox Dynamo,* February 1960.

23. "*Let's Make Love:* A Star-Packed Blockbuster," *Fox Dynamo,* February 1960.

24. Louella Parsons, "I Am Going to Adopt a Baby," *Modern Screen,* January 20, 1960, emphasis in original.

25. Quoted in James Curtis, *Spencer Tracy* (New York: Knopf, 2011), 795.

26. Leaming, *Marilyn Monroe,* 353.

27. Montand, with Hamon and Rotman, *You See,* 317; Leaming, *Marilyn Monroe,* 340, 344.

13. Marilyn

1. Quoted in "Powerful Stars Meet to Play-Act Romance," *Life,* August 15, 1960.

2. Leaming, *Marilyn Monroe,* 340, 343, 352.

3. Quoted in Signoret, *Nostalgia,* 293.

4. Signoret, *Nostalgia,* 294.

5. "A Legend Is Costly, but It's Worth It," *Life,* August 15, 1960.

6. Montand, with Hamon and Rotman, *You See,* 322–23.

7. Montand, with Hamon and Rotman, *You See,* 324.

8. Montand, with Hamon and Rotman, *You See,* 316–20.

9. Pauline Kael, "A Rip-off with Genius," *New York Times,* July 22, 1973.

10. Montand, with Hamon and Rotman, *You See,* 325.

11. Quoted in DeMaio, *Garden of Dreams,* 201–2.

12. "Powerful Stars Meet to Play-Act Romance."

13. Doug Brewer, "The Man Who Almost Destroyed Marilyn Monroe's Marriage," *Modern Screen,* November 1960.

14. Montand, with Hamon and Rotman, *You See,* 324–25.

15. Montand, with Hamon and Rotman, *You See,* 326.

16. Jean-Louis Livi, conversation with the author, July 10, 2021.

17. Montand, with Hamon and Rotman, *You See,* 328, 333.

18. DeMaio, *Garden of Dreams,* 193–94.

19. Quoted in Spoto, *Marilyn Monroe,* 442, and DeMaio, *Garden of Dreams,* 206.

20. Louella Parsons, "The Love Scandal of the Decade," *Modern Screen,* December 1960.

21. Quoted in Montand, with Hamon and Rotman, *You See,* 330.

22. Delahousse, "Alliance(s), couples de pouvoir, Signoret et Montand."

23. DeMaio, *Garden of Dreams,* 204.

24. Montand, with Hamon and Rotman, *You See,* 328–29.

25. Quoted in DeMaio, *Garden of Dreams,* 205.

26. "Marilyn a-t-elle seduit Yves Montand?," *Jours de France,* August 6, 1960.

27. "Marilyn Monroe divorce-t-elle pour Yves Montand?," *Noir et blanc,* November 18, 1960.

28. Signoret, *Nostalgia,* 298.

29. Ivan Levaî in Delahousse, "Alliance(s), couples de pouvoir, Signoret et Montand."

30. Quoted in Spoto, *Marilyn Monroe,* 420.

31. "Enfin Simone et Yves se retrouve pour toujours," *Paris-Match,* November 21, 1991.

32. Brad Darrach, "Yves Montand," *People,* May 16, 1988.

33. Benjamin Castaldi, *Maintenant il faudra tout se dire* (Paris: Albin Michel, 2004), 82.

34. Quoted in Montand, with Hamon and Rotman, *You See,* 389, 334.

35. Quoted in DeMaio, *Garden of Dreams,* 253.
36. Quoted in Montand, with Hamon and Rotman, *You See,* 336.
37. Montand, with Hamon and Rotman, *You See,* 336.
38. Signoret, *Nostalgia,* 302.
39. Quoted in Montand, with Hamon and Rotman, *You See,* 302.

14. Three More for Fox

1. William Faulkner, *Sanctuary* (New York: Modern Library, 1931), vi.
2. E. Pauline Degenfelder, "The Four Faces of Temple Drake: Faulkner's *Sanctuary, Requiem for a Nun,* and the Two Film Adaptations," *American Quarterly* 28, no. 5 (Winter 1976): 544–60, at https://www.jstor.org/stable/2712288.
3. Degenfelder, "The Four Faces of Temple Drake."
4. Bosley Crowther, "The Screen: 'Sanctuary' Adaptation of Faulkner Novels Has Premiere," *New York Times,* February 22, 1961.
5. Degenfelder, "The Four Faces of Temple Drake."
6. Charlotte Chandler, *Ingrid: Ingrid Bergman, a Personal Biography* (New York: Simon & Schuster, 2007), 221; Ingrid Bergman and Alan Burgess, *Ingrid Bergman: My Story* (London: Michael Joseph, 1980), 135.
7. Film Score Monthly Liner Notes, *Goodbye Again* (1961), n.d., at https://www.filmscoremonthly.com/notes/goodbye_again.html.
8. Quoted in Bergman and Burgess, *Ingrid,* 366, emphasis in original.
9. Chandler, *Ingrid,* 222.
10. Quoted in Brad Darrach, "Return of *Psycho,*" *People,* June 13, 1983.
11. Bergman and Burgess, *Ingrid,* 135.
12. Bosley Crowther, "Screen: 'Goodbye Again' at 2 Theaters," *New York Times,* June 30, 1961.
13. Jean de Baroncelli, "Cannes à Paris," *Le Monde,* May 27, 1961.
14. Eugene Archer, "'Butterfly' Film Will Be Comedy," *New York Times,* August 24, 1960.
15. Shirley MacLaine, *My Lucky Stars: A Hollywood Memoir* (New York: Bantam, 1995), 314.
16. Montand, with Hamon and Rotman, *You See,* 337.
17. Quoted in Montand, with Hamon and Rotman, *You See,* 337.
18. MacLaine, *My Lucky Stars,* 310–12.
19. MacLaine, *My Lucky Stars,* 323–24.
20. MacLaine, *My Lucky Stars,* 325–26.
21. "*My Geisha,*" *Variety,* December 31, 1961.
22. A. H. Weiler, "*My Geisha* Arrives," *New York Times,* June 14, 1962.
23. Jean de Baroncelli, "*Ma geisha,*" *Le Monde,* February 24, 1962.
24. MacLaine, *My Lucky Stars,* 328.

15. Mixing Stage and Screen

1. Quoted in "Montand: 'Je ferai ma rentrée à Paris," *France-Soir,* February 18, 1961.

2. Excerpt in an advertisement for the show that is reproduced in Giniès, *Yves Montand,* 75.

3. Quoted in Giniès, *Yves Montand,* 75.

4. Howard Taubman, "Theater: Yves Montand Evokes Paris," *New York Times,* October 25, 1961.

5. "Yves Montand: 'Mon recital d'autumn,'" *France-Soir,* March 15, 1962.

6. "Yves Montand redevient Français," *Paris-Jour,* October 23, 1962.

7. The details here come from the author's telephone conversation with media relations at John F. Kennedy Presidential Library and Archives, Boston.

8. Reproduced in Amiel and Livi, *Yves Montand,* 83.

9. Montand, with Hamon and Rotman, *You See,* 341.

10. Montand, with Amiel, *Montand par Montand,* 128–30.

11. Herb Gardner, *A Thousand Clowns,* in *The Collected Plays* (New York: Applause, 2000), 58.

12. Quoted in Leslie Bennetts, "Most Funny Stuff Is Born of Pain," *New York Times,* June 2, 1985.

13. B. Poirot-Delpech, "*Des clowns par milliers,*" *Le Monde,* December 11, 1963.

14. Montand, with Hamon and Rotman, *You See,* 343–44.

15. Montand, with Hamon and Rotman, *You See,* 344.

16. Konstantinos Costa-Gavras, *Va où il est impossible d'aller—mémoires* (Paris: Points, 2021), 130.

17. James Michael Martin, "'The Sleeping Car Murder (Compartiment tueurs)' by Costa-Gavras," *Film Quarterly* 21, no. 3 (Spring 1968): 44.

18. Bosley Crowther, "Screen: 'The Sleeping Car Murder,'" *New York Times,* March 8, 1966.

19. Costa-Gavras, *Va où il est impossible d'aller,* 137.

20. Costa-Gavras, *Va où il est impossible d'aller,* 132.

21. For Montand on his political films with Costa-Gavras, see *Hexagonal*, France Television, Regions 3 Marseille, May 21, 1978, at https://m.ina.fr/video/I00005146/yves-montand-sur-ses-films-politiques-video.html.

22. Montand, with Hamon and Rotman, *You See,* 346–47.

23. Quoted in Bruce Weber, "Jorge Semprún, Who Blurred Line between Novel and Memoir, Is Dead at 87," *New York Times,* June 10, 2011.

24. Quoted in Weber, "Jorge Semprún."

25. Soledad Fox Maura, *Exile, Writer, Soldier, Spy: Jorge Semprún* (New York: Arcade, 2016), 190–93.

26. Jorge Semprún, *Montand, la vie continue* (Paris: Denoël, 1983), 143.

27. Michel Ciment, conversation with the author, October 15, 2021.

28. Yvonne Baby, "Rêve et révolution," *Le Monde,* May 11, 1966.

29. Montand, with Hamon and Rotman, *You See,* 349–51.

16. The Sixties

1. Quoted in Rémond, *Montand,* 106.

2. Jean Planchais, "*Paris brule-t-il?,*" *Le Monde,* October 26, 1966.

3. Bosley Crowther, "The Screen: 'Is Paris Burning?,'" *New York Times*, November 11, 1966.

4. John Frankenheimer on "Making Of," bonus feature on *Grand Prix* (1966), DVD, Turner Entertainment Co. and Joel Productions, 2006.

5. Jim Russell on "Making Of," bonus feature on *Grand Prix* DVD.

6. Quoted in Bosley Crowther, "Freewheeling Film in Monaco Puts Stars in Grand Prix Cars," *New York Times*, May 20, 1966.

7. Quoted in Rémond, *Montand*, 109.

8. Jean de Baroncelli, "*Vivre pour vivre*," *Le Monde*, September 16, 1967.

9. "*Live for Life*," *Variety*, December 23, 1966.

10. Roger Ebert, "*Live for Life*," *Chicago Sun-Times*, May 8, 1968.

11. Quoted in Rémond, *Montand*, 112–13.

12. Quoted in Rémond, *Montand*, 116.

13. Quoted in Rémond, *Montand*, 119.

14. Quoted in Joseph Harriss, "Something Happened: May 1968," in *About France* (New York: iUniverse, 2005), 155–67.

15. Quoted in Harriss, "Something Happened: May 1968," 166.

16. Quoted in Montand, with Hamon and Rotman, *You See*, 352.

17. Quoted in Montand, with Hamon and Rotman, *You See*, 353.

18. Montand, with Amiel, *Montand par Montand*, 59.

17. "The Best Political Thriller Ever"

1. Quoted in Rémond, *Montand*, 129.

2. Quoted in Maura, *Exile, Writer, Soldier, Spy*, 191.

3. Quoted in Costa-Gavras, *Va où il est impossible d'aller*, 174.

4. Robert D. McFadden, "Mikis Theodorakis, 'Zorba' Composer and Marxist Rebel, Dies at 96," *New York Times*, September 2, 2021.

5. Steven B. Roberts, "Greece Sees 'Z' and Gets Excited," *New York Times*, January 13, 1975.

6. Quoted in Costa-Gavras, *Va où il est impossible d'aller*, 189–90.

7. Vincent Canby, "Screen: Greek Symbols; Costa-Gavras Directs 'Z,'" *New York Times*, December 9, 1969.

8. Roger Ebert, "Z," *Chicago Sun-Times*, December 30, 1969.

9. Wendell Steavenson, "Seven Movies to Watch," *The New Yorker*, December 9, 2013.

10. David Thomson, "Costa-Gavras," in David Thomson, *The New Biographical Dictionary of Film* (London: Little, Brown, 2010), 204.

11. "William Friedkin's Favorite Films of All Time," *Fade In Magazine*, video, June 12, 2013, YouTube, at https://www.youtube.com/watch?v=p-APzEjrklc.

12. "Oliver Stone," *Le Figaro*, July 13, 2021.

13. Quoted in Cannavo and Quiquéré, *Montand*, 226.

14. Montand, with Hamon and Rotman, *You See*, 355.

15. Quoted in Montand, with Hamon and Rotman, *You See*, 357.

16. Montand, with Hamon and Rotman, *You See,* 358–59; Delahousse, "Alliance(s), couples de pouvoir, Signoret et Montand."

17. Jean-Louis Livi, conversation with the author, October 10, 2021.

18. Quoted in Montand, with Hamon and Rotman, *You See,* 360–61.

19. Semprún, *Montand,* 178–80.

20. Danièle Heymann, "Yves Montand vieillit bien," *L'Express,* September 16–22, 1968.

21. Claude Sarraute, "Yves Montand à l'Olympia," *Le Monde,* September 21, 1968.

22. Quoted in Philippe Crocq, *Montand: Qu'est-ce qu'elles avaient à tant l'aimer?* (Paris: Presses de la cité, 2011), 67.

18. The Other Political Films

1. Anne Edwards, *Streisand: It Only Happens Once; A Biography* (Boston: Little, Brown, 1997), 278–79.

2. Crocq, *Montand,* 67.

3. Quoted in Edwards, *Streisand,* 279.

4. Vincent Canby, "Screen: 'On a Clear Day You Can See Forever' Begins Its Run," *New York Times,* June 18, 1970.

5. Quoted in Edwards, *Streisand,* 279.

6. Quoted in Cannavo and Quiquéré, *Montand,* 138, emphasis in original.

7. Quoted in Cannavo and Quiquéré, *Montand,* 125.

8. Quoted in Montand, with Hamon and Rotman, *You See,* 385.

9. Quoted in Montand, with Hamon and Rotman, *You See,* 361.

10. Cynthia Grenier, "The 'Z' People Make a 'Confession,'" *New York Times,* December 6, 1970.

11. Quoted in Montand, with Hamon and Rotman, *You See,* 368.

12. Montand, with Hamon and Rotman, *You See,* 368.

13. Semprún, *Montand,* 198.

14. Vincent Canby, "Film: Costa-Gavras Depicts a Believer's Betrayal by His Belief," *New York Times,* December 10, 1970.

15. Quoted in Montand, with Hamon and Rotman, *You See,* 369.

16. Quoted in Montand, with Hamon and Rotman, *You See,* 370.

17. "Montand à Prague," *Paris-Match,* February 1, 1990.

18. Quoted in Montand, with Hamon and Rotman, *You See,* 370.

19. Quoted in Cannavo and Quiquéré, *Montand,* 223.

20. Rémond, *Montand,* 148, 150.

21. Fonda, *My Life so Far,* 278.

22. Yvonne Baby, "Jean-Luc Godard: Pour mieux écouter les autres," *Le Monde,* April 27, 1972.

23. Quoted in Rémond, *Montand,* 150.

24. Fonda, *My Life so Far,* 278.

25. Quoted in "Yves Montand critique par la CGT pour 'Tout va bien,'" *Le Monde,* August 2, 1972.

26. Carole Amiel, conversation with the author, October 15, 2021.

27. Jean-Louis Livi, conversation with the author, October 10, 2021.

28. Mel Gussow, "Costa-Gavras Elaborates on Politics and Violence," *New York Times,* April 14, 1973.

29. Alan Riding, "Cuban 'Agent' Says US Police Aides Urged Torture," *New York Times,* August 5, 1978.

30. Costa-Gavras, *Va où il est impossible d'aller,* 225.

31. Costa-Gavras, *Va où il est impossible d'aller,* 246–47.

32. Quoted in Rémond, *Montand,* 160.

33. Gary Crowdus, "*State of Siege,*" *Cinéaste* 41, no. 1 (Winter 2015): 56–58.

34. Costa-Gavras, *Va où il est impossible d'aller,* 261; quote from Vincent Canby, "'Siege,' an Angry Muckraker," *New York Times,* April 22, 1973.

35. Theodore Sorensen, "'State of Siege' Speaks 'a Warning to Us All': Movies," *New York Times,* June 24, 1973.

19. From Music Hall to the Met

1. "Augusto Pinochet," *Encyclopedia Britannica* online, updated December 2022, at https://www.britannica.com/biography/Augusto-Pinochet.

2. Chris Marker, dir., *La solitude du chanteur de fond* (1974), DVD, Universal Music France, 2015.

3. Quoted in Montand, with Hamon and Rotman, *You See,* 403–4.

4. Quoted in Montand, with Hamon and Rotman, *You See,* 404.

5. Montand, with Amiel, *Montand par Montand,* 121.

6. Montand, with Amiel, *Montand par Montand,* 119.

7. John T. Correll, "The Euromissile Showdown," *Air Force Magazine,* February 1, 2020.

8. Radio interview on Europe 1, September 1983, quoted in Montand, with Hamon and Rotman, *You See,* 412.

9. Montand, with Hamon and Rotman, *You See,* 429.

10. Semprún, *Montand,* 224.

11. Richard Cannavo, "Un fabuleux coup de poker," *Le Matin,* October 7, 1981.

12. Luc Honorez, "Et la scene?" *Le soir de Bruxelles*, March 4, 1980.

13. Danièle Heymann, "La folie Montand," *L'Express,* March 26, 1982.

14. Danièle Heymann, "Montand à l'heure de Pagnol," *Le Monde,* August 23, 1986.

15. Quoted in Montand, with Hamon and Rotman, *You See,* 409.

16. Charley Marouani, *Une vie en coulisses* (Paris: Fayard, 2011), 147–50.

17. Hodgson, "Yves Montand."

18. Quoted in Hodgson, "Yves Montand."

19. Quoted in Hodgson, "Yves Montand."

20. Frank Rich, "Stage: Montand at the Metropolitan," *New York Times,* September 8, 1982.

21. Jane Boutwell, "Yves Montand," *The New Yorker,* August 29, 1982.

22. Montand, with Hamon and Rotman, *You See,* 434.

23. DeMaio, *Garden of Dreams,* 253, quoting Allégret.

24. Montand, with Hamon and Rotman, *You See,* 388.

25. Quoted in both DeMaio, *Garden of Dreams,* 258, and Montand, with Hamon and Rotman, *You See,* 390.

26. DeMaio, *Garden of Dreams,* 311, 257; Castaldi, *Maintenant, il faudra tout se dire,* 82.

27. Pace, "Simone Signoret Dies in France at 64."

28. Quoted in Pace, "Simone Signoret Dies in France at 64."

29. Castaldi and Massot, *Je vous ai tant aimés,* 260.

20. Montand President?

1. Quoted in Richard Bernstein, "France's Savory Tale of Fate," *New York Times,* June 21, 1987.

2. Danièle Heymann, "Au bonheur des larmes," *Le Monde,* November 2, 1986.

3. Heymann, "Montand à l'heure de Pagnol."

4. Michel Cicurel, "Comme un James Bond," *Le Monde,* February 25, 1984.

5. Quoted in Jacques Amalric, "Yves Montand face à la guerre," *Le Monde,* April 18, 1985.

6. Soviet embassy quoted in "L'ambassade d'URSS dénonce 'l'inaction des autorités françaises' face à cette 'sordide calomnie,'" *Le Monde,* April 20, 1985.

7. Quoted in Dominique Dhombres, "Haro sur 'Yves Mutant' 'renegat' et 'loup-garu,'" *Le Monde,* April 22, 1985.

8. Quoted in Giniès, *Yves Montand,* 148.

9. "Français, si vous changiez," *Paris-Match,* October 23, 1987.

10. John Vinocur, "Yves Montand and the Left at Odds," *New York Times,* October 10, 1983.

11. "La guerre des générations," *Paris-Match,* November 18, 1983.

12. These cover titles are cited in Bruno Frappat, "Bleu, blanc, gris," *Le Monde,* February 27, 1984.

13. John Vinocur, "The French John Wayne," *New York Times,* October 10, 1983.

14. Quoted in Judith Miller, "President Yves Montand? Not Everybody Scoffs," *New York Times,* May 23, 1986.

15. Montand, with Amiel, *Montand par Montand,* 210.

16. Quoted in Michel Gonod, "Montand: Si je crée un parti, ce sera celui du coeur," *Paris-Match,* June 20, 1986.

17. Quoted in Montand, with Hamon and Rotman, *You See,* 425.

18. Jean-Louis Livi, conversation with the author, October 10, 2021.

19. Montand, with Hamon and Rotman, *You See,* 423.

20. Carole Amiel, *Montand, tout simplement* (Paris: Nil, 1997), 52.

21. Carole Amiel, conversation with the author, August 23, 2021.

22. Darrach, "Yves Montand."

23. Amiel, *Montand, tout simplement,* 47.

24. Quoted in DeMaio, *Garden of Dreams,* 312.

25. Amiel, *Montand, tout simplement,* 48.

26. Quoted in Amiel and Livi, *Yves Montand,* 50.

27. Virginie Merlin, "À ceux qui pensent," *Paris-Match,* November 9, 1989.

28. Heymann, "Montand à l'heure de Pagnol."

29. Darrach, "Yves Montand."

30. Quoted in "Ainsi sortent les artistes!" (editorial), *Le Monde,* November 12, 1991.

31. Bonini, *Le veritable Yves Montand,* Kindle ed., loc. 500.

32. Quoted in Noelle Namia, "Beineix raconte Montand," *Paris-Match,* November 19, 1992.

33. Quoted in "Yves Montand, le récit de ses derniers jours," *Téléstar,* February 10, 2016.

34. "Montand la passion," *Paris-Match,* November 21, 1991.

35. Quoted in "Hommage à Yves Montand," *Le Monde,* November 12, 1991.

36. Quoted in "Hommage à Yves Montand."

37. Quoted in Phillips, "France Mourns Montand."

38. Marc Kravetz, "*La voix et les gestes,*" *Libération,* November 12, 1991.

39. "Montand la passion."

40. Quoted in "L'adieu de l'Italie," *Le Monde,* November 12, 1991.

41. Alan Riding, "Yves Montand, Sage Charmer of French Film and Politics, Dies at 70," *New York Times,* November 10, 1991.

42. "Hommage à Yves Montand."

Epilogue

1. "L'exhumation d'Yves Montand," *Le Monde,* November 9, 1997.

2. "La France bouleversée," *Paris-Match,* November 20, 1997.

3. Castaldi, *Maintenant, il faudra tout se dire,* 227–28.

4. Photo caption, *Paris-Match,* May 6, 2004.

5. Catherine Allégret, *Un monde à l'envers* (Paris: Fayard, 2004), 31.

6. Allégret, *Un monde à l'envers,* 31, 96.

7. Catherine Allégret-Livi, *Au non du père* (Paris: Stock, 1998), 138.

8. "L'outrage fait à Montand," *Paris-Match,* October 7, 2004.

9. Catherine Schwaab, "Jean-Claude Brialy," *Paris-Match,* October 7, 2004.

10. Bonini, *Le veritable Yves Montand,* 67–68.

11. Quoted in "Catherine Allégret viole la légende de Montand," *Paris-Match,* October 7, 2004.

Bibliography

Shortly before his death, Yves Montand granted two French journalists, Hervé Hamon and Patrick Rotman, many hours of interviews as well as access to his diaries and other personal documents. First published in French as *Tu vois, je n'ai pas oublié* in 1990, this collaborative work was published in an excellent English translation by Jeremy Leggatt two years later as *You See, I Haven't Forgotten.* It remains the inevitable starting point for any attempt to understand him. I freely acknowledge my debt to it.

Books

Abecassis, Michael, ed. *French Cinema in Close-up.* Dublin: Phaeton, 2015.

Aknin, Alain-Guy, and Philippe Crocq. *Yves Montand: Le temps n'efface rien.* Paris: Albin Michel, 2006.

Alion, Yves. *Claude Lelouch, mode d'emploi.* Paris: Calmann-Lévy, 2005.

Allégret, Catherine. *Un monde à l'envers.* Paris: Fayard, 2004.

Allégret-Livi, Catherine. *Au non du père.* Paris: Stock, 1998.

Amiel, Carole. *Lettres à Montand.* Neiuilly-sur-Seine, France: Lafon, 2006.

———. *Montand, tout simplement.* Paris: Nil, 1997.

———. *Yves Montand: La force du destin.* Paris: Éditions de la Martinière, 2021.

Amiel, Carole, and Valentin Livi. *Yves Montand—Il y a ceux qui rêvent les yeux ouverts et ceux qui vivent les yeux fermés.* Paris: Michel Lafon, 2011.

Andrew, Dudley. *Mists of Regret: Culture and Sensibility in Classic French Film.* Princeton, NJ: Princeton University Press, 1995.

Arnoul, Françoise, with Jean-Louis Mingalon. *Animal doué de bonheur.* Paris: Belfond, 1995.

Austin, Guy. *Stars in Modern French Film.* New York: Oxford University Press, 2003.

Banner, Lois W. *Marilyn: The Passion and the Paradox.* New York: Bloomsbury, 2012.

———. *MM—Personal: From the Private Archive of Marilyn Monroe.* New York: Abrams, 2010.

Barrot, O. *Inoubliables! Visages du cinema francais, 1930–1950.* Paris: Calmann-Lévy, 1986.

Bazin, André. *What Is Cinema?* 1967. Reprint. Berkeley: University of California Press, 1971.

Bergman, Ingrid, and Alan Burgess. *Ingrid Bergman: My Story.* London: Michael Joseph, 1980.

Berteaut, Simone. *Piaf: A Biography.* New York: Harper & Row, 1972.

Blinkhorn, Martin. *Mussolini and Fascist Italy.* London: Routledge, 2006.

Block, Marcelline, ed. *World Film Locations: Marseilles.* Chicago: Intellect Books, University of Chicago Press, 2013.

Bloom, Harold, and Neil Heims. *Arthur Miller.* Philadelphia: Chelsea House, 2003.

Bocquet, José-Louis, and Marc Godin. *Clouzot cinéaste.* Paris: Éditions de la table ronde, 2012.

Bonini, Emmanuel. *Piaf, la verité.* Paris: Pygmalion, 2008.

———. *Le veritable Yves Montand.* Paris: Pygmalion, 2021.

Bonner, Anthony. Introduction to *Songs of the Troubadours,* edited by Anthony Bonner, 1–30. London: Allen & Unwin, 1972.

Bosquet, Norma, and Michel Rachline. *Marlene Dietrich: Les derniers secrets.* Paris: Nouveau monde, 2007.

Bret, David. *Piaf: A Passionate Life.* London: Robson Books, 1998.

Burke, Carolyn. *No Regrets: The Life of Edith Piaf.* New York: Knopf, 2011.

Cannavo, Richard, and Henri Quiquéré. *Montand: Le chant d'un homme.* Paris: Robert Laffont, 1983.

Carné, Marcel. *La vie à belles dents.* Paris: Jean-Pierre Ollivier, 1975.

Carson, Neil. *Arthur Miller.* London: Macmillan, 1982.

Cassati, Sandro. *Yves Montand—le talent d'une vie.* Paris: City Edition, 2011.

Castaldi, Benjamin. *Maintenant, il faudra tout se dire.* Paris: Albin Michel, 2004.

Castaldi, Benjamin, and Frederic Massot. *Je vous ai tant aimés: Montand et Signoret, un couple dans l'histoire.* Paris: Éditions du Rocher, 2021.

Chandler, Charlotte. *Ingrid: Ingrid Bergman. A Personal Biography.* New York: Simon & Schuster, 2007.

Chirio, Maud. "The Other 911." In *France in the World: A New Global History,* edited by Patrick Boucheron, 831–37. New York: Other Press, 2019.

Ciment, Michel, and Jacques Zimmer. *La critique de cinéma en France: Histoire, anthologie, dictionnaire.* Paris: Ramsay, 1997.

Cinquini, Alain. *Montand vu par Cinquini.* Nice: France Europe Editions Livres, 1999.

Collins, Larry, and Dominique Lapierre. *Is Paris Burning?* New York: Simon & Schuster, 1965.

Conard, Mark T., ed. *The Philosophy of Film Noir.* Lexington: University Press of Kentucky, 2007.

Corrigan, Richard W., ed. *Arthur Miller: A Collection of Critical Essays.* Englewood Cliffs, NJ: Prentice-Hall, 1969.

Costa-Gavras, Konstantinos. *Va où il est impossible d'aller—mémoires.* Paris: Points, 2021.

Crackanthorpe, David. *Marseille.* Oxford: Signal Books, 2012.

Crisp, Colin. *The Classic French Cinema, 1930–1960.* Bloomington: Indiana University Press, 1997.

Crocq, Philippe. *Montand: Qu'est-ce qu'elles avaient à tant l'aimer?* Paris: Presses de la cité, 2011.

Curtis, James. *Spencer Tracy.* New York: Knopf, 2011.

Delarue, Jacques. *The Gestapo: A History of Horror.* Translated from the French by Mervyn Savill. London: Frontline Books, 2008.

Delpard, Raphaël. *Le roman d'amour . . . et de vie de Simone Signoret et Yves Montand.* Paris: Éditions de l'histoire, 2021.

DeMaio, Patricia A. *Garden of Dreams: The Life of Simone Signoret.* Jackson: University Press of Mississippi, 2013.

Dimendberg, Edward. *Film Noir and the Spaces of Modernity.* Cambridge, MA: Harvard University Press, 2004.

Dixon, Kathryn. *Marilyn.* Havertown, PA: Casemate, 2013.

Dixon, Wheeler W. *The Films of Jean-Luc Godard.* Albany: State University of New York Press, 1997.

Duggan, Christopher. *Fascist Voices: An Intimate History of Mussolini's Italy.* New York: Oxford University Press, 2013.

Edwards, Anne. *Streisand: It Only Happens Once; A Biography.* Boston: Little, Brown, 1997.

Eisenhower, Dwight D. *Crusade in Europe.* Garden City, NY: Doubleday, 1948.

Faulkner, William. *Sanctuary.* New York: Modern Library, 1931.

Fischer, Harold Henry. *The Communist Revolution: An Outline of Strategy and Tactics.* Stanford, CA: Stanford University Press, 1955.

Fonda, Jane. *My Life so Far.* London: Ebury, 2006.

Gardner, Herb. *The Collected Plays.* New York: Applause, 2000.

Giniès, Michel. *Yves Montand.* Paris: Vade retro, 1995.

Grzesiak, Nathalie. *Yves Montand, Simone Signoret, une passion engagée.* Paris: Acropole, 2001.

Guilcher, Emmanuelle. *Simone Signoret, une vie.* Paris: Le Grand livre du mois, 2005.

Harriss, Joseph. *About France.* New York: iUniverse, 2005.

Heims, Neil. *Arthur Miller.* Philadelphia: Chelsea House, 2003.

Hoyt, Edwin P. *Mussolini's Empire: The Rise and Fall of the Fascist Vision.* New York: Wiley, 1994.

Jackson, Julian. *The Popular Front in France: Defending Democracy 1934–1938.* Cambridge: Cambridge University Press, 1990.

Korb, Stéphane, and Carole Amiel. *Yves Montand.* Paris: Gawsewitz, 2011.

Leaming, Barbara. *Marilyn Monroe.* New York: Crown, 1998.

Lelouch, Claude. *Le dictionaire de ma vie.* Paris: Kero, 2016.

Lemarque, Francis. *J'ai la mémoire qui chante.* Paris: Éditions presses de la cite, 1992.

Lherminier, Pierre. *Signoret Montand: Deux vies dans le siècle.* Paris: Ramsay, 2005.

MacCabe, Colin. *Godard: A Portrait of the Artist at 70.* London: Bloomsbury, 2003.

MacLaine, Shirley. *My Lucky Stars: A Hollywood Memoir.* New York: Bantam, 1995.

Mailer, Norman. *Marilyn: A Biography.* New York: Grosset & Dunlap, 1973.

Marouani, Charley. *Une vie en coulisses.* Paris: Fayard, 2011.

Maura, Soledad Fox. *Exile, Writer, Soldier, Spy: Jorge Semprún.* New York: Arcade, 2016.

McGilligan, Patrick. *Backstory: Interviews with Screenwriters of Hollywood's Golden Age.* Berkeley: University of California Press, 1986.

———. *George Cukor, a Double Life: A Biography of the Gentleman Director.* New York: St. Martin's Press, 1991.

Mégret, Christian. *Yves Montand.* Paris: Calmann-Lévy, 1953.

Merwin, W. S. *The Mays of Ventadorn.* Washington, DC: National Geographic, 2002.

Meyers, Jeffrey. *The Genius and the Goddess: Arthur Miller and Marilyn Monroe.* Urbana: University of Illinois Press, 2010.

Mikkonen, Simo, Giles Scott-Smith, and Jari Parkkinen. *Entangled East and West: Cultural Diplomacy and Artistic Interaction during the Cold War.* Zurich: Springer Nature Switzerland, 2021.

Miller, Arthur. *Timebends: A Life.* New York: Grove Press, 1987.

Miller, Russell. *World War II: The Resistance.* Alexandria, VA: Time-Life Books, 1979.

Monroe, Marilyn. *My Story.* New York: Stein and Day, 1974.

Montand, Yves. *La chansonnette.* Paris: Livre de Poche, 1996.

Montand, Yves, with Carole Amiel. *Montand par Montand, confidences et entretiens, présentés par Carole Amiel.* Paris: Nouveau monde, 2016.

Montand, Yves, with Jean Denys. *Du soleil plein la tête.* Paris: Editeurs français réunis, 1955.

Montand, Yves, with Hervé Hamon and Patrick Rotman. *Montand raconte Montand: Récit recueilli par Hervé Hamon et Patrick Rotman.* Paris: Seuil, 2001.

———. *You See, I Haven't Forgotten.* Translated by Jeremy Leggatt. New York: Knopf, 1992.

Montserrat, Joëlle. *Yves Montand.* Paris: PAC, 1983.

Morgan, Michèle. *Avec ces yeux-là.* Paris: Robert Laffont, 1977.

Moss, Leonard. *Arthur Miller.* Boston: Twayne, 1967.

Office of the Historian, US Department of State. "The Immigration Act of 1924 (the Johnson-Reed Act)." N.d. At https://history.state.gov/milestones/1921-1936/immigration-act.

Pessis, Jacques, and Jacques Crépineau. *Le Moulin rouge.* Paris: Hermé, 1989.

Phillips, Gene D. *Fiction, Film, and Faulkner: The Art of Adaptation.* Knoxville: University of Tennessee Press, 2001.

Piaf, Edith. *Au bal de la chance.* Paris: L'Archipel, 2003.

———. *My Life.* London: Penguin, 1992.

Pound, Ezra. *A Walking Tour of Southern France.* New York: New Directions, 1992.

Rajsfus, Maurice. *La police de Vichy: Les forces de l'ordre françaises au service de la Gestapo, 1940/44.* Paris: Cherche midi, 1995.

Rémond, Alain. *Montand.* Paris: Henri Veyrier, 1982.

Riding, Alan. *And the Show Went On: Cultural Life in Nazi-Occupied Paris.* New York: Knopf, 2010.

Ridley, Jasper. *Mussolini.* London: Constable, 1997.

Robson, Mark. *Italy: Liberalism and Fascism, 1870–1945.* London: Hodder & Stoughton, 2000.

Rosenberg, Justus. *The Art of Resistance: My Four Years in the French Underground.* New York: William Morrow, 2020.

Rotman, Patrick. *Ivo et Jorge: Roman.* Paris: Grasset, 2021.

Saad, Shirine. *Marseille.* London: Phaidon Press, 2015.

Sagan, Françoise. *Aimez-vous Brahms?* London: John Murray, 1960.

Semprún, Jorge. *Montand, la vie continue.* Paris: Denoël, 1983.

Shirer, William. *The Collapse of the Third Republic: An Enquiry into the Fall of France in 1940.* New York: Simon and Schuster, 1969.

Signoret, Simone. *Nostalgia Isn't What It Used to Be.* Translated by Harper & Row. London: Weidenfeld and Nicolson, 1978.

Spoto, Donald. *Marilyn Monroe: The Biography.* New York: HarperCollins, 1993.

A Study Guide for Herb Gardner's A Thousand Clowns. Farmington Hills, MI: Gale Group.

Taraborrelli, J. Randy. *The Secret Life of Marilyn Monroe.* New York: Grand Central, 2009.

Temple, Michael, and Michael Witt, eds. *The French Cinema Book.* London: British Film Institute, 2004.

Thomson, David. *The New Biographical Dictionary of Film.* London: Little, Brown, 2010.

Weber, Eugen. *The Hollow Years: France in the 1930s.* New York: Norton, 1994.

Welland, Dennis. *Arthur Miller: The Crucible.* Harlow, UK: Longman York Press, 1980.

Wood, Eon. *Dietrich: A Biography.* London: Sanctuary, 2002.

Young, Daniel. *Made in Marseille.* New York: HarperCollins, 2002.

Periodical Articles

Amalric, Jacques. "Yves Montand face à la guerre." *Le Monde,* April 18, 1985.

Archer, Eugene. "'Butterfly' Film Will Be Comedy." *New York Times,* August 24, 1960.

Baby, Yvonne. "Jean-Luc Godard : Pour mieux écouter les autres." *Le Monde,* April 27, 1972.

———. "Rêve et révolution." *Le Monde,* May 11, 1966.

Bennetts, Leslie. "Most Funny Stuff Is Born of Pain." *New York Times,* June 2, 1985.

Bergquist, Laura. "The Lives and Loves of Simone Signoret." *Look,* August 1960.

Bernstein, Richard. "France's Savory Tale of Fate." *New York Times,* June 21, 1987.

"Billboard Year-End Hot 30 Chart for 1953." Music Outfitters, n.d. At https://www.musicoutfitters.com/topsongs/1953.htm.

Blumenfeld, Samuel. "Cannes 2017: 'Le salaire de la peur.'" *Le Monde,* May 19, 2017.

Boutwell, Jane. "Yves Montand." *The New Yorker,* August 29, 1982.

Brewer, Doug. "The Man Who Almost Destroyed Marilyn Monroe's Marriage." *Modern Screen,* November 1960.

Campbell, Kenneth. "Theater: Yves Montand; Gallic Actor-Singer Opens One-Man Show." *New York Times*, September 23, 1959.

Canby, Vincent. "Film: Costa-Gavras Depicts a Believer's Betrayal by His Belief." *New York Times,* December 10, 1970.

———. "Review/Film: Clouzot's 'Wages of Fear' Version Complete." *New York Times,* October 18, 1991.

———. "Screen: Greek Symbols; Costa-Gavras Directs 'Z.'" *New York Times,* December 9, 1969.

———. "Screen: 'On a Clear Day You Can See Forever' Begins Its Run." *New York Times,* June 18, 1970.

———. "'Siege,' an Angry Muckraker." *New York Times,* April 22, 1973.

Candide. "La peine et l'argent." May 22, 1967.

Cannavo, Richard. "Un fabuleux coup de poker." *Le Matin,* October 7, 1981.

Cicurel, Michel. "Comme un James Bond." *Le Monde,* February 25, 1984.

Correll, John T. "The Euromissile Showdown." *Air Force Magazine,* February 1, 2020.

Crowdus, Gary. "*State of Siege.*" *Cinéaste* 41, no. 1 (Winter 2015): 56–58.

Crowther, Bosley. "Freewheeling Film in Monaco Puts Stars in Grand Prix Cars." *New York Times,* May 20, 1966.

———. "Screen: French 'Crucible.'" *New York Times,* December 9, 1958.

———. "Screen: 'Goodbye Again' at 2 Theaters." *New York Times,* June 30, 1961.

———. "The Screen: 'Is Paris Burning?'" *New York Times,* November 11, 1966.

———. "The Screen: Milton Berle Steals Show in 'Let's Make Love.'" *New York Times,* September 9, 1960.

———. "The Screen: 'Sanctuary' Adaptation of Faulkner Novels Has Premiere." *New York Times,* February 22, 1961.

———. "Screen: 'The Sleeping Car Murder.'" *New York Times,* March 8, 1966.

Darrach, Brad. "Return of *Psycho.*" *People,* June 13, 1983.

———. "Yves Montand." *People,* May 16, 1988.

De Baroncelli, Jean. "Cannes à Paris." *Le Monde,* May 27, 1961.

———. "*Ma geisha.*" *Le Monde,* February 24, 1962.

———. "*Le milliardaire.*" *Le Monde,* October 12, 1960.

———. "*Le salaire de la peur,* un coup de foudre." *Le Monde,* April 17, 1953.

———. "*Les sorcières de Salem.*" *Le Monde,* May 2, 1957.

———. "*Vivre pour vivre.*" *Le Monde,* September 16, 1967.

Degenfelder, E. Pauline. "The Four Faces of Temple Drake: Faulkner's *Sanctuary, Requiem for a Nun,* and the Two Film Adaptations." *American Quarterly* 28, no. 5 (Winter 1976): 544–60. At https://www.jstor.org/stable/2712288.

Delye, Hélène. "Mémoires pour Simone." *Le Monde,* October 14, 2013.

Dhombres, Dominique. "Haro sur 'Yves Mutant' 'renegat' et 'loup-garu.'" *Le Monde,* April 22, 1985.

Ebert, Roger. "*Live for Life.*" *Chicago Sun-Times,* May 8, 1968.

———. "*Z.*" *Chicago Sun-Times,* December 30, 1969.

Le Figaro. "Oliver Stone." July 13, 2021.

———. "Signoret–Montand, le couple mythique du cinéma français aurait cent ans." March 25, 2021.

Film Score Monthly Liner Notes. *Goodbye Again* (1961). N.d. At https://www.filmscoremonthly.com/notes/goodbye_again.html.

Fox Dynamo. "*Let's Make Love:* A Star-Packed Blockbuster." February 1960.

France-Soir. "Montand: 'Je ferai ma rentrée à Paris.'" February 18, 1961.

———. "Yves Montand: 'Mon recital d'autumn.'" March 15, 1962.

Frappat, Bruno. "Bleu, blanc, gris." *Le Monde,* February 27, 1984.

Gonod, Michel. "Montand: Si je crée un parti, ce sera celui du coeur." *Paris-Match,* June 20, 1986.

Grenier, Cynthia. "The 'Z' People Make a 'Confession.'" *New York Times,* December 6, 1970.

Gussow, Mel. "Costa-Gavras Elaborates on Politics and Violence." *New York Times,* April 14, 1973.

Heymann, Danièle. "Au bonheur des larmes." *Le Monde,* November 2, 1986.

———. "La folie Montand." *L'Express,* March 26, 1982.

———. "Montand à l'heure de Pagnol." *Le Monde,* August 23, 1986.

———. "Yves Montand vieillit bien." *L'Express,* September 16–22, 1968.

Hodgson, Moira. "Yves Montand: From the Music Hall to the Met." *New York Times,* September 5, 1982.

Honorez, Luc. "Et la scene?" *Le soir de Bruxelles,* March 4, 1980.

Jours de France. "Y-a-t-il un secret Marilyn Monroe–Yves Montand?" August 6, 1960.

Kael, Pauline. "A Rip-off with Genius." *New York Times,* July 22, 1973.

Kemp, Robert. "*Les sorcières de Salem.*" *Le Monde,* December 18, 1954.

Kravetz, Marc. "*La voix et les gestes.*" *Libération,* November 12, 1991.

Life. "A Legend Is Costly, but It's Worth It." August 15, 1960.

———. "Powerful Stars Meet to Play-Act Romance." August 15, 1960.

Loos, Ted. "The Most Suspenseful Movie Ever Made." *Esquire,* November 2005.

Magnan, Henry. "*Les portes de la nuit.*" *Le Monde,* December 6, 1946.

———. "Yves Montand à l'Étoile." *Le Monde,* September 25, 1946.

———. "Yves Montand montreur d'images." *Le Monde,* March 10, 1951.

Martin, James Michael. "'The Sleeping Car Murder (Compartiment tueurs)' by Costa-Gavras." *Film Quarterly* 21, no. 3 (Spring 1968): 44–46.

McFadden, Robert D. "Mikis Theodorakis, 'Zorba' Composer and Marxist Rebel, Dies at 96." *New York Times,* September 2, 2021.

Merlin, Virginie. "À ceux qui pensent." *Paris-Match,* November 9, 1989.

Miller, Arthur. "Why I Wrote 'The Crucible.'" *The New Yorker,* October 21 and 28, 1996.

Miller, Judith. "President Yves Montand? Not Everybody Scoffs." *New York Times,* May 23, 1986.

Le Monde. "L'adieu de l'Italie." November 12, 1991.

———. "Ainsi sortent les artistes!" (editorial). November 12, 1991.

———. "L'ambassade d'URSS dénonce 'l'inaction des autorités françaises' face à cette 'sordide calomnie.'" April 20, 1985.

———. "L'exhumation d'Yves Montand." November 9, 1997.

———. "Hommage à Yves Montand." November 12, 1991.
———. "Yves Montand critique par la CGT pour 'Tout va bien.'" August 2, 1972.
Namia, Noelle. "Beineix raconte Montand." *Paris-Match,* November 19, 1992.
Noir et blanc. "Marilyn Monroe divorce-t-elle pour Yves Montand?" November 18, 1960.
Pace, Eric. "Simone Signoret Dies in France at 64." *New York Times,* October 1, 1985.
Paris-Jour. "Yves Montand redevient Français." October 23, 1962.
Paris-Match. "Catherine Allégret viole la légende de Montand." October 7, 2004.
———. "Enfin Simone et Yves se retrouve pour toujours." November 21, 1991.
———. "La femme de sa vie." November 21, 1991.
———. "Français, si vous changiez." October 23, 1987.
———. "La France bouleversée." November 20, 1997.
———. "La guerre des générations." November 18, 1983.
———. "Montand à Prague." February 1, 1990.
———. "Montand la passion." November 21, 1991.
———. "L'outrage fait à Montand." October 7, 2004.
Parsons, Louella. "I Am Going to Adopt a Baby." *Modern Screen,* January 20, 1960.
———. "The Love Scandal of the Decade." *Modern Screen,* December 1960.
Phillips, John. "France Mourns Montand." *The Times* (London), November 11, 1991.
Planchais, Jean. "*Paris brule-t-il?*" *Le Monde,* October 26, 1966.
Poirot-Delpech, B. "*Des clowns par milliers.*" *Le Monde,* December 11, 1963.
Rich, Frank. "Stage: Montand at the Metropolitan." *New York Times,* September 8, 1982.
Riding, Alan. "Cuban 'Agent' Says US Police Aides Urged Torture." *New York Times,* August 5, 1978.
———. "Yves Montand, Sage Charmer of French Film and Politics, Dies at 70." *New York Times,* November 10, 1991.
Roberts, Steven B. "Greece Sees 'Z' and Gets Excited." *New York Times,* January 13, 1975.
Rotman, Patrick. "Il était d'abord un solitaire." *Paris-Match,* November 21, 1991.
Sarraute, Claude. "À l'Étoile." *Le Monde,* October 8, 1958.
———. "Yves Montand à l'Olympia." *Le Monde,* September 21, 1968.
Schwaab, Catherine. "Jean-Claude Brialy." *Paris-Match,* October 7, 2004.
Skouros, Spyros P. "Design for Perpetuity." *Fox Dynamo,* February 1960.
Sorensen, Theodore. "'State of Siege' Speaks 'a Warning to Us All': Movies." *New York Times,* June 24, 1973.
Steavenson, Wendell. "Seven Movies to Watch." *The New Yorker,* December 9, 2013.
Taubman, Howard. "Theater: Yves Montand Evokes Paris." *New York Times,* October 25, 1961.
Téléstar. "Yves Montand, le récit de ses derniers jours." February 10, 2016.
Tynan, Kenneth. "Direct from Paris." *The New Yorker,* October 3, 1959.
Variety. "*Let's Make Love.*" December 31, 1959.
———. "*Live for Life.*" December 23, 1966.
———. "*My Geisha.*" December 31, 1961.

Vinocur, John. "The French John Wayne." *New York Times,* October 10, 1983.

———. "Yves Montand and the Left at Odds." *New York Times,* October 10, 1983.

Weber, Bruce. "Jorge Semprún, Who Blurred Line between Novel and Memoir, Is Dead at 87." *New York Times,* June 10, 2011.

Weiler, A. H. "*My Geisha* Arrives." *New York Times,* June 14, 1962.

Audio-Visual

"1984: Vive la crise!" Video, February 22, 1984. Dailymotion. At https://www.dailymotion.com/video/xa95yp.

Bilalian, Daniel. "Signoret's Death." France 2 newscast, September 30, 1985. At https://www.youtube.com/watch?v=g28asB031ps.

Bonini, Emmanuel. Interview. *L'invité du jour,* November 9, 2021. At https://www.youtube.com/watch?v=vJALQ9q6If4.

Carsson TV. "Yves Montand: Un heritage d'outre tombe." December 3, 2021. YouTube. At https://www.youtube.com/watch?v=5HwtuHLKKZs.

Delahousse, Laurent, announcer. "Alliance(s), couples de pouvoir, Signoret et Montand." Video. *13h15 le Dimanche,* France 2 (television), September 6, 2020. At https://www.francetvinfo.fr/replay-magazine/france-2/13h15/13h15-du-dimanche-6-septembre-2020_4078813.html.

Hexagonal. Montand on his political films with Costa-Gavras. France Television, Regions 3 Marseille, May 21, 1978. At https://m.ina.fr/video/I00005146/yves-montand-sur-ses-films-politiques-video.html.

Job, Guy, dir. *Montant International.* Documentary on Montand's 1982 international tour. France Y. M. Aries ATVF, 1983. At https://www.youtube.com/watch?v=z_Z8Schg-Pk.

Leprince, Chloé. "Rafle à Marseille en 1943: Un quartier rasé et le petit rire de Pétain." Video. France Culture, June 6, 2019. At https://www.franceculture.fr/histoire/rafle-a-marseille-en-1943-les-images-de-la-verrue-de-leurope-et-le-petit-rire-de-petain.

"Making Of." Bonus feature on *Grand Prix* (1966), DVD. Turner Entertainment Co. and Joel Productions, 2006.

Marker, Chris, dir. *La solitude du chanteur de fond* (1974). DVD. Universal Music France, 2015.

Montand, Yves. Guest appearance on *The Dinah Shore Chevy Show.* November 15, 1959. At https://m.ina.fr/video/CAF88034264/yves-montand-aux-usa-ok-mister-montand-video.html.

"Obsèques d'Yves Montand." Video of Montand's funeral, November 13, 1991. At https://www.ina.fr/ina-eclaire-actu/video/cac91061831/obseques-d-yves-montand.

Pascal, Victor. "'Les feuilles mortes,' parcours d'un titre culte." Video. France Musique, October 14, 2021. At https://www.francemusique.fr/culture-musicale/les-feuilles-mortes-parcours-d-un-titre-culte.

Revon, Jérôme, dir. *Nous nous sommes tant aimés.* Documentary. FR3, January 5, 2015. At https://www.francedimanche.fr/actualites/yves-montand-il-voudrait-tant-que-l -on-se-souvienne.

"Simone Signoret Wins Best Actress: Oscars 1960." Video, n.d. At https://www.oscars.org/videos-photos/32nd-oscars-highlights.
"William Friedkin's Favorite Films of All Time." *Fade In Magazine,* video, June 12, 2013. YouTube. At https://www.youtube.com/watch?v=p-APzEjrklc.
Yves Montand Is Singing. Documentary on Montand's Russian tour, 1956. At https://www.net-film.ru/en/film-4886/?search=qyves%20montand%20is%20singing.

Index

Screen Classics

Screen Classics is a series of critical biographies, film histories, and analytical studies focusing on neglected filmmakers and important screen artists and subjects, from the era of silent cinema through the golden age of Hollywood to the international generation of today. Books in the Screen Classics series are intended for scholars and general readers alike. The contributing authors are established figures in their respective fields. This series also serves the purpose of advancing scholarship on film personalities and themes with ties to Kentucky.

Series Editor
Patrick McGilligan

Books in the Series

Olivia de Havilland: Lady Triumphant
Victoria Amador
Mae Murray: The Girl with the Bee-Stung Lips
Michael G. Ankerich
Harry Dean Stanton: Hollywood's Zen Rebel
Joseph B. Atkins
Hedy Lamarr: The Most Beautiful Woman in Film
Ruth Barton
Rex Ingram: Visionary Director of the Silent Screen
Ruth Barton
Conversations with Classic Film Stars: Interviews from Hollywood's Golden Era
James Bawden and Ron Miller
Conversations with Legendary Television Stars: Interviews from the First Fifty Years
James Bawden and Ron Miller
They Made the Movies: Conversations with Great Filmmakers
James Bawden and Ron Miller
You Ain't Heard Nothin' Yet: Interviews with Stars from Hollywood's Golden Era
James Bawden and Ron Miller
Charles Boyer: The French Lover
John Baxter
Von Sternberg
John Baxter
Hitchcock's Partner in Suspense: The Life of Screenwriter Charles Bennett
Charles Bennett, edited by John Charles Bennett
Hitchcock and the Censors
John Billheimer
A Uniquely American Epic: Intimacy and Action, Tenderness and Violence in Sam Peckinpah's The Wild Bunch
Edited by Michael Bliss

My Life in Focus: A Photographer's Journey with Elizabeth Taylor and the Hollywood Jet Set
Gianni Bozzacchi with Joey Tayler
Hollywood Divided: The 1950 Screen Directors Guild Meeting and the Impact of the Blacklist
Kevin Brianton
He's Got Rhythm: The Life and Career of Gene Kelly
Cynthia Brideson and Sara Brideson
Ziegfeld and His Follies: A Biography of Broadway's Greatest Producer
Cynthia Brideson and Sara Brideson
Eleanor Powell: Born to Dance
Paula Broussard and Lisa Royère
The Marxist and the Movies: A Biography of Paul Jarrico
Larry Ceplair
Dalton Trumbo: Blacklisted Hollywood Radical
Larry Ceplair and Christopher Trumbo
Warren Oates: A Wild Life
Susan Compo
Improvising Out Loud: My Life Teaching Hollywood How to Act
Jeff Corey with Emily Corey
Crane: Sex, Celebrity, and My Father's Unsolved Murder
Robert Crane and Christopher Fryer
Jack Nicholson: The Early Years
Robert Crane and Christopher Fryer
Anne Bancroft: A Life
Douglass K. Daniel
Being Hal Ashby: Life of a Hollywood Rebel
Nick Dawson
Bruce Dern: A Memoir
Bruce Dern with Christopher Fryer and Robert Crane
Intrepid Laughter: Preston Sturges and the Movies
Andrew Dickos
The Woman Who Dared: The Life and Times of Pearl White, Queen of the Serials
William M. Drew
Miriam Hopkins: Life and Films of a Hollywood Rebel
Allan R. Ellenberger
Vitagraph: America's First Great Motion Picture Studio
Andrew A. Erish
Jayne Mansfield: The Girl Couldn't Help It
Eve Golden
John Gilbert: The Last of the Silent Film Stars
Eve Golden
Strictly Dynamite: The Sensational Life of Lupe Velez
Eve Golden
Stuntwomen: The Untold Hollywood Story
Mollie Gregory
Jean Gabin: The Actor Who Was France
Joseph Harriss
Yves Montand: The Passionate Voice
Joseph Harriss
Otto Preminger: The Man Who Would Be King, updated edition
Foster Hirsch
Saul Bass: Anatomy of Film Design
Jan-Christopher Horak

Lawrence Tierney: Hollywood's Real-Life Tough Guy
Burt Kearns
Hitchcock Lost and Found: The Forgotten Films
Alain Kerzoncuf and Charles Barr
Pola Negri: Hollywood's First Femme Fatale
Mariusz Kotowski
Ernest Lehman: The Sweet Smell of Success
Jon Krampner
Sidney J. Furie: Life and Films
Daniel Kremer
Albert Capellani: Pioneer of the Silent Screen
Christine Leteux
A Front Row Seat: An Intimate Look at Broadway, Hollywood, and the Age of Glamour
Nancy Olson Livingston
Ridley Scott: A Biography
Vincent LoBrutto
Mamoulian: Life on Stage and Screen
David Luhrssen
Maureen O'Hara: The Biography
Aubrey Malone
My Life as a Mankiewicz: An Insider's Journey through Hollywood
Tom Mankiewicz and Robert Crane
Hawks on Hawks
Joseph McBride
John Ford
Joseph McBride and Michael Wilmington
Showman of the Screen: Joseph E. Levine and His Revolutions in Film Promotion
A. T. McKenna
William Wyler: The Life and Films of Hollywood's Most Celebrated Director
Gabriel Miller
Raoul Walsh: The True Adventures of Hollywood's Legendary Director
Marilyn Ann Moss
Veit Harlan: The Life and Work of a Nazi Filmmaker
Frank Noack
Harry Langdon: King of Silent Comedy
Gabriella Oldham and Mabel Langdon
Mavericks: Interviews with the World's Iconoclast Filmmakers
Gerald Peary
Charles Walters: The Director Who Made Hollywood Dance
Brent Phillips
Some Like It Wilder: The Life and Controversial Films of Billy Wilder
Gene D. Phillips
Ann Dvorak: Hollywood's Forgotten Rebel
Christina Rice
Mean . . . Moody . . . Magnificent! Jane Russell and the Marketing of a Hollywood Legend
Christina Rice
Fay Wray and Robert Riskin: A Hollywood Memoir
Victoria Riskin
Lewis Milestone: Life and Films
Harlow Robinson
Michael Curtiz: A Life in Film
Alan K. Rode

Ryan's Daughter: *The Making of an Irish Epic*
Paul Benedict Rowan
Arthur Penn: American Director
Nat Segaloff
Film's First Family: The Untold Story of the Costellos
Terry Chester Shulman
Claude Rains: An Actor's Voice
David J. Skal with Jessica Rains
Barbara La Marr: The Girl Who Was Too Beautiful for Hollywood
Sherri Snyder
Buzz: The Life and Art of Busby Berkeley
Jeffrey Spivak
Victor Fleming: An American Movie Master
Michael Sragow
Aline MacMahon: Hollywood, the Blacklist, and the Birth of Method Acting
John Stangeland
My Place in the Sun: Life in the Golden Age of Hollywood and Washington
George Stevens, Jr.
Hollywood Presents Jules Verne: The Father of Science Fiction on Screen
Brian Taves
Thomas Ince: Hollywood's Independent Pioneer
Brian Taves
Picturing Peter Bogdanovich: My Conversations with the New Hollywood Director
Peter Tonguette
Jessica Lange: An Adventurer's Heart
Anthony Uzarowski
Carl Theodor Dreyer and Ordet: *My Summer with the Danish Filmmaker*
Jan Wahl
Wild Bill Wellman: Hollywood Rebel
William Wellman Jr.
Harvard, Hollywood, Hitmen, and Holy Men: A Memoir
Paul W. Williams
The Warner Brothers
Chris Yogerst
Clarence Brown: Hollywood's Forgotten Master
Gwenda Young
The Queen of Technicolor: Maria Montez in Hollywood
Tom Zimmerman